INTO THE STORM

Lessons in Teamwork
from the Treacherous Sydney
to Hobart Ocean Race

DENNIS N.T. PERKINS
WITH **JILLIAN B. MURPHY**

ᴬAMACOM

American Management Association
New York • Atlanta • Brussels • Chicago • Mexico City • San Francisco
Shanghai • Tokyo • Toronto • Washington, D.C.

Bulk discounts available. For details visit:
www.amacombooks.org/go/specialsales
Or contact special sales:
Phone: 800–250–5308
E-mail: specialsls@amanet.org
View all the AMACOM titles at: www.amacombooks.org
American Management Association: www.amanet.org

This publication is designed to provide accurate and authoritative information in regard to the subject matter covered. It is sold with the understanding that the publisher is not engaged in rendering legal, accounting, or other professional service. If legal advice or other expert assistance is required, the services of a competent professional person should be sought.

Library of Congress Cataloging-in-Publication Data

Perkins, Dennis N. T., 1942–
  Into the storm : lessons in teamwork from the treacherous Sydney to Hobart ocean race / Dennis N. T. Perkins, with Jillian B. Murphy.
     p. cm.
  Includes bibliographical references and index.
  ISBN 978-0-8144-3198-6 (hbk.)
  1. Teams in the workplace. 2. Leadership. 3. Management. 4. Yacht racing—Australia—Case studies. I. Murphy, Jillian B. II. Title.
  HD66.P4275 2013
  658.4'022--dc23
                             2012031538

Excerpts from *SOFTWAR* by Matthew Symonds, with commentary by Larry Ellison. Copyright © 2003 by Matthew Symonds and Larry Ellison, used by permission of The Wylie Agency LLC. Excerpts reprinted with the permission of Simon & Schuster, Inc. from *SOFTWAR: An Intimate Portrait of Larry Ellison and Oracle* by Matthew Symonds with commentary by Larry Ellison. Copyright © 2003 by Matthew Symonds and Larry Ellison.

About AMA

American Management Association (www.amanet.org) is a world leader in talent development, advancing the skills of individuals to drive business success. Our mission is to support the goals of individuals and organizations through a complete range of products and services, including classroom and virtual seminars, webcasts, webinars, podcasts, conferences, corporate and government solutions, business books, and research. AMA's approach to improving performance combines experiential learning—learning through doing—with opportunities for ongoing professional growth at every step of one's career journey.

Printing number

10 9 8 7 6 5 4 3 2 1

To the Heroes of the Hobart

Contents

Sydney to Hobart Race Course

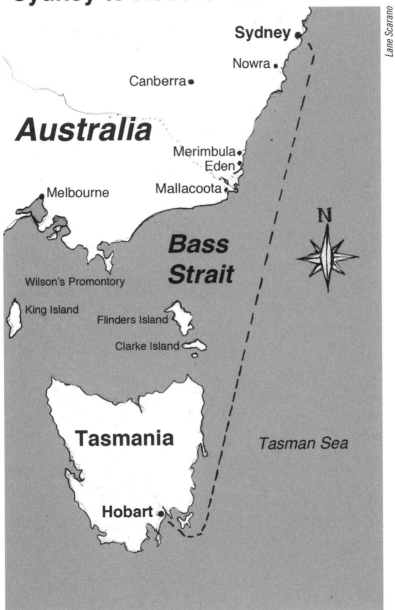

Lane Scarano

Sydney

Nowra

Canberra

Australia

Merimbula
Eden
Mallacoota

Melbourne

Bass
Strait

Wilson's Promontory

King Island

Flinders Island

Clarke Island

N

Tasmania

Tasman Sea

Hobart

Preface:
At *The Edge*

Dusk was coming on and I was at the end of my tether and thinking to myself, "If this continues, I can't keep going like this. And there's no one else that can steer this damn boat, so we're in serious trouble."
        —Ed Psaltis, Skipper, *AFR Midnight Rambler*

The Sydney to Hobart Race is unknown to many Americans, but it is an iconic event for Australians. Held every year on Boxing Day—the day after Christmas—this 628-nautical-mile,[1] (723-statute-mile) deepwater challenge is often called the "Everest" of offshore ocean racing. With unpredictable weather and seas, the Sydney to Hobart Race is considered one of the toughest in the world. It is always a challenging race. But in 1998, conditions were extraordinary. Extraordinarily dangerous.

In the fifty-three years leading up to the 1998 race, more than 35,000 sailors on 4,465 boats participated in "the Hobart." Only two died from injuries during the race, and no one had ever been lost overboard. In the fifty-fourth year, everything changed.

In 1998, 115 boats and 1,135 sailors crossed the starting line. By the time the race was over, only forty-four boats reached the finish line. Five had sunk, seven were abandoned at sea, twenty-five crewmen were washed overboard, and fifty-five sailors were rescued in an operation involving twenty-five aircraft, six vessels, and approximately 1,000 people. It was the largest search-and-rescue operation in the history of Australia.

In the wake of such tragedy, one story went largely untold: the incredible achievement of the Overall Race Winner, the *AFR Midnight Rambler*. This is their story, and the story of the Sydney to Hobart Race. It is a story of teamwork and triumph at *The Edge*.

■

What is it that enables leaders and teams to succeed under conditions of great adversity? What are the qualities and behaviors that can turn hardship into victory? These are questions I have thought about for years, but finding solid answers seems especially critical today. Organizations have always encountered tough challenges, but the turbulence, ambiguity, and uncertainty we face today seem unprecedented.

My research on leaders and teams has convinced me that there are *core principles proven to help organizations thrive under conditions of extreme challenge.* These strategies work for organizations struggling to survive, for organizations that simply aspire to do better, and for organizations racing to outperform their competitors.

As a young Marine I was faced with life-and-death decisions in combat. I was a leader and a team member in situations where survival depended on seamless collaboration. Later, as an academic, I tried to understand teamwork from a different perspective—that of an organizational psychologist. After I left the academic world, I found myself in the role of a consultant working with beleaguered executives—leaders who were often facing the metaphorical equivalent of a firefight. To be effective, I needed to connect with people whose tumultuous daily lives left little time for academic theories.

This challenge led me to explore stories of adventure and survival as a way of communicating a set of critical leadership and teamwork strategies. I discovered that compelling accounts of groups in life-threatening situations helped people understand how they could work together to overcome adversity.

I have studied hundreds of stories of individuals and teams pressed to the limits of human endurance—a place I have come to call *The Edge.* I examined epic adventures of polar exploration, such as the Amundsen-Scott race to the South Pole. I studied contemporary stories, including the *Apollo 13* lunar mission and the 1996 Everest Expedition chronicled in Jon Krakauer's bestseller, *Into Thin Air.*

Drawing on my research, I wrote *Leading at The Edge*—a book that highlights the story of Ernest Shackleton and his epic expedition to Antarctica. Using Shackleton and others as case studies, I outlined ten critical strategies for leaders facing daunting challenges.

As I continued my work with leaders and teams, another question arose. Were there stories of teams that triumphed at *The Edge*—but in situations where the leader was less prominent than Shackleton? Was there a story in which leadership was more visibly shared among team members? The search for answers to those questions led me to the extraordinary story of the *AFR Midnight Rambler.*

The *AFR Midnight Rambler*

The 1998 Sydney to Hobart Race proved to be the most perilous in the event's sixty-five-year history. As the fleet sailed down the coast of Australia, boats were hit by an unexpected *weather bomb*—a massive storm that created 80-foot waves and 92-knot (105-mile-an-hour) winds. While many crews tried to maneuver around the storm, the 35-foot *AFR Midnight Rambler* chose to head directly into its path. After battling mountainous waves and hurricane force winds in the Bass Strait, the tiny boat arrived safely in Hobart, three days and sixteen hours later.

Their decision to head into the eye of the storm—along with extraordinary tenacity, optimism, courage, and teamwork—enabled this crew of amateur sailors to beat professionals on much larger and better financed boats. The skipper, Ed Psaltis, and his crew of six were proclaimed the Overall Winners and awarded the coveted Tattersall's Cup. They were the smallest boat in ten years to win the race.

A number of books have been written about the 1998 Sydney to Hobart Race, but most focused on the tragedy and loss of life. The spotlight was on death and destruction. When I looked further, however, I found that the story of the *AFR Midnight Rambler* had been almost completely overlooked.

I immersed myself in the saga of the *Midnight Rambler* and the Sydney to Hobart Race. I contacted Ed Psaltis, and the more I heard about his philosophy—and the way the crew worked together—the more engaged I became. It was clear to me that the success of the *AFR Midnight Rambler* was not a fluke or mere luck. It was the result of a consistent set of exemplary practices that embody the concept of *Teamwork at The Edge.*

In the years following my initial contact with Ed, I spent considerable time studying the *AFR Midnight Rambler* crew and the Sydney to Hobart Race. I made numerous trips to Australia and conducted extensive interviews with members of the crew. I also spoke with other accomplished sailors who had won the famed race. Finally, with some trepidation, I sailed the race myself so that I would understand as much as I possibly could about the Everest of ocean racing.

To be clear, the story of the *Midnight Rambler* is not the only story that can be told about teamwork in the Sydney to Hobart Race. The lessons in this book incorporate insights from conversations with many extraordinary sailors. Roger Hickman, skipper of *Wild Rose,* is one of Australia's most experienced offshore ocean racers. "Hicko," who won the 1993 race and many other trophies, was exceptionally generous with his observations about effective teamwork.

Adrienne Cahalan—navigator of *Wild Oats*—holds five world speed sailing records and is a veteran of nineteen Sydney to Hobart Races. Adrienne shared her insights from years at sea on a diverse array of boats and crews. Neville Crichton, owner and skipper of the "super maxi" *Alfa Romeo,* also took time from his busy schedule to speak with me. And, though most of my conversations took place with Australian sailors, I was able to get some "Yankee insights" from the crew of *Rosebud*—including Jim Slaughter and Malcolm Park. *Rosebud* was the first American winner of the Sydney to Hobart Race in thirty years.

Each of these sailors contributed important ideas about teamwork that are incorporated ino this book. As is the case of *Leading at The Edge,* however, I felt that the best way to talk about the strategies was to focus on one story. In my previous book, that story was the saga of Ernest Shackleton and the crew of the *Endurance.* In this book, I chose the story of the *AFR Midnight Rambler.*

There are a number of reasons why the metaphor of ocean racing can help teams facing today's tough challenges. Let's look at some of the core characteristics of the sport:

- Ocean racing is a complex team endeavor.
- It's a test of endurance and tenacity involving a journey into the unknown.
- Like today's business environment, racing is characterized by constant change. The weather can be sunny one minute, with gale force winds the next.
- Ocean racing is competitive, stressful, and anxiety-provoking.
- While there is a skipper in charge of the boat, leadership can be distributed among other members of the crew.
- A team that fails to execute flawlessly can lose a race. There are winners and losers in the sport.
- Winning a sailing race requires clear vision, a cohesive and committed team, and the ability to learn and adapt.

The demands placed on a crew of ocean racers are strikingly similar to those faced by any team working to overcome tough challenges. And I believe that, by understanding the things that make ocean racers successful, we can draw useful insights for a broad range of team challenges.

Having a superb team doesn't guarantee success, and every challenging adventure involves an element of chance. But I believe that the kind of teamwork exhibited by the best ocean racing teams changes the odds. Every race will still involve rolling the dice, but the dice can be weighted in favor of teams that strive to get everything right—crews that excel in *Teamwork at The Edge.*

After sharing the story of the *AFR Midnight Rambler* and the 1998 Sydney to Hobart Race, I'll explore the strategies that I believe provide the foundation for their success, and for the success of other ocean racers. Then I'll suggest ways that these *Teamwork at The Edge* strategies can be applied to your own challenges.

The Role of the Leader

My primary goals for this book are to highlight the role of teamwork in organizations facing adversity and to explore ways in which leadership can be shared by team members. In today's challenging environment, the burden of leadership can be extraordinarily heavy—often more than one person alone can shoulder.

An additional goal is to explore how expectations about the nature of leadership and teamwork may have evolved since Shackleton's age of exploration. Team members in today's organizations are likely to be far better educated than they were in 1914, and perceptions of hierarchy are different. People are more informed, and they expect to play a greater role in decision making than they might have even a decade ago.

The story of the *AFR Midnight Rambler* seemed to be an ideal laboratory for understanding new forms of *distributed leadership*. For one thing, the culture of the Ramblers was inherently more egalitarian than that of the crew on the *Endurance* Expedition. In addition, the contemporary nature of the story enabled me to study the roles and personalities of the team members in considerable depth. I could do more than read expedition journals; I could personally interview each member of the team.

In my zeal to shift focus from leadership to teamwork, however, I encountered an unexpected hitch. The issue was framed perceptively by a friend and colleague, Chuck Raben. Chuck was concerned about the absence of leadership in my approach. As Chuck put it in an e-mail:

> Exceptional teams do not emerge naturally or in a vacuum. Someone, notably the leader or skipper in this case, sets the tone and starts the ball rolling in so many ways. How can you go from "all about Shackleton" to almost "nothing about Psaltis"? I realize that you're focusing on teams in this piece, but the role of the leader was conspicuously absent.

Chuck was right. I had been looking at the world in a binary way, as if leaders have the choice between being Ernest Shackleton—a charismatic, legendary figure—and something far more pedestrian. With this alternative view, the leader was more of a group facilitator than an Ernest Shackleton.

These insights led to a lively discussion about a well-known author who has argued that the word *leadership* was no longer needed in today's world. I attended a seminar in which this expert proclaimed that *leadership* should be expunged from the dictionary in contemporary society. Leaders weren't needed because work would be accomplished by *self-organizing systems.* These systems would evolve over time, and groups would essentially lead themselves.

For people who have spent time at *The Edge* in life-and-death situations, this view seems hopelessly naïve. For me, the thought of a Marine rifle company in combat evolving as a self-organizing system was both ludicrous and terrifying.

Listening to this expert, it also seemed inconsistent that the speaker who was railing against leadership was, in fact, leading the group: calling on individuals to speak, setting time boundaries, establishing breaks, offering expert opinions, and making pronouncements.

As I reflected on Chuck's comment and my own experience, I decided that I needed to be less rigid in thinking about teamwork. My perspective on *Teamwork at The Edge* needed to be one that acknowledged the reality that leaders—including skippers on boats—have a very special role.

There is no requirement that the leader must be as prominent as Ernest Shackleton. For that matter, in my previous book I did not suggest that every leader try to become "The Boss." But I do believe that the skipper has a special role to play. In Part Two of the book I will point out specific ways in which leaders can help ensure that their teams are able to succeed at *The Edge.*

PART ONE

The Story of the *AFR Midnight Rambler* and the Sydney to Hobart Race

1

The Everest of Ocean Racing

This has the reputation of being the toughest race in the world, and it is. It's considered to be the Everest of sailing and no race is more difficult on men or the boats.

—George Snow, Owner and Skipper, *Brindabella*

F or those unfamiliar with ocean races, they may all seem pretty much like the one described in a satirical article published in *The Onion*. Emblazoned with the title "Rich Guy Wins Yacht Race," the piece features a photo of a smiling, self-satisfied sailor with a caption reading "The rich guy who defeated an estimated 75 other rich guys in Monday's Regatta."

Some sailing races do, in fact, fit the stereotype. There are some races—such as the America's Cup—that really do cater to rich guys, because it takes a lot of money to build the boats and find the sailors capable of winning the competition.

The America's Cup originated in 1851 with a race between the schooner *America* and seventeen British boats. It is still governed by pretty much the same rules that applied when *America* first brought home the trophy. The winner of the cup picks the race venue, and challengers engage in a survival-of-the-fittest process until one boat remains to take on the winner.

Though the America's Cup is the oldest international sporting trophy in the world, only a wealthy person could ever hope to claim it. The expenses are enormous. Marketing, salaries for champion sailors, research and development, and boat construction require millions of dollars. Many, many millions of dollars.

A single sail can cost hundreds of thousands of dollars, and the contest doesn't always take place on the water. The 2007 race set off a bitter legal battle between billionaires Larry Ellison and Ernesto Bertarelli, two of the richest men on the planet. Bertarelli, a biotech heir, took home the cup, but Ellison was unhappy with the winner's proposed rules for the next race. Thus ensued a nearly three-year court battle that had many race enthusiasts shaking their heads.

While the America's Cup may be the iconic race for many people, not every ocean race is a rich guy's sport. The Rolex Fastnet Race, for example, is a different kind of competition. Held in the United Kingdom, the Fastnet is a challenging technical race covering 608 nautical miles. The race begins in Cowes, on the southern coast of England, rounds the Fastnet Rock off the southwest of Ireland, and finishes at Plymouth in the south of England.

The rules of the classic Fastnet Race are different than those of the America's Cup, and it doesn't take the same level of wealth to compete. That's because the Fastnet Challenge Cup is awarded to the overall winner based on *corrected time.* Each boat is given a handicap based on a mathematical calculation of its potential speed, and the boat with the best corrected time based on its handicap is the winner.

Of course, there will always be a boat that makes it over the finish line first. Winning *line honors* is not an insignificant accomplishment, and sailors compete to be first. But winning line honors is different than being the *overall winner.*

Like the America's Cup, the first boat to finish will undoubtedly be an expensive boat with the latest technology. Anyone with enough money to build a state-of-the-art boat and hire a world-class crew has a chance at being first across the line. Enough money, perhaps, and maybe enough Dramamine. But the handicap system of the Fastnet levels the playing field, and it gives great sailors on smaller boats a chance to take home the Challenge Cup.

The Fastnet is a tough race. It also gained a worldwide reputation for being a dangerous race when, in 1979, 303 yachts were hit by 60-knot winds. The unexpected storm slammed into the fleet, bringing 40-foot waves that smashed into boats and sailors, ultimately claiming fifteen lives.

The Fastnet is a demanding race that's not just for rich guys. It takes skill to win, and it can be a treacherous undertaking. But there is another race that's not just for the wealthy. It is a race that many call the Everest of ocean racing. That event is the Sydney to Hobart Race.

The Sydney to Hobart Race

The Sydney to Hobart Race may not be widely known throughout the world, but most Australians are familiar with "the Hobart," and many are at least acquainted with its history. In 1945, Peter Luke and several Australian sailing enthusiasts who had formed the Cruising Yacht Club invited Captain John Illingworth, a visiting British Naval Officer stationed in Sydney, to accompany them on a cruise to Hobart. Illingworth thought it was a superb idea but persuaded them to make the cruise a race, and so the Sydney to Hobart was born.

The Sydney to Hobart soon became an annual event. It was exciting and could be dangerous. The Sydney to Hobart soon took its place alongside England's Fastnet and America's Newport to Bermuda as one of the three "majors" in offshore racing. All three events demand the highest skill and endurance no matter what the conditions. Australians come out in the hundreds of thousands to watch the start in Sydney Harbour, and sailors throughout the world watch for news of the race with great anticipation. As one newspaper put it, "It's a disease, not a yacht race."

How Ocean Races Are Classified

Ocean races are classified by categories that calibrate them according to the degree of difficulty. The most challenging are *Category 0 races,* defined as:

> Trans-oceanic races, including races which pass through areas in which air or sea temperatures are likely to be less than 5° C other than temporarily, where yachts must be completely self-sufficient for very extended periods of time, capable of withstanding heavy

storms and prepared to meet serious emergencies without the expectation of outside assistance.

The Volvo Ocean Race is a *Category 0* race. Although the route may vary, boats sail some 37,000 miles through some of the world's most treacherous seas. Crews have no fresh food and take only one change of clothes. It is not for the fainthearted.

Neither is the Sydney to Hobart Race, which is a *Category 1* competition. It is not considered transoceanic, and temperatures are not below 5°C "except temporarily," but it is long distance and well offshore. The rest of the description is precisely the same as a *Category 0* race. *Category 1* competitions include:

Races of long distance and well offshore, where yachts must be completely self-sufficient for extended periods of time, capable of withstanding heavy storms and prepared to meet serious emergencies without the expectation of outside assistance.

A race like the Fastnet is a tough, demanding race, and it can be perilous. Some believe it is the most technically demanding race in the world. But it is a *Category 2* race, held "along or not far removed from shorelines or in large unprotected bays or lakes . . ." A high degree of self-sufficiency is required of the yachts, but it is different than an offshore race in which boats have to be prepared to deal with serious problems with no outside help.

The Race Track

The path of the 628-mile Sydney to Hobart Race runs from its start line in Sydney Harbour to the finish line in Hobart, Tasmania. As I discovered, the race really ends in one of the many drinking establishments in Hobart—most particularly, The Shipwright's Arms.

The *rhumb line*—the most direct path, having nothing to do with alcohol—angles down the eastern coast of Australia and crosses the Bass Strait, a body of open water that separates the continent of Australia from the island of Tasmania.

Many people are familiar with Tasmania only because of the Looney Tunes Tasmanian Devil. But there is more to this island than the cantankerous, spinning cartoon character. The island is noted for its wines and is an attractive destination for vacationers. Hobart, Tasmania's capital, is a lovely, scenic spot. It's easy to get to Tasmania by airplane but not so easy by boat.

Sailors traveling south can take advantage of the East Australian Current—an ocean current that moves warm water down the coast of Australia. Some Americans are likely to have heard of the current only because of *Finding Nemo.* In the Disney/Pixar film, fish and sea turtles use the current as a highway to rescue Nemo, and ocean racers can take advantage of the current's movement in much the same way. Although the current can flow as fast as about 7 knots, it provides only a 2- to 3-knot advantage in most races. But 2 to 3 knots is a huge benefit in sailing, and skilled navigators carefully calculate the gains of sailing east to catch the current against the alternative of hugging the coast.

As sailors pass the southeast tip of Australia marked by Gabo Island, they enter the notorious Bass Strait. Named for the surgeon-explorer George Bass, the reputation of this dangerous stretch of water is created by three different forces of nature. First, the East Australian Current creates a vortex in the Tasman Sea separating Australia from Tasmania. The water of the East Australian Current collides with the West Wind Drift.

The second factor is the Antarctic Circumpolar Current, the largest of ocean currents, driven by strong westerly winds from the Southern Ocean that begin at a latitude of about 40°. Because there is little land to blunt the force of the air, the Roaring Forties in the Southern Ocean are fierce and have a well-deserved reputation for being turbulent.

Both of these forces make the Bass Strait's 130-mile stretch of water formidable, but there is a third feature that makes the conditions truly unique. The Bass Strait is shallow, and big waves from the Southern Ocean plow into the strait, like waves hitting the beach. These waves move quickly from a depth of 3,280 feet to around 150 feet, and the bottom of the wave slows dramatically. The result can be a maelstrom of flat back waves that create a dangerous cocktail for sailors. Each year, racers feel the anticipation of leaving the safety of the Australian mainland and dashing across the strait.

Those who make it to Flinders Island encounter the third leg of the race down the East Coast of Tasmania. They're closer to shore, but anything can happen with the wind. It can be cold, I discovered, because you are sailing toward Antarctica. It is unpredictable, and the wind can be fickle. Boats have the relative safety of land, but they can fall into a "hole" and be slowed to a near halt by heavy air. Or they can be propelled like a rocket, all depending on the whim of Huey—the Australian weather god.

In the final stretch, sailors are treated to the stunning sight of the Tasmanian Organ Pipes—columns of dolomite stone that do indeed look like the pipes of a giant organ. And then there's the hard right turn into Storm Bay and up the Derwent River.

The Derwent. Safety. The race is almost over. But it's far from finished. Now the wind gets even more temperamental, and sailors who have their eyes set on the Tattersall's trophy know that their fate can be determined in the last few hours of the home stretch. They can see the lights of Hobart in the distance as they pass the famous lighthouse called the Iron Pot. But seeing the lights of Hobart is not the same as crossing the finish line.

All sailors know the times they need to win and where their archrivals are located. Tensions rise at the end as sailors will their boats across the finish line, trying to pick exactly the right sail to match each gust of wind. In a long race, in theory, no mile is more important than any other mile. But it doesn't seem that way to a crew in contention to become the overall winner of the race. Minutes can crawl like hours as the boats edge toward the finish line near Battery Point.

Crossing the finish line brings a sense of accomplishment and success, but crews are tired, sleep deprived, and physically exhausted. Gear must be stowed and the boat squared away, but those mundane tasks are often accompanied by cases of beer brought aboard by friends and family.

The Prize

From the beginning, the Sydney to Hobart Race has always had an *Overall Handicap Winner.* Like the Fastnet, each boat is given a handicap rating based on a calculation of its estimated potential performance. The boat's actual time is multiplied by its handicap number to produce a corrected time. For example, if a boat took two days to complete the race and its handicap was 1.5, the corrected time would be three days. The boat with the best corrected time is the Overall Winner.

Mark Richards—skipper of *Wild Oats,* a boat that has won both line honors and overall—shares a view held by many sailors: "It's a bigger thrill for a boat to win on handicap than to get line honors. Line honors . . . is between four or five boats, really. Handicap is between the whole fleet . . . From the sailor's point of view, that is the real trophy, to win the Tattersall's Cup."

The Tattersall's trophy—more formally known as the George Adams Tattersall's Cup—has been presented to the overall winner of the Sydney to Hobart Race ever since the second contest in 1946. The name of the original race winner in 1945, *Rani,* was later engraved on the trophy.

The Tattersall's trophy, designed by an Australian silversmith, is a beautifully ornate trophy adorned with mermaids and sea horses. At its top is a mermaid on the crest of a wave calling up the winner. After the presentation ceremony, the Tattersall's Cup is held in a place of honor in the trophy cabinet at the Cruising Yacht Club of Australia (CYCA).

In addition to having the names of their boats engraved on the Tattersall's Cup, half models of the overall winners are placed on the wall of the CYCA Members' Bar. These models show the distinctive hull, keel, and rudder shapes over the years. They provide a visual history showing the evolution of ocean racing yacht design.

History aside, having models of their boats memorialized means something more personal: The overall winners of the Sydney to Hobart Race can look up at the wall of the CYCA and see a symbol of their victory in the Everest of ocean racing.

The Boats

Because the Tattersall's Cup is awarded on the basis of a handicap, the race is a democratic contest. It is open to anyone who owns a boat that meets the safety requirements for a *Category 1* race. In the early years of the competition, this often meant boats that were primarily designed for cruising. As the race became more popular, however, boats became faster and relied more on high technology, including Kevlar and carbon sails and carbon fiber masts.

The Sailors

The sailors who cross the starting line in Sydney are even more diverse than the boats they sail on. Some are millionaires, but many are blue-collar workers. Some are serious and dedicated amateurs. Others are consummate professionals who make their living by racing. They're essentially professional athletes who are very, very good at what they do.

Among the professionals, there are also individual sailors often referred to as *rock stars.* These are crew members who have developed a reputation as champion sailors in high-visibility events—at the Olympics, for example—and are recruited because of their special and unique abilities.

Though they are outstanding sailors, the term is often used pejoratively. Rock stars frequently have little interest in working as members of a team. As the term implies, they want to stand out, to be unique, and to express their opinions loudly. And they're sometimes given special privileges in *jewel positions.* As a result, rock stars make unique contributions, but their personalities and privileges can disrupt the functioning of a team.

For many who enter the Sydney to Hobart Race, the event has nothing to do with money or fame. These sailors compete simply because of their passion for the sport, and they enter year after year. Among these veteran racers, one legendary figure stands out.

I heard about John Walker on my first trip to Australia. Fascinated by his reputation, I was eager to meet John in person and find out what drew him to the race. He shared his story in the living room of his beautiful home, high on a hill north of Sydney. One side of the home was nothing but windows that framed an extraordinary view of his boat, *Impeccable,* resting gently at anchor down the slope.

John was born in Prague, Czechoslovakia, of Jewish ancestry. A talented athlete, he became his country's national figure-skating champion in 1938. Then, during the Nazi occupation of Prague, he was imprisoned in the concentration camps of Auschwitz and Buchenwald.

John spent almost four years in the camps, learning to survive under conditions more horrific than any I could imagine. He emerged from the concentration camps, finished his degree in mechanical engineering, and helped rebuild his family business. The business thrived until Czechoslovakia's Communist Government nationalized the company and took possession of the family's assets.

Desperate to escape from a second totalitarian existence, John was faced with another challenge. As he attempted to leave the country, John was told that he could not get a passport until he paid off all the mortgages on the property that had been confiscated. John and his family managed to scrape together enough money to escape. They immigrated to Australia in 1949, and John eventually established a successful timber business.

I was surprised to learn that John had only begun ocean racing at age 60. He found that he loved the sport and eventually gathered a *sailing family* to complement his *natural family* and his *business family*.

Named Ocean Racing Veteran of the Year on three occasions, John has won awards in almost all of Australia's major ocean classics, and he has come in second and third in the Sydney to Hobart Race.

On the advice of his cardiologist, John skipped the Sydney to Hobart Race the year he had a triple bypass, electing to do a less challenging event. The year I did the race he had just turned 84, and skippered *Impeccable* for his twenty-third trip to Hobart—equaling the record for the oldest skipper.

John's wife, Helen, was not so enthusiastic about his sailing, and a year later I inquired about his plans. I received an e-mail in return saying, "Surprise, surprise, I will be doing the Hobart again. I have to do it while I am young."

Sure enough, John sailed the Hobart again at age 85, and once more at 86, to become the oldest skipper ever in the history of the Sydney to Hobart Race.

John sailed into Hobart after four days at sea showing no sign of fatigue, his hand firmly on the tiller. The Commodore of the Cruising Yacht Club of Australia presented him with a cake, and reporters asked questions about his exploits. In his quiet sophisticated way, John summed up his feelings: "It was special because of the crews that have been with me for many years. I never set out to create any records. I sail because I love it, the camaraderie with my crew and everything that goes with it."

John Walker is truly one of the most charming, thoughtful, and kind individuals I have ever met. I keep a photo in my office of John at the helm of *Impeccable* wearing his red foul-weather gear. For me, and many others, he will always be an inspiration.

2

The Patriarch
of a Sailing Family

Bill Psaltis started sailing just about the time of the first Sydney to Hobart Race. In those days the Cruising Yacht Club of Australia was little more than one in a row of boat sheds and fishing shanties. Bill kept a small boat about two sheds down from the club.

Bill was an inquisitive guy with an accounting background, and he became interested in the Club's finances. At an annual meeting, he pointed out that the Club had more liabilities than assets. Faced with a problem that no one wanted to touch, one of the sailors commented, "All right, wise guy, why don't you be the treasurer?" And with that, Bill Psaltis became Treasurer of the Cruising Yacht Club of Australia at age 22.

The promotion got Bill closer to offshore ocean racing, and—in his first Hobart in 1956—Bill's boat came in second. Bill Psaltis had caught the disease.

> I enjoyed it. It motivated me. And apart from the pleasure of being at sea and seeing the sunrise and the sunset, there's that feel that you're achieving something. Comradeship was marvelous in those days.

Four years after that, Bill was sailing on a 54-foot boat—a pretty big vessel for a thirty-year-old. His passion for sailing continued unabated, and he had his eyes set on becoming Commodore of the Cruising Yacht Club of Australia.

In keeping with tradition, becoming Commodore meant that you needed to sail your own boat to Hobart. So Bill bought a famous ocean racing boat called *Lass O'Luss* and sailed her for a number of years in the Hobart. Bill developed his skills as a sailor, and his leadership aspirations were realized as well: Accountant Psaltis became Commodore Psaltis.

It's not surprising that Bill's passion for sailing infected his three boys. Every Friday, Bill would be home from work by 5:30 in the evening. Then he, his wife, Margaret, and their three boys were off to spend most of the weekend on the boat.

There were cruises up and down the coast with the Royal Sydney Yacht Squadron. The Psaltis family was in the advanced *Spinnaker division,* restricted to those who would use the big parachute-like sails to catch the wind from behind. The boys were young—10, 8, and 6—but they were capable, and they learned quickly.

All three boys sailed, but Ed and Arthur seemed especially committed to the sport. Bill recalled:

> I've got photos of Edward as a little boy and he's always holding a boat. He was always into boats, and Arthur tagged along. It's hard to remember, but looking at the photos, Ed is always sitting next to me on the boat, wherever it may be.

Though he loved sailing, Bill's passion for the sport was almost extinguished in 1968. Sailing in a Hobart race he thought couldn't have been any worse, Bill suddenly found himself in the water, gasping for air, with his boat capsized over him. He remembers praying to God and saying: *If I ever escape this and get out with my life, I will never sail again.* When he got back, he sold *Lass O'Luss.* He had had enough. He would never go sailing again.

That resolve lasted for about a year— until Bill decided to find a boat that could take anything. He spent a week in the United States at Sparkman & Stephens, a famous yacht design firm. Working with top designers, Bill was intent on creating a boat that would be unsinkable—absolutely unsinkable. It had to be able to right itself. It couldn't let water in. And it had to win the Hobart race.

The boatbuilders were good, but they weren't magicians. Bill still has a copy of the letter he received with the discouraging news: "You want the boat to win and you want it to be unsinkable. You can have one or the other, but we can't promise both. Which do you want?"

Shivering at the memory of his brush with death in the Bass Strait, he answered without hesitation. Given the choice, Bill Psaltis wanted to be certain that he would come home on an unsinkable boat. And that's exactly what he got.

Bill got a very good, solid boat named *Meltemi,* after the Greek wind. According to mythology, Meltemi is controlled by Boreas, the god of the North Wind. It blows from the north and sweeps across Greek waters, sometimes swamping small craft and wreaking havoc along the beaches. *Meltemi* was a good racing boat, and Bill did well. He came in second in his division, but he never won the Hobart race. He took away something even more important than a trophy:

> The Hobart taught me when things are hardest, that's when you work hardest. When things are easy, you don't take it easy, you think about the next thing you're going to have to do and work it all out before it happens.[1]

Bill Psaltis retired from racing after twenty-three Hobarts, but the story of the Psaltis family was not over. It was, in fact, just beginning.

3

Nuzulu and the Start of a Winning Team

E d Psaltis has been sailing since he was two months old, and it's not surprising he shares his father's passion for the sport. As a six-year-old he looked up to his father as a "hero of the Hobart," and he became immersed in the drama of it all—following races on the radio and television.

From the beginning, Ed dreamed of sailing in a real Sydney to Hobart Race, but his father forbade it until Ed turned 18. Bill had taken Ed's older brother, Charles, when he was 18, then it was Ed's turn, and finally the turn of his younger brother, Arthur. But Bill was careful never to have all three sons on board at the same time.

In Bill's accountant way of looking at things, he worried to himself: *Boy, the whole family could disappear in one go.* He knew too well that there is always a danger for sailors venturing into offshore waters. He was willing to take chances, but he was intent on minimizing the danger: "When conditions are good it's great, but you may have to fight it out and hope for the best." Like a good accountant, Bill wasn't taking any chances.

In 1979 Ed finally got his first chance to do the Hobart, sailing with his father on the unsinkable *Meltemi*. His first race was pretty scary. Ed had heard horror stories about the Bass Strait, and he knew the race was a fairly difficult thing to do. He was excited but also apprehensive about whether he could handle it.

With the help of his father, his personal hero of the Hobart, Ed stepped up to the challenge. At the finish of the race, he walked triumphantly into the Customs House in Hobart, where he was further inspired by the walls covered with photos of the *sailing greats*—ocean racers who had met the Sydney to Hobart challenge and won. Ed had learned from one of the best, an excellent seaman and sailor who had shown him the way. Now it was up to him.

As he grew older, Ed crewed on a number of well-known yachts, gaining experience and confidence. He came to realize that he knew at least as much about sailing as many owners and decided it was time to strike out on his own.

In 1988, Ed bought his first boat, *Chameleon*. It was too light to compete offshore, but *Chameleon* became a regular challenger in Sydney Harbour winter series races. In the process, Ed began to hone his style of skippering a boat. He stripped the boat of weight wherever he could, floorboards included. His Spartan approach worked: Ed and his crew came from behind in the last race to clinch victory in their division.

Ed was hungry for a more competitive boat, one that could participate in the offshore *main event*—the Hobart. After a careful search, he found a 30-footer called *Nuzulu* and purchased it in partnership with Michael "Mix" Bencsik and another sailor, Peter Ward. Mix's knack for organization was perfect for managing the tangle of ropes and lines that inhabit the cockpit of a racing boat. They were another step closer to building a winning team.

The Birth of the Ramblers

Nuzulu was the picture of aggression. The boat's black and red color scheme was highlighted by Assegai spears along her sides. The distinctive spear—designed by the legendary Zulu king, Shaka—revolutionized tribal warfare in Southern Africa. It was the perfect symbol for Ed Psaltis and his determined crew. With her raked mast, *Nuzulu* just looked fast. And over the next five years, she was going to prove that she was.

To race in the Hobart, Ed needed a navigator. His eye caught the name of one prospect who had posted on a notice board at the Cruising Yacht Club. Bob Thomas was a commercial captain and a master mariner.

He had also done two Hobarts, and that was important. But Bob had another quality that helped differentiate him from the hundreds of aspiring sailors who wanted to do the Hobart.

The deal was sealed when Ed learned that Bob was still playing competitive rugby at the age of 39. To top it off, Bob was playing in the front row. Front rowers are sometimes the butt of rugby jokes, with the reputation of being slow, unskilled, and often a bit thick. But no one doubts that front row rugby players are tough, and Ed was looking for tough as well as smart.

Bob joined the team and was impressed by what was to become Ed's signature style of preparation. They trained for two weeks around Sydney Harbour and capped their groundwork with a trip to Bird Island. It was only 90 miles to Bird Island and back, but the journey gave the team valuable experience on the boat in nighttime conditions.

Sailing in the dark is far different than a day sail, and Ed wanted to use that difference to their advantage. Limited vision, fatigue, and lack of familiarity with a boat make everything more difficult at night, so a racing crew can be exceptional in the daylight but falter when the sun goes down. Ed and his team practiced until they had achieved an intimate knowledge of everything aboard *Nuzulu*. Sails, fittings, lines, and hatches became as familiar in pitch blackness as they were in bright sunlight.

The crew's ability to excel in every condition, along with their unceasing attention to detail, began to emerge as a core capability of the team. And there was another essential characteristic that would distinguish the team: There were *No Rock Stars.*

Though Ed had numerous chances to bring in superior sailors, he refused to push a crew member off the boat to accommodate a *heavy*—a top sailor with rock star credentials. This policy meant that the crew would come to know each other intimately. They would learn each other's strengths, as well as their limitations. Eight years later, this knowledge would contribute to their racing success. More important, it would be essential to their survival.

Three forces converged to create a cohesive *Nuzulu* team. First, their bonding was undoubtedly accelerated by shared experiences in team sports, especially rugby. The fact that most were front rowers—tough guys turned sailors—was one ingredient in their esprit de corps.

Second, the *No Rock Stars* policy cemented their bond. Everyone who consistently showed up for practice and gave their all was assured a place on the boat. There would be no Darwinian selection process. The fundamental assumption was that every competent sailor had a spot on the team. Individually they might not be sailing rock stars, but collectively they had the potential to be a *Rock Star Team*.

Finally, there was Ed Psaltis. Ed was the skipper, a superb sailor, and also the team leader. He was prone to losing his temper and could get so excited in tense situations that he would forget people's names. But Ed was a skipper who understood the power of a rock-solid team, and he worked to build that foundation from the very beginning. Loyalty from both sides, owners and crew, became the unspoken norm. And while Ed exercised leadership, he also assumed the role of player-coach, taking on the toughest jobs. Ed never asked anyone to do what he wouldn't do himself.

The weather during the 1990 Hobart, the team's inaugural race, turned out to be typical for the Hobart, but the finish was atypical for most of the crew. To Bob's great surprise, the team was awarded third place in its division. His initial ambition in racing to Hobart had been to one day crew on a vessel that placed in the top twenty. *Nuzulu* placed fifteenth overall in the race, beating many of the more favored competitors. Bob was excited. But what he didn't know was that the team was destined for accomplishments that would exceed even his wildest dreams.

Three months later, *Nuzulu* was back racing again, this time in another classic Australian challenge, the Mooloolaba Race. Held along the East Coast of Australia, the race from Sydney to Mooloolaba—an aboriginal word meaning "black water snake"—is not the Hobart; nevertheless, the 469-mile course is exceptionally demanding.

Nuzulu battled its sister ship, *Pemberton III*, tooth and nail the whole way. After *Nuzulu* recovered from a disastrous first night, rarely more than a mile separated the two boats. *Nuzulu* crossed the line first and was proclaimed overall winner. It was a tremendous victory.

Ed would have received the trophy along with Peter Ward, except for a rather long drinking session with the skipper and crew of *Pemberton III*. Although absent at the awards ceremony, Ed was eventually found curled up, fast asleep, nestled next to a coconut palm at the front entry of the club. The crew was disappointed at Ed's absence. Everyone was convinced his acceptance speech would have been exceptionally entertaining.

Nuzulu went on to win another Mooloolaba in 1994, and, though the team didn't win every race, they regularly finished among the top boats in the event. Ed and his crew were developing a reputation, and they were buoyed by the confidence that came from consistent success.

It soon became clear that the team's ability to win wasn't restricted to any particular race or any unique set of racing conditions. They were consistently placing in all the major offshore races. The somewhat esoteric race names—like *Blue Water Pointscore* and *Short Ocean Pointscore*—may seem abstract to nonsailors. But in the sailing community, Ed's standing as a talented skipper with a talented team continued to grow.

One of their proudest moments came in the 1991 Sydney to Hobart. The team had done everything right and was leading the race on handicap for quite some time. A hundred miles from the finish line, they could taste victory. All they needed to win was for Huey, the weather god, to keep smiling on them. Even a slow pace would do if the wind stayed in.

It didn't. The wind died down to nothing in Storm Bay, about 60 miles from the finish. It was their first taste of things to come when helicopters and the media swamped the boat as they reached the finish. The crew was delighted at the rousing, warm ovation from the other competitors. They had won their division and were eighth overall.

The team was on a roll, and the sky seemed to be the limit. But their real test was to come with the fiftieth Hobart. It would be their finest moment and their greatest disaster.

Rogue Wave: The Challenge That Forged a Team

The moment of truth for *Nuzulu* came in 1994. The fiftieth Hobart race brought out the largest number of boats in its history—371 yachts showed up for the event. Boats had come from every corner of the globe, and two start lines were needed to accommodate the mammoth fleet.

Nuzulu was one of the smallest entrants, a tiny boat in a big crowd. And there was one other twist to the race. The handicapping system had been changed entirely that year, so boat designs shifted to accommodate the new rating standard. This effectively meant that *Nuzulu* was in its competitive twilight. The team had a chance to perform really well, but it was also their last shot at the Tattersall's Cup on *Nuzulu*. This was a really big year.

There were other developments as well. Ed's brother Arthur had just come back from working in the United Kingdom and joined the crew for the first time in a long while. Arthur had been away for four years, and he felt like a bit of an outsider because the crew had scored so many successes in his absence. Though part of Arthur felt like a rookie, he also felt connected to the core team.

Years before, Ed, Arthur, and Mix had sailed for hours at a time on the Parramatta River near the Psaltis home. Ed would steer, barking out orders, with Arthur and Mix serving mostly as ballast and sobbing because they were afraid of getting wet. They got more and more adventurous, sailing to nearby islands. In their youthful imaginations, these journeys were smaller versions of the Sydney to Hobart Race. Not like the real thing, of course, but it was all preparation.

Joining the two Psaltis brothers was Ed's brother-in-law, John Whitfeld. "Jonno" was given the unenviable job of *forward hand,* or bowman. As the name implies, the station of the forward hand is in the very front of the boat, where waves come over the highest and hardest. In this position, Jonno was responsible for making sure sail changes went smoothly and for organizing and running the front end of the boat—most of which was underwater much of the time.

The forward hand has, by most accounts, the toughest job on an ocean racing crew. It's much like being a gymnast or a rock climber: Balance, strength, speed, and the ability to think ahead under pressure are all essential skills. Not only is the job difficult, but being a forward hand on *Nuzulu* was even tougher than on one of the big maxis. On a small boat, the bowman is constantly underwater and relentlessly knocked around as the boat careens through the waves.

Forward hands are carefully selected on a racing boat, and Jonno was one of the best. Not only was he nimble, he also demonstrated an unusual ability to withstand and absorb pain. Somehow, Jonno just handled whatever came his way and kept going without complaint. Among a collection of tough guys, he was one of the toughest.

Jonno's value as bowman was impossible to overstate, but one of his most important duties began after the race was over. He was the official crew *exchequer,* responsible for handling the communal drinking funds for the celebration in Hobart. It was a much easier job and a lot more fun than being the forward hand.

The crew was excited to be sailing out of Sydney Harbour, surrounded by a forest of white sails. It was an extraordinary sight. *Nuzulu* got a great start, and it looked like it was going to be a fun bash and a nice run down the Tasmanian coast. It didn't turn out that way.

They had a fairly light crossing through the Bass Strait, which was unusual. *Nuzulu* made it two-thirds of the way across and was one of the top boats in her division. Then a major line squall, a cigar-shaped cloud, hit *Nuzulu* in the late afternoon.

As they sailed into the night, the crew was constantly changing the sails to accommodate the uncertain wind. When the wind speed increased, they *reefed* the sails. The reef points allowed the crew to pull down the mainsail—the big sail behind the mast—effectively creating a smaller triangle exposed to the wind. When the wind slacked, they had to take out the reefing lines. On again and off again, they *flogged* the main as the sail snapped back and forth in the wind.

Nuzulu was well into the race, just north of Tasmania and in a very good handicap position, when things started to go seriously wrong. It happened as they sailed through the southernmost part of the Bass Strait, in a treacherous stretch of water called the Banks Strait. Named for an early British botanist, Joseph Banks, his legacy waters were known to be dangerous and, as the sailors sometimes put it, "confused."

Nuzulu was sailing on a knife's edge with two reefs in the mainsail. The wind was blowing hard—a steady 40 knots, with higher gusts. It was a lot of wind, though not so unusual for the Hobart. As a precautionary measure, however, they decided to take down the big mainsail and replace it with a *storm trysail*.

The storm trysail is a small sail that, as the name implies, is intended to be used in very heavy weather. The sail is small, but the job of rigging it in strong winds is not. All hands were needed for this cumbersome task, and Arthur and Mix were called up from below to help.

Before they could get their wet-weather gear on, Arthur and Mix heard Ed call out, "Bad wave!" And it *was* a bad wave. The incoming tide, pushing against the southwesterly wind, had created a *rogue wave*. It was big, but its size wasn't the only problem. The shape was the ugly part. It went straight up about 20 feet and was covered with white water and foam at the top.

The crew could feel the boat being moved by the mass of water long before the wave hit. Down below, Arthur and Mix heard the crashing noise of the water as the wave broke over them. The wave hit *Nuzulu* from the side, and the boat slid down the face of the wave and nearly turned turtle—almost completely upside down. Water rushed through the open cockpit hatch. The mast was submerged, and the keel of the boat—the weighted fin designed to keep it upright—was up in the air.

Ed was steering and, because of the heavy weather, was wearing a harness for safety. But the ironically named safety harness had wrapped around the tiller used to steer the boat. Ed was trapped, drowning and wondering when and if *Nuzulu* would right itself. Arthur and Mix were in the water as well, stuck below and kneeling on the overhead of the cabin, which had now become the floor. Arthur's mind raced: *What would happen next? Would the mast break? Would they be rolled again? Please come up*, he thought, with a silent prayer.

Up on deck, Bob was in the water just like everyone else but was his usual unflappable self. Floating in the water, he estimated the angle of *Nuzulu's* capsize to be about 130 degrees. He remembered that the life raft was securely stored in the cockpit, where it could be retrieved in case the boat failed to right itself. Then Bob thought through what might happen next.

There were three possible scenarios. First, they could be rolled 360 degrees, and the boat could fill with water and sink. Second, the mast could be ripped out by the force of the sea, with the same result. Finally, it was possible that the sail could rip from the pressure. If this happened, the boat would recover and flip back upright.

It seemed like hours, but in a matter of minutes *Nuzulu* gave a shudder and chose the last of the three options. She popped right side up, though filled with lots of water. Water was everywhere, shooting down the mast and through the hatch, and showering everyone below.

Soon everyone was on deck, coughing, spluttering, and swearing. They looked around, expecting that the mast would be gone completely, but it was still in position. The outline of the sail was perfectly in place but—with the exception of the tape at the edges—there was absolutely nothing left of the brand-new sail.

All the reefing and flogging the night before had weakened the Kevlar material so much that when the wave hit, the sail simply vanished. Had it not given way, the mast would have been ripped out of its base. In theory, the boat might eventually right itself, but that could take a long time. Then the crew would have had no choice but to dive for the life raft in the cockpit and hope for rescue. In view of the alternative, losing the sail was a sacrifice but a small price to pay.

The crew took stock of their situation. Arthur commented dryly that viewing the boat from the inside while upside down was interesting. Bob surveyed the cockpit and was reassured to see the life raft securely in place. Then he realized that the knife they would have had to use to cut the restraining line was gone.

When *Nuzulu* capsized, the knife must have slipped out of its pouch and fallen to the bottom of the Banks Strait. If they had needed to cut the lashings, they would have had to use their teeth—and the knots holding the raft could not be undone easily. Dismissing that unpleasant thought, Bob resolved to tape the knife to the life raft casing in the future.

Then Bob looked down below. Everything was in complete shambles. Bags were scattered everywhere, and the contents of his navigation station had been emptied when *Nuzulu* was unceremoniously upended. Bob saw that his precious sextant—the one he used to find their position by the sun and the stars—had come out of its case and was floating around the bottom of the boat.

Their shot at the Tattersall's Cup was over, gone. A feeling of deep disappointment settled over the crew. With no spare mainsail, they knew they had no chance of winning the race. It was a harsh realization. But their mood turned quickly from disappointment to resolve.

Arthur, in particular, felt the shift. He had pulled out of two Hobarts before, and he wasn't going to make this a third. The loss of the mainsail now became a challenge. How could they finish the race? If they weren't going to quit, what could they do so that they would be able to say that they finished the fiftieth Hobart?

No one wanted to pull out of the race, but they needed a sail that would power the boat. Then Huey smiled, and the winds shifted so that they could put up their spinnaker—a sail that ballooned out in front of the boat like a parachute, pulling *Nuzulu* along behind. Boats were passing them that never would have under normal circumstances, but *Nuzulu* was still sailing.

Then the wind shifted again and started coming directly from the front—hard on the nose. They were 40 miles from Tasman Island, with 110 miles to go. Without their large triangular mainsail, *Nuzulu* was helpless. They zigzagged across the face of the wind, but they weren't making any ground. They couldn't go forward; they could only go sideways. They were losing ground, and, at points, they were actually sailing backward.

The puzzle of how to finish the race became more complex. They had to devise a way to get power to the back part of the boat where the mainsail used to be. They had no sail material, and it seemed hopeless. Desperate, they tried a number of jury-rigged contraptions, but the sail dynamics weren't right. Even with these concoctions, their forward speed was less than half a knot. At this rate, they would have been lucky to finish the race on the 3rd of January, and it was the 29th of December. They were patient and determined, but not that patient.

The crew tried for hours, experimenting with every contraption they could think of, but nothing worked. Arthur was persistent to the point of aggravating everyone. He kept suggesting idea after idea. Ed was discouraged. *No, that won't work. No, that's no good. No, no, no. Forget about it. We're done.* But Arthur kept experimenting until he came up with a solution. In the end, it was so simple. Simple, but nobody had even considered it.

They had a small sail with a series of eyelets down the front. The holes were designed for severe conditions. If the sail were to pull out of its track, the crew could lash the sail in place. It occurred to Arthur that the eyelets could be used in a different way: With short pieces of line and knots on each end, the sail could be inserted into the track that ran up the mast. It wasn't pretty, but it worked. They started sailing and were going faster. They weren't going to win the race, but they weren't going to drop out either.

It wasn't going to be easy. Every time they changed course, the wind would shift as well. It was always on their nose. It was as if Huey was testing them. In Arthur's mind, Huey was saying, *I'm going to make an example out of you fellows.*

Arthur would not give in. He was not going to fail the test. There were only another, maybe, twenty-four hours to go, and he resolved to stick it out. *Yes,* he thought, *boats are passing us, but let's put that out of our minds. It doesn't matter. Just finishing the race will be great. We have to say that we finished the fiftieth Hobart race.*[1]

Still, it seemed so unfair. The wind kept shifting, and the more the wind changed, the more frustrated the crew became. It was tempting to give up. They were all thinking, *We can be at the pub having a beer in twelve hours or we can continue the race. At this pace, it could be three days with no trophy. We don't need to do all this. We've finished other races, and we will finish future races. Why kill ourselves?*

Even Ed was tired of it. He knew that there was a shortcut to Hobart—through the Schouten Passage then down into the Denison Canal. But taking the shortcut would mean dropping out of the race. Ed turned to Bob and said, "Look, I've had enough of this. I can't handle it anymore with these boats passing us. We're going to be the back end of the fleet, so let's forget it."

Mix, standing nearby, overheard the conversation. It was his third Hobart, and he had pulled out of the first two. He wasn't about to relinquish the third. Mix stared ahead and said, "Don't even think about pulling out of this race. I won't forgive you. We have got this far and we have to finish this race. If we do, we will remember this as one of our proudest moments."

With his unremitting resolve, Mix shook Ed out of his funk. And as hard as it was, they did keep going. This had become more than a sporting event; it was a nearly impossible psychological challenge. The team had become used to racing at the top of their game, and they had no chance of winning with their jury-rigged sail. It was demoralizing watching other boats pass them, and in the home stretch on the Derwent River things got even worse.

It was one thing to sail across the Bass Strait, where they had room to maneuver. It was another to navigate a constricted channel with limited control, trying to reach the finish line. By the time they completed the race, more than seventy boats had passed them. It was the only time in the five years of racing that *Nuzulu* was defeated by an equivalent boat in a major offshore race.

In spite of their poor performance, the Commodore of the yacht club in Hobart came out with his family to welcome them. Crews of other boats found them as well, and they knew what the crew of *Nuzulu* had accomplished. That was the victory. It was not about winning the race. It was about setting a goal and never deviating from it.

It was a defining moment in the history of the team. Though they did not win the race, they accomplished something even more important. They worked together and solved a huge problem. The experience of having finished the race using their skills and resources gave them a new sense of pride. It galvanized a spirit that the crew would need later—and upon which their survival would depend.

After the race was over, the team sat down over a drink for an intensive postmortem, reviewing everything that had happened over the last few days. Ed was feeling his age after the ordeal. He remarked, half seriously and half sarcastically, "We're getting a bit long in the tooth for a thirty-footer." Bob laughed. He was ten years older than Ed, so a logical conclusion would be that he had been too old for *Nuzulu* all along.

No one argued with Ed—they were ready for a larger and more competitive boat. But what would it take to get a boat that would give them a shot at the Tattersall's Cup? Their new challenge was to find an answer to that question.

4

The *Midnight Rambler*— A One-Off Boat

t took Ed and Bob a long time to find the right boat. They had always admired a yacht commissioned by a fellow sailor from Melbourne, Bruce Taylor. Taylor's boat, appropriately named *Chutzpah,* had been custom-built with one thought in mind: winning the Sydney to Hobart Race. Taylor was moving on to a more modern boat, so *Chutzpah* was up for grabs.

The boat had some unique features that made it just what the crew wanted in their Christmas stockings. It was sturdy and beautifully balanced, and it had a relatively short, stout mast. Taylor had lost *Chutzpah's* "stick" twice before doing the Hobart and decided it wouldn't happen again.

While the shorter mast could be a liability in the lighter winds east of Tasmania, it would be a huge asset when the going got tough. A boat like this would give them the confidence they needed to match any competitor in the rough conditions they would inevitably encounter in the Bass Strait. *Chutzpah* was much more seaworthy than anything they'd ever had before. It was a one-off boat.

They bought the boat on the 6th of December, and the Hobart was the 26th. That gave them a little less than three weeks to get the boat prepared for the race. A number of old salts told them categorically that it couldn't be done, but they were determined that the boat would be ready in time.

Through a series of fortunate coincidences and financial machinations, they got the new boat up to Sydney quickly. It arrived just in time to begin the prodigious task of getting it ready for the Hobart. There were mountains of safety, measurement, radio, and crew qualification checks. And to compound the challenge, they had to quickly familiarize themselves with the boat in Sydney. The alternative would be doing a crash course during the race—far from an ideal option.

The first time Bill Psaltis heard about the boat was a frantic call from Ed. "Dad, I bought a new boat. It's arriving from Melbourne, and I'm tied up at work. Can you go down and pick it up?"

Bill agreed to help, but when he saw the boat he was appalled. Unlike the boats he was used to, the bottom was flat with a fin hanging off "like a wind surfboard." As far as he was concerned, it was not a boat to go to Hobart, and there was not enough time to turn it into one.

Bill called Ed, and he was adamant. "You're crazy to try to get ready," he insisted. "I've done enough Hobarts to know you can't get a boat ready in three weeks. This is madness—don't do it." Bill knew his boys well, and he wasn't concerned about their competence. But he was concerned about what the sea could do to a boat, and this new one looked like a Windsurfer.

To the surprise of no one, Ed was just as stubborn as his father. He was absolutely convinced they could do it. Ed told his father he was confident that they could be ready, and his optimism was infectious. Everyone set to work preparing for the big race. Even Ed's wife, Sue, got involved in getting the new boat ready. And Bill, once he realized his son was really going to do the race, was as committed as everyone else to getting the boat set to go.

The sails were desperately in need of replacement. Almost all the *wardrobe* needed to be renewed, and coming up with the money for new sails wouldn't be easy. Looking for divine intervention, Ed approached the *Australian Financial Review*—Australia's equivalent to the *Wall Street Journal*—to ask for help. The paper agreed to sponsor the boat, and, backed by *The Fin,* they scraped together enough money for a new set of sails.

With a sponsor like the *Australian Financial Review,* Ed and Bob now had a solid financial platform that would allow them to play in the big leagues. But they were concerned about more than sails. The rigging was a problem, too.

Lines called *runners* hold up the mast, especially when the wind is coming from behind, and, if the runners fail, everything comes crashing down. No one was sure how much torture the original runners had been put through. Leaving nothing to chance, Ed decided to have new runners fabricated. It was a decision that, with the benefit of hindsight, may have saved their lives.

Beyond the sails and rigging, one other thing needed to be renewed: The boat needed a name. *Chutzpah* was a great name, but it was Bruce Taylor's selection. The decision was Ed's to make, and the choice was easy. Their new boat would be called the *AFR Midnight Rambler*. The "AFR" came from their sponsor, and the "Midnight Rambler" came from their history.

The crew always sailed well at night. In most races, that's when they jumped ahead in the standings, and their exceptional nighttime performance was a direct payoff from their diligent practice. They were good midnight sailors, so the name was a logical fit.

Midnight Rambler was a logical choice, but it was an emotional choice as well. Ed Psaltis was a devoted Rolling Stones fan—so much so that the crew speculated that his firstborn son might be named Keith, after Keith Richards. They were relieved when Ed and Sue chose Ben instead of Keith, but Ed's devotion to the Stones was undiminished. He still wanted to pay homage to the band, and there was another consideration as well. Naming the new boat *Midnight Rambler* would justify playing the Stones at maximum volume all night, every night, even while docked at the Cruising Yacht Club.

Not every member of the crew was as enthusiastic about the Rolling Stones as Ed Psaltis. But they were all excited about sailing the *AFR Midnight Rambler* in the next Hobart race. With new sails, new rigging, and a new name, the Ramblers were ready for the Hobart.

5

The Ramblers—Run-Up to the Race

The crew in the '98 race included two relative newcomers to the *Midnight Rambler* team—Chris Rockell and Gordon Livingstone. Chris was the resident "Kiwi." He was untested, but New Zealanders came equipped with reputations for being superb sailors.

This would be Chris' second Hobart race. Chris' boat had pulled out the previous year, retiring with damage. Not only was Chris a sailor, he also played front row on a provincial New Zealand rugby team. And he was the picture of what people might imagine a rugby player would look like—or maybe a Marine on a recruiting poster.

Behind his rugged good looks, Chris exuded toughness. He was strong and dependable, and he followed orders without question. Although not an experienced sailor, what Chris lacked in technical ability he made up in determination, strength, and reliability.

Chris was warm and friendly at the bar, but his tough-guy demeanor was not an act. Over drinks, he matter-of-factly shared a school-day story of being bullied by an older classmate. Years later, in a New Zealand rugby game, Chris encountered the same boy who had bullied him as a child. This time, however, Chris was all grown up and the odds were even. As he reflected on that game, he looked pensively at a scar on his knuckle. With a slight grin he noted, "I've still got the scar where his tooth got stuck in my fist."

Gordon Livingstone—"Gordo"—was the second new member of the team. He had known Arthur from their workdays at Coopers & Lybrand, and was eager to join the crew. In his first sail on the *Midnight Rambler,* however, Gordo was intimidated by Ed's singular focus and passion.

Gordo's baptism by fire took place several years before the '98 race. His initiation came during a short race off the Sydney Heads—the high cliffs that mark the entrance to the harbor. As a rank amateur, Gordo was given a relatively simple job at the back of the boat near Ed. Unfortunately for Gordo, he kept making mistakes with his relatively straightforward assignment. And Ed, who confesses to a heightened level of excitability during races, shouted at Gordo nonstop for hours.

In spite of this rough start, Ed saw in Gordo a desire to learn, and he invited him back. Others might have balked at the invitation, but Gordo was not a quitter. He wanted to give it another go, and he was drawn to Ed's passion. Gordo was also attracted by the strength of the bonds that held the team together and by their staunch commitment to getting things right. Gordo liked what he saw, and he was willing to do whatever it took to become a part of the *AFR Midnight Rambler* crew.

Though both Gordo and Chris were new kids on the block, there were no inner and outer circles. There were "no Hollywood boys," as Ed put it. Everyone was respected, and all seven crew members were treated as equals.

Everyone brought a unique combination of skills. Gordo was a witty guy who could break the ice by cracking a joke. Sometimes his jokes were told at the expense of others, but he delivered the punch lines in a way that took the edge off difficult situations. Chris brought his strength and determination, and both he and Gordo believed in *the cause*—the team's commitment to teamwork and excellence.

Their assimilation into the team was accelerated by Mix, who brought his own unique style. Mix's formal role on the boat was in *the Pit.* Stationed in the cockpit, he was responsible for organizing the *halyards*—ropes that are fed in from the mast to raise and lower the sails. Without organization, the halyards and the backstays supporting the mast could easily become a tangled mess. Not only would the snarl interfere with performance. It could also become a dangerous trap for sailors trying to move around the boat in heavy weather.

Mix was a great pitman, but his informal role was equally important. Mix patiently translated Ed's sometimes frantic instructions to new members of the crew. He was a buffer between Ed—who could get so carried away that he would yell obscenities—and the rookies, who were eager to perform but confused about what they were supposed to be doing.

With Mix as an intermediary, Chris and Gordo came to understand that Ed's outbursts were nothing personal. It was simply that Ed was extraordinarily focused and emotional about sailing. Once that became clear, Ed's intensity took on a different light. Instead of a liability, it became a huge asset. It was one of the reasons people loved sailing with Ed as a skipper.

Polishing the Stove

The crew also came to appreciate Ed's methodical approach to preparing for the Hobart. The routine never changed. Before each race, Ed created an extensive checklist that inevitably ran to many pages. Each item was assigned to a crew member, and everything had to be checked before the start of the race.

Ed's wife, Sue, matter-of-factly describes him as obsessive about making sure that all the items on the list are in place and done properly. Sue was responsible for rounding up first aid kits, fire extinguishers, and other safety equipment. She was as devoted as Ed to flawless preparation. If something was missing, it needed to be replaced. If something had expired, it needed to be changed. Nothing was left to chance.

The crew went through *AFR Midnight Rambler* with a fine-tooth comb. They got to know every inch of the boat, inside and out. And as always, they stripped out every ounce of excess weight. At one point, Ed instructed Bob to count the number of bolts. Even an extra screwdriver in the toolbox required special permission.

Bob understood Ed's zealous devotion to eliminating extra weight, but Ed's determination also amused him. Flawless preparation was functional, but it was one of the skipper's idiosyncrasies.

Bob delights in recounting one occasion on which Ed was allegedly caught violating his own rule. On a previous voyage, Ed had given Bob considerable grief in a dispute about a plastic sextant. Bob wanted to take the sextant as a backup for navigation in case their electronic instruments failed. The sextant weighed all of 2 ounces. But Ed complained about the unnecessary weight, and he was so insistent that Bob finally acquiesced and left the sextant behind.

Later, according to Bob, he discovered a men's magazine in Ed's sailing pack. Bob took great pains to point out that the magazine weighed three times as much as the sextant. Ed denies ownership of the magazine, insisting that it was part of a "goody bag" given to each boat. Whatever the truth of the matter, the incident provides ammunition for ongoing banter between Bob and Ed.

Part of the crew's preparation involved cleaning everything that they could get their hands on, and one of Gordo's assignments was polishing the boat's kerosene stove. The task involved taking the stove out of its storage spot in the cabin and polishing the stainless steel until it glistened.

The task was clear-cut, and Gordo had no question about what was expected: The stove had to look like it was just out of the box from the store. Gordo dutifully took on the assignment, but he thought the task was somewhat odd. He had enough sailing experience with Ed to know food preparation is a low priority during a race, and he doubted that the stove would ever be used.

Puzzled, Gordo kept wondering why he had been assigned the task. He finally came to realize that polishing the stove was simply an icon. It was part of the mental preparation, and an integral part of Ed's conditioning program.

The Hobart would be tough on both the crew and the equipment, and Ed's goal was to instill confidence. Before an important race, they needed to be sure that the boat was prepared. They needed to know that every nook and cranny on the boat was as tight and shipshape as it could possibly be. Nothing could be ignored, and the gleaming stove was a symbol of their devotion to preparation. At the time, no one knew that their lives would soon depend on this meticulous attention to detail.

Getting the equipment ready was important, but preparation involved more than just the boat and its gear. Team members had to be ready as well, both physically and mentally. Each crew member engaged in a personalized program of physical training. They ran, they swam, and they lifted weights. Anticipating the demands of the race, they pushed themselves to increase their strength and stamina.

Seamless Teamwork

Along with individual preparation, the crew worked to develop their capacity for seamless teamwork. Some of their training took place in the relative protection of Sydney Harbour, but much of it occurred outside Sydney Heads and far offshore.

They spent time on tasks that were very basic. They practiced, for example, reefing the mainsails. Reefing involves using short pieces of rope to pull down the bottom of the sail and reduce the area exposed to the wind. The job of reefing isn't technically complicated, and it is unnecessary in light winds and sunshine. But in heavy weather and rough seas, their ability to reef the sails could be critical.

Onlookers who saw the team performing these maneuvers in good weather were often amused. Many wondered, *Why bother?* But each time the crew went through the process, the steps became more familiar. The Ramblers practiced these routines repeatedly until they could hardly stand them. Then they would go through the steps again, making sure that the patterns were completely ingrained.

As a result of their exhaustive preparation, the crew learned to work with seamless precision under all conditions. It was tedious, uncomfortable, and boring. But the time would come when they would be thankful for their effort.

6

The Aussie Competitors

The Ramblers were not the only ones preparing for the Sydney to Hobart Race in 1998. As usual, the fleet comprised a diverse mix of vessels—including one venerable boat that had been competing since the first race in 1945.[1]

The *Winston Churchill* was a strong wooden boat, and Jim Lawler, a close friend of Bill Psaltis, was on the crew. Jim was one of the finest sailors that Bill had ever met, and the *Winston Churchill* was the kind of boat that Bill felt good about. If he had been asked to sail on it that year, he would have done it in a flash.

Richard Winning, the owner of the boat, had spent a quarter of a million dollars rebuilding the famous yacht. Since its inaugural race, the *Winston Churchill* had sailed in fifteen Hobarts and circled the world twice. Built in Hobart in 1942, the yacht symbolized classic sailing at its best.

With its teak deck, brass fittings, and white hull, the boat stood in stark contrast to the *Rambler*'s fiberglass surfboard. With the latest modifications—including a heavy timber mast fitted with a lighter aluminum section and a brand-new set of sails—the *Winston Churchill* seemed to represent the best of the old and the new. Bill Psaltis would have been much more confident had his boys been aboard a boat like that instead of their sleek racing machine.

Winston Churchill was an imposing boat, but its real power came from its distinguished crew. In addition to Jim Lawler, John "Steamer" Stanley was aboard. Stanley had sailed in fifteen Hobarts and had quite a record. He began his sailing career at age 11, sailed in numerous long-distance races, and had crewed in the America's Cup. He worked for six months on restoring the vintage boat, and Steamer had recruited others to form a first-rate crew. Two of Richard Winning's childhood friends, John Dean and Michael Bannister, had even joined the crew for the race.

Although a huge amount of time and money had been poured into the boat, the restoration effort may have been imperfect. A former Navy sailor, Greg Bascombe, had just finished scrubbing the bottom of several boats when he noticed something unusual along the waterline of the *Winston Churchill*. Bascombe—aka "Mega" because of his 300-pound weight—swam closer to examine the boat more carefully. To his practiced eye, it appeared that a small section of caulking, used to seal the wooden planks, was missing.

Bascombe was alarmed at the sight of what seemed to be a flaw in the *Churchill's* watertight integrity. Though the gap was small, perhaps a quarter of an inch, it could expand in heavy weather. He got out of the water and walked over to the *Churchill's* dock. Approaching several men he thought were members of the crew, he warned, "There's some caulking missing. You should make sure the owner knows about it." Bascombe then left, satisfied that he had shared his concerns with the crew. Richard Winning, however, never got the message. Later, no one who sailed on the boat could recall the conversation.

The *Sword of Orion,* owned by Rob Kothe, was a very different design. It lacked the classic lines of the *Winston Churchill,* but it was a superb racing boat. Like Richard Winning, Rob Kothe was a successful entrepreneur. Unlike Winning, however, Kothe was a relative newcomer to the world of sailing.

Kothe bought his first boat in 1997 and achieved some measure of success in that year's Hobart. Buoyed by a second place in his division, Kothe was eager to join the ranks of the sailing greats that he had heard about as a small child. Kothe purchased the *Sword* with the intent purpose of taking home the Tattersall's Cup.

On the surface, there were a number of similarities between *Sword of Orion* and *AFR Midnight Rambler. Sword* was longer—43 feet to the *Rambler's* 35—but both boats were *balsa core* fiberglass construction with Kevlar sails. They were typical of the modern boat designs that worried Bill Psaltis.

As on the *AFR Midnight Rambler,* some members of *Sword*'s crew were expert racers with extensive sailing experience. Like Ed Psaltis, Rob Kothe insisted on a disciplined regimen of training and preparation. *Sword*'s schedule included at least two races and one practice sail each week. Kothe required crew members to be on time, to exercise, and to lose weight. And like Psaltis, Kothe was focused on everything that might add a few additional pounds to the boat. He replaced the *Sword*'s brass barometer case with a plastic one, and he was always looking to improve the boat's equipment. Finally, like Ed Psaltis, Rob Kothe was a perfectionist. The similarities ended there.

Kothe not only lacked sailing experience, he was also new to the world of team sports. He had flown gliders in airborne regattas, which he saw as similar to sailing because it was competitive and because gliders rely on the wind. But gliding is an individual sport. The pilot controls everything, and the aircraft obeys the pilot's commands without question. Ocean racing is an entirely different sport, one that demands the highest level of coordination among team members with diverse roles.

Though Kothe may not have fully grasped the importance of teamwork, he understood the need for sailing talent. Kothe recruited Darren "Dags" Senogles to take care of the *Sword,* and used his athletic skills in the demanding position of bowman.

Even more important than a talented bowman, *Sword* needed an experienced helmsman. In late September, just months before the race, a mutual friend introduced Kothe to Steve Kulmar.

Kulmar had the kind of sailing pedigree that Kothe was after. Kulmar had been sailing since childhood and had won Australian and world championships. He had done seven Fastnets and seventeen Hobarts—including three in which his boat had won the Tattersall's Cup. The two seemed to hit it off, and Kulmar agreed to join *Sword* as its principal helmsman.

Kulmar wanted to win as much as Kothe, and he aggressively sought additional talent. In 1997, Kulmar had sailed in the U.K. Admiral's Cup with an enthusiastic Olympic sailor named Glyn Charles.

Charles was an accomplished sailor who had aspirations of representing Britain in the Sydney Olympics and eventually winning an Olympic medal. He had impressed Kulmar with both his sailing ability and his personality. Charles' specialty was small boats. But he had competed in four Admiral's Cups, and he had sailed on boats ranging from dinghies to ocean racers.

In 1998, Charles was headed to Australia as a sailing coach for the British Olympic team. As soon as Kulmar found out that Charles was going to be in Sydney, he e-mailed him an invitation to join the crew. Charles replied with a tentative acceptance, to be finalized after discussions in Sydney.

On December 10, just a little over two weeks from the start of the race, Glyn Charles arrived from London. The morning he landed, Charles met Kulmar and Kothe at the Cruising Yacht Club in Sydney. After an extended conversation, the British sailor said he would think about it, and two days later agreed to join the crew. Because of prior commitments, however, he would not be able to train with the crew until December 22—just four days before the race. This would be his first Hobart.

Kothe's decision to bring Charles on board was not universally acclaimed. One young sailor, Tracy Roth, had planned to do the Hobart on *Sword*. She was an accomplished sailor who had done five Atlantic crossings, but she was not a sailing heavy like Glyn Charles. Tracy was cut from the crew, a casualty of Kothe's search for rock stars.

Others who remained on the team were also upset by the decision to bring Kulmar and Charles on board. These crew members had sailed together to train for the event, and they had followed Kothe's strict rules. They hadn't even met the new rock stars.

Their status on *Sword* had now been altered, and there were disagreements about decisions that had already been made. Should they take two mainsails, or stick with one? Should they use a two-watch system in which half the crew was on duty and the other half free, or should they use a three-watch system in which only a third of the crew would be completely free to rest?

The crew of the *Sword* would begin the race with disagreement about these and other questions. Opinions were split. Perhaps most critically, they would sail with unanswered questions about who was really in charge of the boat. Was it Kothe, the official skipper and owner? Or was it Steve Kulmar, the sailing rock star? And where did Glyn Charles fit into the decision-making hierarchy?

By race time on the 26th, 115 boats had registered for the Sydney to Hobart Race. Their names were as assorted as the design of the boats themselves: *Atara, Business Post Naiad, Miintinta, Pippin, Renegade, Siena, Solo Globe Challenger, Team Jaguar Infinity III, T42 Solandra, VC Offshore*

Stand Aside, and *Secret Men's Business*. Bearing a name that would later cause heartbreak and confusion during the race, a boat called the *Midnight Special* would be competing alongside *AFR Midnight Rambler*.

As in every race, the biggest boats—the maxis—would be competing for line honors, trying to be the first to cross the finish line. The largest boat in the fleet was *Nokia,* an 83-foot maxi ketch. Almost every other boat in the race was rigged as a sloop, with two triangular sails. *Nokia* had three, with an extra mast and small sail in the back.

One local favorite was *Brindabella,* skippered by Australian financial executive George Snow. Snow had begun sailing on a man-made lake in Canberra and had moved to Sydney so he could be closer to the water. He developed a reputation as a tough competitor who truly enjoyed the camaraderie of the team sport. A coach as well as a skipper, he was dedicated to ocean racing and had persisted despite setbacks.

In the 1996 race, *Brindabella* did so well that it appeared she would win the esteemed trifecta: crossing the line first with line honors, being declared overall winner on handicap, and breaking the race record with the shortest time to Hobart. When all seemed to be going so well, the mast broke and *Brindabella* was out of the race. Although discouraged, the next year George Snow was back. And in 1997, he achieved what had been a lifetime dream. *Brindabella* crossed the finish line first.

At 75 feet, *Brindabella* was more than twice the size of the *AFR Midnight Rambler.* Like the crew of the *Rambler,* however, Snow's team of twenty-one comprised primarily amateur sailors. They were not novices, and many in the crew had done the Hobart before. But Snow did not hide his disdain for other skippers who might show up at the last minute to step onto a boat consisting of paid professionals. For Snow, "buying the team" was not an option.

Others in the race did not share Snow's reservations about using wealth to buy hired guns and rock stars. *Brindabella's* biggest threat to a second line honors win was anything but amateur. The crew of *Sayonara* consisted of twenty of the best professional sailors in the world.

7

Sayonara—
The Big Yank Tank

arry Ellison became reacquainted with sailing relatively late in his
life.[1] In 1994, Ellison was working out on a StairMaster alongside
a friend, David Thompson, who casually asked Ellison if he sailed.
The question got Ellison's attention. He had been an avid sailor, but had
given up the sport.

Ellison first learned to sail when he came to California in the mid-60s.
He took to sailing right away, and his enthusiasm led him to remark that
he attended the University of California and "majored in sailing." Ellison
began with a tiny 14-foot "plastic boat," later graduating to a 24-foot
boat, and finally a 34-foot racing sloop.

Ellison also read stories about sailing. He was fascinated by people
like Robin Lee Graham, who sailed his 24-foot boat, the *Dove*, around
the world. And Ellison loved sailing enough to borrow $25,000 to pur-
chase the 34-foot *Galilee Hitchhiker*. His sailing adventures ended rather
abruptly, however, when his first wife, Adda, came close to going overboard during a California race.

It wasn't just that incident that created problems. Adda was so worried about the money that Ellison was spending on his sailing habit that
she sought counseling to deal with her anxiety. Ellison was finally forced

to sell the boat, having concluded that "eating came before sailing in Maslow's hierarchy of needs."

All that changed when Oracle went public in 1986. The lower-order needs of safety and security had reached an entirely different level. Ellison was now rich, and he could afford to buy whatever toys he found appealing. He proudly proclaimed, "I'm now world-class at buying things. I moved from Rolex to Patek Philippe. I still have a Mercedes, a couple of them actually, plus the new BMW Z8, a McLaren F1, and a Bentley. It took me a while to learn how to spend money, but once I got started, I discovered I have a real talent for it."[2]

Ellison had acquired considerable talent for buying things, but purchasing another sailboat never entered his mind until Thompson's question. Then, when the conversation turned to racing—and when his friend raised the possibility of sailing on one of the ultrafast maxi boats—everything changed. With money no longer an object, the world of sailing reentered Larry Ellison's life.

It could have been something else, of course. Ellison had contemplated buying the New York Yankees but gave up the idea because he couldn't play on the team. With sailing, it would be different. He would own the boat and he would hire the crew. And if Larry Ellison wanted to drive, nobody would tell him it was against the rules or that he wasn't qualified.

Ellison was not a person to do things halfway, and he set about using his money to buy the best of everything. He found Bruce Farr, a world-famous yacht designer in Annapolis, Maryland. He signed up Mike Cookson and Steve Wilson in New Zealand, known for their expertise with sails and rig design. Ellison found what he considered to be the best in every aspect of sailing and put his team to work building what he hoped would be the fastest maxi in the world. His new boat, *Sayonara,* was "designed as an all-out race boat whose only purpose was winning."[3]

Ellison hired an experienced sailor, Bill Erkelens, who agreed to live in New Zealand for the six months that it would take to build this extraordinary boat. And when *Sayonara* was finally launched, Erkelens became Ellison's *campaign manager,* accompanying him on races as he got the feel of the 80-foot racing machine.

Ellison immediately set his sights on "winning" the 1995 Sydney to Hobart Race. He was not concerned about being declared the overall winner, holding the Tattersall's Cup, or having *Sayonara*'s hull on the wall of the Cruising Yacht Club. These were things that passionate sailors with smaller boats might aspire to, but Ellison wanted to cross the finish line first. The distinction between line honors and overall winner was not an issue. If *Sayonara* made it to Hobart first, Ellison could forever say—without qualification—that he had won the Sydney to Hobart Race.

Sayonara did take line honors in '95, and the taste of victory only whetted Ellison's appetite for more. No matter that the overall winner that year was a boat from Victoria named *Terra Firma*—half the size of *Sayonara*—and that Scott Carlile and Dean Wilson had been awarded the Tattersall's Cup. Larry Ellison had been first across the line, so he had won the Sydney to Hobart Race. And he was ready to do it again in 1998.

In '95, Ellison was a novice and far from an accomplished helmsman. Winning line honors a second time would prove that Ellison had achieved his rightful status as a sailing heavy. It would show just how much he had improved as a driver. It would give him the ability to showcase his skills. It was the perfect chance to prove himself.

Then there was one other reward. It would also give Ellison a chance to steal the race record from Hasso Plattner, a fellow software mogul who had sailed his boat, *Morning Glory,* to line honors victory in 1996. Ellison and Plattner had a much less than friendly competition, as evidenced by one regatta in which Plattner was said to have saluted *Sayonara* by dropping his pants and displaying his posterior for all to see. Plattner later denied that the incident ever happened, but it became fodder for an ongoing feud between the two competitors.[4]

Altogether, it is easy to see why the 1998 race had such appeal to Ellison. It was a unique opportunity to demonstrate his sailing skills, to set a new race record, and—symbolically, at least—to return Plattner's backside insult. It was a win-win-win, with little downside risk.

Of course, there was the reputation of the Hobart as the Everest of offshore ocean racing. But Ellison had little concern about physical danger. Though the Hobart was a demanding race, in Ellison's view, it was "one of those events that everyone thinks is cool because it's dangerous. But it's not really a dangerous race. I mean, it's not life-threatening, it's just a hard, demanding race. You have to be reasonably fit to cope with the pounding in Bass Strait, but it's pretty unlikely you'll get hurt."[5]

So the stage was set for Ellison's victory in the '98 race, but his formula for winning was incomplete. Though he felt that his skills had improved greatly, Ellison left nothing to chance. He had the best boat in the world as his platform, but he couldn't sail *Sayonara* by himself. He would need more than skill and Bill Erkelens. He would need a world-class team, the best that money could buy. And he found that team in New Zealand.

With his talent for spending money, Ellison hired a crew that included ten members of the New Zealand America's Cup team—the same crew that had sailed *Black Magic* to victory in 1995 and who took the trophy back from the Americans. Ellison was willing to pay top dollar for talent, and he was fully prepared to pay hundreds of thousands of dollars to have the sailing equivalent of the New York Yankees at his command.

Ellison now had the best boat and, in his view, the best crew in the world. All he had to do was to get *Sayonara* to Sydney by December 26. As he did in '95, Ellison solved that problem with a container ship that transported *the Big Yank Tank*—as Australian sailors derisively nicknamed *Sayonara*—across the Pacific.

Poised for victory, Ellison arrived in Sydney a week before the race, accompanied by his then girlfriend, Melanie Craft. Craft did not share Ellison's confidence that the Sydney to Hobart Race was simply a demanding event that others perceived to be dangerous. There was some talk that a major storm could be brewing, and she tried—as she had done repeatedly before—to discourage Ellison from competing.

Larry Ellison brushed aside her concerns, confident that the Sydney to Hobart Race was only perceived to be dangerous and that there was nothing to worry about. He was going to do the race, and it was going to be cool. Very cool.

8

Uncertain Weather— Buster or Bomb?

It was a busy time in the Psaltis household. Sue Psaltis and the other spouses and companions of the crew were engaged in a frenzy of activity. One of the biggest jobs was organizing meals for the race. Everything had to be frozen, and the menu was worked out well in advance so the food would be ready on December 26. When the meals were done, Sue made sure that she had a complete crew list with contact numbers in case messages had to be passed along to people at home.

Ed and Bob were preoccupied with getting the new boat in top condition and taking care of the last-minute details that always precede a big race. As he did every year, Bob also set up Sue's computer so she could track the progress of the *Rambler* on the Cruising Yacht Club's website.

At 9 a.m. on the 23rd of December, Ed and Bob attended a compulsory weather briefing at the club. A Bureau of Meteorology representative talked about various computer models and described some of the things that might happen over the next four days leading up to the race.

The forecast[1] at the briefing was for a quick ride down the coast, but with a gale, at the least, in the Bass Strait. Bob thought, *If we add a 50 percent fudge factor, which is pretty reliable, we'll likely be in strong gale to storm conditions.* Ed remembers one model predicting a chance of an *East Coast Bomb*—a weather pattern in which a cold front moving north combines with a warm front heading south. If that happened, the result would be a mini cyclone off the southeast coast of Australia. In any case, both Ed and Bob left the briefing thinking they would encounter strong gale to storm conditions. It might be a tough race—but they had done tough Hobarts before.

Christmas Day was an exciting time for the children but not a particularly relaxed time for their parents. It was a mixture of fun and opening presents, combined with poring over charts and finalizing last-minute details of who was going to do what on which watch.

Sue was nervous. Some races, like the Mooloolaba, were okay. They were relatively close to shore, with no big offshore stretch like the Bass Strait. If anything went wrong, the crew could be rescued. But the Lord Howe and the Hobart were different. They were more frightening because the boats were farther away from shore.

Sue felt she could relax a bit after the start, but until they passed the Sydney Heads she would be more stressed than any of the crew in the race. Once they were out of Sydney Harbour, she could, as her mother-in-law used to joke, " 'Ease off the backstay' and let out a big sigh that they've gone."

The day after Christmas, Boxing Day, was the kickoff. Once the crew bags and food had been delivered to the boat, it was Bob's job as navigator to meet with the Bureau of Meteorology rep and hear detailed weather information firsthand. Traditionally, the department would set up a table at the Cruising Yacht Club with printed reports and projected summary weather analyses. As Bob approached the table, however, it was obvious that something had recently changed. He watched as the "Met officer" picked up an entire stack of paperwork and threw it into the trash can beside him.

The meteorologist was shaking his head back and forth as he spoke matter-of-factly: "All our predictions are now obsolete. Everything has changed. You are heading into some very nasty weather." What had started out as a strong wind forecast had now increased to a gale and could even become a storm. It wasn't clear exactly what was going to happen, and nothing was mentioned about the size of the waves.

Bob returned to the *Rambler* and gave Ed the news. "Forget all the stuff about an easy race," he said. "This is going to be a very tough one. We've got some major s—t happening down the track."

The two talked it over, and finally Ed said, "Okay, it's going to happen and we've been here before, we'll just have to handle it." The two partners were aligned. The crew usually did very well when things got tough. They had planned for rough weather and prepared their boat for bad conditions. They knew from the initial forecast that it would be a "hard" Hobart, but both felt confident they could make it, even if conditions worsened.

Will it be A, B, or C?

Not surprisingly, Larry Ellison had much more detailed information about the weather. He had purchased the services of a weather expert, a private forecaster named Roger "Clouds" Badham. Clouds, who had been forecasting for sailboat racers since 1977, had a distinguished client list. Now he was focused on helping *Sayonara,* another maxi yacht, *Wild Thing,* and other boats that could afford his services.

A week before the race, Clouds began studying an array of computer models and developing scenarios of what might happen. There was the American model, which predicted the most dangerous outcome. There was the Australian model, which seemed less threatening. And there was the European model, which had been most accurate in the past and was of less concern.

Clouds typically ranked the models A, B, or C, in accordance with his assessment of how likely they were to be right. This year, it was a gamble. But twelve hours prior to the start of the race, Clouds decided to go with the regional Australian model, which predicted that the oncoming low-pressure area would be south of the Bass Strait. There was still some uncertainty, however, and he made that clear to his clients at a last-minute briefing on Saturday morning.

Not everyone had the budget to afford Clouds' services, but word of a worst-case scenario started to spread. John Mooney, skipper of the 38-foot *Avanti,* saw Clouds talking to one of his clients.[2] Mooney maneuvered into a position to eavesdrop on their conversation. He learned that one of the models was predicting more than a southerly buster. It was forecasting a southerly *bomb,* with much higher wind speeds. Clouds hastened to add that this was not the most likely option, and he thought that the fleet would get winds of 40 to 50 knots. But the possibility of a weather bomb had Mooney's attention.

Putting aside any thoughts of the days ahead, the crew of the *AFR Midnight Rambler* began stowing provisions. Water bottles were frozen so no ice would be needed. The meals, which consisted of sandwiches and precooked cold dinners, were packed and marked in chronological order of serving. Had weather forecasting been an exact science, however, they would have saved themselves the trouble of thinking about meals. Food would be a very low priority during the next thirty hours.

9

AFR Midnight Rambler— And They're Away!

The morning of the race, Ed and Bob were down at the boat early. One by one, the other Ramblers showed up. Chris was first, as usual, followed by Mix, and then Gordo, then the smiling Jonno. Well after the designated arrival time of 11 a.m., all the remaining crew had arrived. Everyone, that is, except for Arthur.

Arthur had planned to catch a flight from a family Christmas vacation in the town of Dubbo, in central New South Wales, over 300 miles away. It would be a tight schedule in a perfect world, and travel from the outback is far from perfect. Now Arthur was late and everyone started to get concerned. Ed was particularly upset. Just as Bob was about to ask Ed if he should be worried about a coronary, Arthur showed up. He walked briskly up to the boat and enthusiastically asked, "What's all the fuss about?"

With that hurdle crossed, the crew stowed their bags, a relatively simple task. In keeping with Ed's "travel light" philosophy, only one spare shirt was allowed. After the foul-weather gear was hung up, the nearly empty bags were stowed at predetermined spots, where their almost negligible weight would be of greatest value as ballast.

With everything stowed, the crew said the first of their good-byes to family and friends, then gravitated to the Cruising Yacht Club for the last hot cup of coffee they would enjoy for days.

With that final taste of civilization, the crew headed to the boat, which was conveniently docked right in front of the clubhouse. There were the usual additional farewells, and Ed's father, Bill, gave his traditional rousing pep talk. Then the Ramblers cast off the dock lines and began their journey, playing a game of "dodgem-boats" through the marina and out into the harbor.

Sue Psaltis and the others waved good-bye from the dock. She continued to wave as the boat motored out into Sydney Harbour. She watched as her husband, her brother, her brother-in-law, and her good friends disappeared from view. Sue relaxed a little, but the relief was mixed with worry.

In previous years, Sue would then drive out to the Sydney Heads and watch the start of the race. She liked seeing the panorama of sails making their hard right turn and heading south. This year she had a one-year-old and a two-year-old, and it was too complicated to make the trip. It also felt like saying good-bye twice, and once was enough.

Sue headed over to the home of Mix and his wife, Annabel—whom everyone called "Tink." The two wives watched the start of the race on television. As always, it was a somewhat disappointing show. The TV cameras focused on the big maxis, and especially *Sayonara.* The smaller boats were not so spectacular and got much less attention.

Out of sight of the cameras, *AFR Midnight Rambler* made its way through the armada of spectator craft that would dog them all the way through to the *exclusion zone* where nonracers were prohibited. Despite the dedication of the police, a few spectator boats always created challenges with their unexpected maneuvers and the accompanying close calls.

The race hadn't started, but the maneuvering required concentration. It would be a nightmare to have some lunatic ruin the race before they even made it to The Heads. Months of labor, sacrifice, and expense would all be down the drain.

Finally, the *Rambler* broke through to open water and had enough room to hoist the new mainsail. It went up without any major snags, and the sail looked terrific with the logo of the *Australian Financial Review* emblazoned in bold letters. After the race, Bob mused that "if the sail had known what it was going to be in for, it would probably have tried to stay hidden in its bag."

Though the TV cameras were largely focused elsewhere, there was one bit of good fortune. Just as they raised their new spinnaker, the television helicopter flew by, and the black sail blossomed—displaying the logo of the *Australian Financial Review* for all to see. The Ramblers were pleased by the timing, and so were their sponsors at The *Fin.*

With ten minutes to go, activity at the starting line was at a fever pitch. Navigators and tacticians were focused on their stopwatches. Adrenaline was pumping. All 115 boats were jockeying for the most advantageous position, and it seemed to Bob that everyone wanted to be exactly where the *AFR Midnight Rambler* was located.

Even if they were in a perfect position at the start, *Sayonara* or some other maxi could roll over them with their superior speed. But there was little that could be done about that problem. It was simply one of the many disadvantages that the smaller competitors had to tolerate. All they could do was to fight for a good opening position, and they were intently focused on doing exactly that.

The five-minute gun was the harbinger of the mayhem that was about to unfold. Yacht racing starts are both the best and the most stressful part of the competition. They match any sport for the sheer adrenaline rush, and the Ramblers were feeling the surge.

Almost every boat in the southern hemisphere seemed headed toward the *Rambler,* which was sparring with competitors on the right-hand side of the line. Being small was their one asset, because it made them so maneuverable. They were able to weave through openings between the larger craft, while staying close to the starting line. This bobbing and weaving was much more difficult for the maxis.

A perfect start would mean reaching the starting line just as the canon signaling the beginning of the race went off. That's what the Ramblers were hoping for, but they began their run to the starting line too early. In addition, they had let too many boats get on their windward side—the direction from which the wind was blowing—and they were getting turbulent air from the other sails. This uneven flow of wind created problems, making it harder to adjust their own sails.

Every boat was preoccupied with the same challenge of maneuvering to be in a perfect position, but not crossing the line prematurely. Boats that were too quick off the mark would be given a significant penalty with an adjustment to their handicap. It was a disadvantage that everyone tried to avoid.

Nokia and *Sword of Orion* had been playing cat and mouse, with *Sword* cast in the role of mouse. Less than a minute before the gun, *Nokia* headed directly to *Sword* on a collision course. According to sailing rules of the road, *Sword* had the "right-of-way." But it was only at the last minute that the maxi swerved, making a sudden turn to avoid collision.

The turn came too late, and *Nokia*'s bow crashed into the rear of the smaller boat. Nokia scraped its way up the side of *Sword* with the cringe-inducing sound of steel against fiberglass. The crew of *Sword* was enraged, as one crew member took out a knife and threatened to cut down *Nokia*'s sails. Kothe raised a red protest flag, and Dags attempted to repair the damage to the stanchions that support the lifelines.

Nokia's sudden turn forced all the boats on the right side of the starting line to take evasive action. They escaped the collision, but it was like a highway pileup. The air was filled with screams and obscenities as boats took desperate actions to avoid crashing into each other.

Nokia blamed *Sword,* saying the collision resulted because the smaller boat came in too close and the maxi couldn't maneuver. At the moment, it was a huge source of contention. Robert Kothe sent an e-mail to the CYCA, reporting that *Sword of Orion* had sustained "severe damage" and that there was a "compression crease" in the mast.

Later in the afternoon, Kothe realized that what appeared to be serious damage to the mast was simply a rub mark. And when the race was over, no protest would be filed. The events of the next days would dwarf the importance of the collision.

The *Sword* had been damaged and other boats delayed, but the Ramblers received a gift. The confusion had provided them with a much appreciated clean run to the starting line. Watching the melee, Bob thought, *I'll have to buy that bloke a beer in Hobart. Then again, I probably won't see him because he'll be four days in the protest room being hung and quartered.*

At 1 p.m. the final gun went off, and the 54th Sydney to Hobart Race had begun. One hundred fifteen boats and their eager crews fought their way to the starting line.

The *AFR Midnight Rambler* was in a perfect position—on the far right end of the line, with clean air. And the Ramblers had a plan. They would make a right turn out of the Sydney Heads, then it was a straight shot to Tasmania—only 628 miles to go.

Within limits, they could control their own destiny by sailing right on the edge of the spectator boats. Then, once they made it to Watsons Bay, the course would widen just enough to make it easier to avoid the larger boats. They would round the first mark and speed straight for the famous marker "Z" offshore.

That was the plan, but plans go awry. After *AFR Midnight Rambler* passed the Z, a 50-foot pleasure boat came out of nowhere, spoiling the wind and creating turbulent air. They could see the skipper was annoyed that a small yacht was in his way, but he was soon gone. *He's probably sailing northeast to Caledonia*, thought Bob. The pleasure boat was more fortunate than he could know, given what lay ahead for the sailors headed south.

10

Sayonara—The Best Professional Sailors on the Planet

As *AFR Midnight Rambler* maneuvered before the starting gun, Larry Ellison had his own concerns.[1] This was his moment. He was standing proudly in the limelight at *Sayonara*'s wheel, the focus of hundreds of thousands of spectators and television cameras. This was his chance to prove that he had arrived as a world-class ocean racer. But it wouldn't be easy. Ellison would have to constantly tack the boat. A tacking maneuver—changing direction so the bow of the boat passes through the wind and the sails swing to the opposite side—requires timing and coordination. Zigzagging through hundreds of other boats was dicey, and a collision could mean the end of the race.

Ellison was surrounded by some of the finest sailors in the world, but there were two other amateurs aboard *Sayonara*—Phil Kiely and Lachlan Murdoch. Kiely, the head of Oracle's Australian operations, had grown up in Sydney and had done two Hobarts. His experience was on smaller boats, but he wasn't a complete novice.

Lachlan Murdoch is the son of news mogul Rupert Murdoch. The elder Murdoch had been aboard *Sayonara* in 1995 and had shown some spunk when he lost the tip of his finger during a practice sail. After the missing piece was reattached, Murdoch declared himself fit to sail, served coffee during the race, and shared Ellison's line honors victory. Murdoch topped off the race by buying drinks for the crew in Hobart.

Now it was Lachlan's turn, but this was a new adventure for the young scion. He was a risk taker and a rock climber, but not a professional sailor. Though he had sailed his own boat in the 1997 Hobart, he was not at the level of Ellison's hired guns. The opportunity to sail on *Sayonara* arose when he met Ellison at a friend's Fourth of July party. Rupert Murdoch was also there, and Ellison extended an invitation. Rupert couldn't do the race, but he suggested his son. Ellison agreed, and Lachlan enthusiastically accepted.

Except for Lachlan and one other guest, Ellison was surrounded by a superb crew of professional sailors drawn from the ranks of Olympic medalists and New Zealand's national ocean racing team. At least on the water, Ellison was aware of his limitations: "I love working with the *Sayonara* crew . . . because I'm not the star. I'm just a pretty good amateur driver. The rest of the *Sayonara* crew are the best professional sailors on the planet. These guys are unbelievably good at what they do. They're the best."[2]

At the top of the hierarchy of professional sailors was Chris Dickson. Dickson was as intensely competitive as Ellison, with an uncompromising commitment to winning. He had won three *International Sailing Association Youth World Championships* and had skippered the first New Zealand yacht to compete in the America's Cup. He had completed numerous America's Cup campaigns and competed in the 1993 Round the World Whitbread Race. Ellison's search for "the best sailors in the world" led him straight to Dickson, who would be responsible for sailing *Sayonara* and managing the crew.

Dickson had a reputation as an uncompromising taskmaster, and *Sayonara*'s crew had practiced just as relentlessly as *AFR Midnight Rambler*. Like Ed Psaltis, Dickson was a perfectionist. With the exception of Ellison, Dickson would scream at anyone who failed to meet his expectations. Unlike Psaltis, however, Dickson was not known for making up after harsh words. His reputation was that of a fanatical perfectionist, unforgiving of himself and others.[3]

Ellison was at the wheel, but Dickson was standing right behind him shouting out orders. Ellison was doing what he was told, and so far things were going just as planned. The weather was perfect, warm and sunny,

not a storm cloud in the sky. The breeze was light and they were surrounded by spectacular scenery. Then things took a turn for the worse.

In spite of the amount of money that Ellison had invested in *Sayonara,*
not all of the high-tech equipment was working perfectly. During one
maneuver a special carbon fiber gear broke in one of their main winches.
The winch is a critical part of a sailboat. Lines running from the sails
wind around the circular drum and enable sailors to quickly adjust the
angle of the sail to the wind for maximum speed. Without a winch it
would be an impossible task, especially on a boat the size of *Sayonara.*

Dickson was furious. "How the hell can we break one of our main
winches before the goddamn race's even started?"[4] Ellison was relieved
that he didn't bear the brunt of Dickson's wrath, but there was no time
to repair the winch before the start of the race. Maneuvering had to be
done slowly and carefully, compounding the challenge of getting a good
start.

Dickson made it clear that they should stay away from *Nokia,* because
of their record of colliding with other boats. All *Sayonara* wanted was a
good start, and that's what they got. Ellison was thrilled:

> It was a good start. We rounded the first mark ahead of the rest the
> fleet. . . . It was just about as perfect sailing as we could get. We had
> no idea what was going to happen to us over the next three days.
> If we had, we would've turned left and gone up north to the Great
> Barrier Reef. That's where all the sensible people having sensible
> Christmas holidays go. Instead we turned right and raced down the
> Australian coast toward the island of Tasmania.[5]

With George Snow and *Brindabella* close on Ellison's heels, *Sayonara*
was the first boat to sail out of the harbor. With hundreds of thousands
of people watching and television cameras focused on the Big Yank Tank,
Ellison had made the most of his moment.

11

AFR Midnight Rambler— Smokin'

T he *Rambler* was free of the crowd, but the water in the first hours of the race was, as Bob put it, "disturbed." There were waves going in every direction. The confused sea state had nothing to do with the racing boats but rather an obstacle created by the topography of the coast. The sheer cliffs created a backwash that made sailing difficult for everyone, and especially for a tiny boat.

In spite of the rough water, *AFR Midnight Rambler* rounded the Z Mark, made a sharp right, and headed due south. The rhumb line—the most direct course to Tasmania—was 185 degrees on the compass, and no more maneuvering would be required except to compensate for the wind. *A few days from now,* Bob thought, *we'll be drinking Cascade Lager in Hobart*. He had no idea what a wonderful sight Tasmania would be—all they had to do was get there.

With a predicted nor'easter that afternoon, they knew the boat would accelerate throughout the day, especially once they could hoist *the kite*—the big spinnaker that would enable them to catch the wind. In the meantime, they headed away from shore, pointing as directly into the wind as the boat could sail. By midafternoon their new spinnaker was flying high and the *Rambler* was rapidly moving down the coast. Once again, seemingly out of nowhere, another pleasure boat appeared. This time was even more infuriating. The boat was motoring and adorned with bikini-clad passengers who were out for a good time in the sun.

The rules of the road are very clear in this situation: A sailing vessel always has the right-of-way, regardless of whose bikinis are on deck. Oblivious to any concerns about rules of the road, the spectator boat nearly crashed into the *Rambler.* Angry shouts were exchanged as passengers on the cruiser spilled their martinis and the Ramblers made sarcastic comments. A furious Arthur nearly climbed over the railing to board the other vessel, shouting, "What the hell? Do you have the IQ of a jellyfish?" Then, as quickly as it had begun, the encounter was over.

There was so much free-floating adrenaline on the boat that no one could sleep. Jonno and Mix went below to get some rest, collapsing on the taut polyethylene berths, out of the sun. But Bob's work had just begun. He had charted a course to a point near Jervis Bay about 100 miles south of Sydney. But as always, there was a trade-off. They wanted to sail offshore to the East Australian Current so they could take advantage of the "oceanic conveyer belt." But they didn't want to waste time sailing unnecessary miles. Bob's plan was to strike just the right balance.

For once, the presence of one of the maxis was a help, not a burden. The navigator on one of the faster boats had the same idea of finding an optimal course, and the big boat zipped past them. Eventually it disappeared, but Ed steered toward its huge sail until the maxi gradually faded from view over the horizon.

Hour by hour, the Ramblers began to understand just what their new boat could do. Although their last boat was 5 feet longer, they were moving much faster than in previous years. Unbelievably, they were now almost keeping up with rivals that would've left them far behind in other races. Even Bruce Taylor's brand-new *Chutzpah*—a larger and more high-tech boat—was within reach. Crew morale skyrocketed. The boat was everything they had hoped for.

As the crew settled into their racing routine, giving Ed a break was the first priority. He had been at the helm steering since well before the start—through the melee in Sydney Harbour, and now down the coast for a long stretch. Arthur took over, steering for three hours or so. Mix followed suit before sunset. They were sailing smoothly, still with the large black spinnaker up, and conditions were improving every minute.

The speed of the wind is a fundamental consideration in sailing, but the significance of wind direction is not quite so obvious. Boats can't sail directly into the wind, but a really good boat can sail at an angle of 20 to 30 degrees to either side. As the wind swings more toward 90 degrees—directly to the left or right—handling becomes easier and speeds increase dramatically. Most boats don't respond well when the wind comes directly behind them, but an ideal wind comes at an angle from the rear—say, 45 degrees to either side. This perfect direction is precisely what evolved as the day progressed.

AFR Midnight Rambler was screaming down the coast of New South Wales. Combining weather predictions and their current pace, Bob figured that they would make it to the Bass Strait by the next afternoon. This would be a spectacular run for the 35-foot sailboat, about 260 miles in one day.

By dusk the nor'easter was building and growing stronger. It continued to rotate until it was finally blowing directly behind the boat. This made steering *AFR Midnight Rambler* even more challenging. Keeping the boat on course required intense focus and constant adjustment of the tiller. Two hours at the helm was all that anyone could take. As they did earlier, the Ramblers continued to share the load, rotating those responsible for steering the boat.

They were flying down the coast at an ever-increasing rate. The wind was at their back, they were in the East Australian Current, and the combined forces were driving them south. It was all good. And the 4-knot current, along with the northerly breeze, created another advantage. The wind and current flattened the seas, so the *Rambler* had a clear runway to Tasmania.

With the strong wind and level surface, *AFR Midnight Rambler* took off like a Jet Ski as it flew across the water. As the bow cut through the ocean, streams of white water shot into the air on either side. A huge rooster tail of water spewed out the back of the boat, and everyone on the crew was grinning from ear to ear. It was the most exhilarating sailing that they had ever done.

The speed of the new boat was amazing. They were doing over 22 knots. It was a surreal experience, as they sailed into the pitch-black night. There were thunderstorms with lightning everywhere. Jonno was hypnotized by nature's light show and by the sensation of the boat traveling so fast. *We're just smokin'*, he said to himself.

They had never sailed the new boat in heavy weather like this, and part of the excitement was wondering what would happen next. With the wind from behind and the spinnaker out front, the bow of the *Rambler* began to dive into the water. They realized that they would need to put weight in the stern of the boat to keep the nose out of the water and the rudder in the water. It was quite a picture: six crew lined up in the rear of the boat, with one continuous smile, ear-to-ear and face-to-face. "This is awesome," yelled Chris.

The coastal communities of Ulladulla and Batemans Bay flew by, and the boat was proving eminently steerable. In just under twenty-four hours, they were south of Gabo Island, after a "rollicking spinnaker run." As exciting as the start was, there was nothing more exhilarating than going that fast in calm seas and being in complete control. That is, in control most of the time.

There were points at which Ed felt control slipping away. With his exceptional ability as a helmsman, Ed could almost always make small corrections that would stabilize the boat. But twice, even his remarkable seamanship didn't work and their knife-edge sailing turned into a broach.

When a sailboat broaches, it violently turns into the wind and flips onto its side. It's like an automobile that suddenly stops, throwing the passengers forward. Anyone on deck needs to swim, hang on, and scramble to avoid getting washed under the rails. People below are thrown out of their berths or pinned to the side of the boat that has suddenly become the floor.

Broaching can be an extraordinarily disruptive and frightening experience, and especially for an unprepared crew. But the Ramblers knew that broaches would likely occur, and they had faith that the boat would recover. As Ed pumped the tiller—the stick that controls the rudder—the crew watched calmly as he shook *AFR Midnight Rambler* back onto her feet.

Everyone moved back into their positions, and minutes after the broach, *AFR Midnight Rambler* was racing again. They were not only recovering quickly, but they were doing it at night. *All that practicing in the dark is paying off*, thought Gordo. *Onward and upward!*

There was no serious damage, but Ed realized they needed to put up a smaller sail with the increasing wind. They would still use a spinnaker, but now they would use a smaller one designed for storm conditions. Seconds after Ed shouted the familiar command "All hands on deck!," Arthur scrambled through the hatch onto the deck.

Eager to answer Ed's call, Arthur didn't stop to put on his wet-weather gear. He climbed onto the deck just as the boat flew down one wave and straight into the back of the next. The *Rambler* was submerged, and

Arthur was saturated from head to toe. With no spare clothing, he would stay encrusted with brine until they arrived in Hobart.

With the storm spinnaker up, *AFR Midnight Rambler* was roaring down the waves. The sound of the wind and water was deafening, but their new boat was showing her stuff. They broached a second time, but once again the boat took the punishment and recovered, as if to say, *There's plenty left in me!* It was clear to everyone that they had a tough little craft. They were pressing the limits of the boat and the team, and both were passing the test.

12

Sayonara—Temporary Humility

*A*FR *Midnight Rambler* was flying down the coast, but *Sayonara* was far ahead. With Ellison at the helm, the Big Yank Tank made a spectacular showing with its name emblazoned in kanji script on its spinnaker. George Snow on *Brindabella* was close behind, but there was no question about who was leading the fleet. There were 114 boats in *Sayonara's* wake.

Big puffs of wind would hit the sail, lifting up *Sayonara* and propelling her through the water, creating excitement and adrenaline for everyone, but especially for Ellison. Then it happened. An incredibly strong gust of wind ruptured the sail. The chute was gone—ripped to pieces, taking *Sayonara's* lead with it.

While Ellison's world-class sailors were hoisting a new and smaller spinnaker, *Brindabella* caught up to *Sayonara* and took the lead. Ellison saw his victory escaping and wondered whether the blown sail was his fault. If he had turned the boat a few degrees, could he have saved the chute? He concluded he had been sailing the boat at too high an angle, putting too much pressure on the spinnaker. Thinking he may have been getting tired, he decided he should relinquish the wheel to a professional. Brad Butterworth, who had been Team New Zealand's winning tactician, took over the helm.

Once again *Sayonara* took the lead, and the big maxi was moving close to 20 knots. Ellison was looking back, checking his distance from *Brindabella,* when he heard another explosion. It was the sound of another sail blowing apart. *What the hell was happening?* The wind was gusting to 30 knots, and increasing. They decided to fall back on their sail of last resort—the smallest, strongest, mini spinnaker. This one was indestructible. It was so strong that Ellison was sure the mast would give way before the sail.

Ellison got back on the wheel, alternating driving with Butterworth. *Sayonara* was hitting extraordinary speeds of 22, 24, then 26 knots. A pace like that was unheard of for a boat this size, and *Sayonara* seemed on its way to setting a new race record. In twelve hours they had gone twice as far as the previous record set by Ellison's rival, Hasso Plattner, in 1996. That was the good news. *The bad news,* thought Ellison, was *Why the f—k are we going 26 knots?*

Ellison's question was immediately followed by an extraordinary blast of wind. It hit *Sayonara* with tremendous force, so hard that it appeared to destroy the indestructible spinnaker. Ellison was dumbfounded. *That's impossible,* he thought, *the sail is unbreakable.* It couldn't be happening.

Ellison was right. The sail didn't break, but the pole that held it to the mast had come apart and was thrashing around. The force of the wind was so great that the metal fitting for the high-tech carbon spinnaker pole had failed. A three-quarter-inch metal alloy thread had been dislodged from the pole with incredible force. Ellison speculated that the wind power must have been around 100,000 pounds.[1] Now what?

Conditions were changing. The wind that had been blowing from behind was now swinging to their side, so they gave up on the spinnaker. With their remarkable speed, *Sayonara* had almost reached the Bass Strait. Now they had to deal with the familiar southerly buster, a well-known weather occurrence for boats sailing south to Tasmania. The wind rotated from northeast to southeast, and *Sayonara* was sailing as closely hauled, or as directly into the wind, as its advanced design would allow.

As they entered the Strait's shallow water, things got dramatically worse. The flat-backed waves crashed against the bow of the boat, and Ellison struggled to maintain course. The rain and salt spray hit him in the face. It felt like being stabbed with an ice pick.

To Ellison, the faces of 25-foot waves looked like rows of three-story glass office buildings. This was different than the '95 race, and this time it was not feeling as cool to be doing the Hobart. *It's a lot worse than last time,* thought Ellison, *but I can do it.*[2]

Still, the wind continued to build. There was blackness everywhere. The sky was black, the ocean was black, and the horizon was nonexistent. Most of the waves were now obscured by rain and spray, but the waves that Ellison could see were huge. As he steered up the walls of water, the wind would increase dramatically when he reached the top.

Just as Ellison tried to turn the boat toward the wind to adjust, *Sayonara* would slide down into the trough of the wave. In the valleys between the waves, the wind speed would drop and the boat's angle to the wind had to be adjusted again. It was a helmsman's nightmare, especially for an amateur.

Ellison could see almost nothing, and the instruments were no help. Butterworth was trying to help by shouting instructions, but it was no use. After repeated tries, Ellison was beaten. He screamed, "I can't do it, Brad! Take it! Take it! You take it!" Butterworth grabbed the helm. Ellison felt defeated. Less than a day into the race, he felt overwhelmed and routed by the Southern Ocean. He had wanted to find his limits, and he found them in the Bass Strait.

While Ellison was lamenting his limitations as a sailor, the horrific conditions suddenly took a turn for the better. The wind dropped to a much more manageable 10 knots. The waves were still Bass Strait monsters, but the sky, stars, and the horizon had reappeared. Relieved, Ellison relaxed, thinking they were now safe on the other side of the brutal front that had gotten the best of him.

His confidence back, Ellison was ready to race again. But their small storm sails were still up, and *Sayonara* was moving slowly. Ellison was eager to get the big sails up and get moving. Butterworth was more cautious, but the two finally reached a compromise. They would hoist the big jib—the triangular sail forward of the mast—but leave the smaller mainsail in position. With that resolved, at 3 a.m. on Sunday, Ellison went below to check the weather.

Like most of the larger ocean racing boats, *Sayonara*'s navigation station was crammed back in the rear of the boat. Ellison made his way to the cramped bench where Mark Rudiger, the boat's navigator, was sitting. Rudiger was intently studying the satellite images that were slowly appearing on his computer screen. Line by line, images appeared, starting with the Australian coast and finally filling the screen to *Sayonara*'s position.

Ellison was once again dumbfounded. What he saw appeared to be an enormous cloud formation, rotating clockwise. It looked like a target, and *Sayonara* was right in the bull's-eye. Ellison asked Rudiger if he had seen this pattern before. There was no response. Rudiger just stared at the screen, shaking his head. Ellison kept talking. "Well, I have. It was on the Weather Channel. It was called Hurricane Helen! We're in the middle of a f—ing hurricane!"

Above deck, Ellison heard Butterworth screaming for the crew to get the big jib down. In less than a minute, the wind had gone from a leisurely 10 knots to more than 50. What Ellison had thought was a passing front was actually the eye of a massive storm.

13

An Ominous Forecast— Storm Warning

The computer weather models used by Bureau of Meteorology forecasters were a veritable alphabet soup. There was the ECMWF model, created by the European Center for Medium-Range Weather Forecasts; the JMA model, from the Japan Meteorological Agency; and the LAPS, from The Australian Limited Area Prediction System. Another Bureau model with higher resolution was the MESO-LAPS. The U.K. global model was UKMO, while the U.S. model was called, simply, US. Finally, there was the Global Assimilation and Prediction model—appropriately called GASP.

Even with all these advanced systems, prior to the start of the race there was no consensus about exactly what was going to happen. Computer modeling of the atmosphere had improved since the development of the first operational systems more than forty years ago, but it is still an inexact science. On December 23, three days before the race, the computer models were forecasting a wide range of expected weather patterns. The European model was forecasting moderate to "fresh" northeasterly winds around Gabo Island at the entrance to the Bass Strait. Other models predicted winds of around 25 to 40 knots from the south.

The next day, the European model forecast southwesterly winds of about 30 knots, not "fresh" northeasterly winds. Other models, including

GASP, were suggesting light and variable winds. By Friday, Christmas Day, the models were beginning to agree that a low-pressure system would develop over the Tasman Sea, but they disagreed about its exact location.

There did seem to be some consensus that the winds would be from the south or southwest, with wind speeds between 15 and 30 knots, but significant differences remained. As late as the early morning hours on Saturday, the highest prediction for wind speed was about 35 to 40 knots, with the most detailed LAPS model forecasting a moderate 25.

Around 8 a.m. Saturday, a meteorologist named Peter Dunda examined the latest satellite photographs taken the night before and compared them with the computer model generated by the supercomputer at the Bureau's headquarters.

The forecaster wasn't surprised by the appearance of the *southerly buster* that was common for the Hobart. But he was concerned about a low-pressure area that seemed to be forming east of the Bass Strait. While most of the fleet would be safely out of the way of the system, boats at its perimeter could encounter very strong winds.

About an hour later, Dunda issued a *priority gale warning* to race organizers. He also posted the warning on the website and other public systems, and predicted that winds of 30 to 40 knots would strike the southeast coast of Australia by Sunday night. Shortly before the race began—and unbeknownst to many sailors—that prediction changed.

Around noon, all the global models reached consensus. They were forecasting the development of a deep low that would bring southwesterly winds of about 45 knots—near the high end of the gale force range. And at 1 p.m., precisely the start of the race, the high-resolution MESO-LAPS model predicted westerly winds of 55 knots. The storm would be centered directly on the path that the fleet would be following into the Bass Strait. With the latest computer data, it looked as if the American model—characterized as "bullish" by Clouds Badham—was going to prove right. This was going to be more than a gale.

Forecasters from the Bureau of Meteorology watched the start of the race on television, and they were worried. At 2:14 p.m. on the 26th, just over an hour into the race, the Sydney Bureau office upgraded the *gale warning* to a *storm warning*. This meant that the average wind speeds would be 45 to 55 knots. There were 115 boats sailing into the storm, and if the fleet was caught in these winds without warning, the Bureau would look very bad.

An alert was transmitted by fax to Australia's marine broadcast service, commercial radio and television stations, the Royal Australian Navy, and the Cruising Yacht Club. Beyond the official warnings, some Bureau forecasters took it upon themselves to spread the word.

Meteorologist Kenn Batt had friends in the race, and he was so upset that he became physically ill. Batt understood what the forecast could mean. He had done the 1993 Hobart and had encountered some of the worst weather conditions in the history of the race. That year, only 38 of 104 boats made it to Hobart. And as bad as the weather was in '93, this storm looked significantly worse.

Fearing that the race could turn into a "massacre," Batt and his colleague Brett Gage, though off duty, continued to sound the alarm, contacting Australian Search and Rescue. *The worst that could happen,* thought Gage, *would be a false alarm and interrupted holidays for rescue personnel.* The alternative would be exposure to enormous criticism if the Bureau failed to predict a perilous weather event.

The forecasters had issued a *priority storm warning,* but meteorologists have a technical language that can be very confusing to the uninitiated. According to the Australian Bureau of Meteorology, a *gale warning* is issued for average wind speeds between 34 and 47 knots. A *storm warning* is issued for wind speeds in excess of 48 knots.

Hurricane warnings apply to average wind speeds in excess of 63 knots. But in 1998, the term *hurricane* was not used for the waters off southeastern Australia. A *storm warning* was the highest level of alert, and storms were considered to be open-ended. The minimum speeds would average more than 48 knots, but the maximum speeds experienced during a storm warning could be anything above that.

Experts at the Bureau of Meteorology were familiar with these distinctions, but many sailors were not. Those who had done the Hobart before knew that big waves—and high, gusty winds—were part of the package. The label put on bad weather didn't make that much difference.

In fact, a number of sailors thought that the *gale warning* issued earlier sounded more extreme than the *storm warning* sent after the start of the race. And few realized that they could encounter *maximum gusts up to 40 percent greater* than the predicted average wind speeds. With the *storm warning,* gusts of 70 knots—more than 80 miles an hour—were to be expected. A storm warning at sea is a frightening forecast, even if the full danger was not well understood by many racers.

The sailors' difficulty in comprehending the weather was further complicated by the complexity of the sea state predictions. Again, more arcane terminology. The term *wind waves* refers to waves generated by local prevailing winds, but the term *swell waves* refers to waves generated by winds from a distant weather system. *Sea state* is the combination of both.

Forecasts of waves also vary according to their location. Coastal wave forecasts are given in meters and use phrases such as *significant wave height*—the average height of the highest one-third of the waves. Forecasts for the high seas use descriptive terms such as *slight, moderate,* and *rough.* Sailors would need a separate table to relate these descriptive terms to the heights they represent. And to clearly understand the forecast, they would need to know that—in open water—a wave of 1.86 times the significant wave height can be expected in every 1,000 waves.

During the race, the storm warning for coastal waters predicted wave heights of about 13 to 23 feet. Storm warnings for the high seas mentioned "rough" seas and "moderate to heavy" swells, which could be expected to result in a combined significant wave height of 23 feet. This meant that individual waves almost twice that size could be expected. And that was not the worst of it.

Sustained winds blowing over open water create patterns that converge in unpredictable ways. Monstrous waves—described as *kings, freaks,* or *rogues*—are created when wind waves, or swell waves, or a combination, join to create a massive wall of water. These rogues can be much, much higher than 1.86 times the predicted wave height. And a boat caught by one of these freak waves can easily be rolled or dismasted.

Sailors who could assemble all the pieces of the weather puzzle would face a menacing forecast. The fleet could expect to be hit with winds of more than 70 knots and waves almost 43 feet high. Boats could be exposed to other waves that were higher than 43 feet, and these rogue waves would arrive unexpectedly. Confronted with this intimidating scenario, a racer might decide to turn back to shore. But to fully grasp what might happen, a sailor would need to have received the updated weather forecast, understood the implications of a *storm warning,* and be able to process the torrent of information and put the puzzle together.

Sayonara was equipped with fax machines, computers, and state-of-the-art technology. Not only did Ellison and his crew receive the storm warning, they could also see the cyclonic weather pattern taking shape on the screen in front of their eyes. And they had a secret weapon: Clouds Badham. He saw the maelstrom unfolding and alerted Ellison and his other clients.

AFR Midnight Rambler had no such warning. Bob Thomas had returned from the weather briefing before the race knowing only that it was going to be a bad blow. But that was nothing new for the Hobart. In the afternoon and early evening the Ramblers had been treated to an extraordinary electrical storm with lightning and thunder, but they were streaking south and were relatively unconcerned about the weather.

At 8 p.m., Bob was first alerted to the deteriorating weather during the first race *sked*. Skeds—short for "schedules"—are check-ins designed to establish the position of each boat. Boats are required to report their positions in alphabetical order, indicating their latitude and longitude.

The *storm warning* broadcast during the sked essentially reinforced what Bob already knew: The next day was not going to be pretty. A pre-frontal trough, or small front, would pass that evening, and the next day after lunchtime they would be getting into the main storm.

Boats were allowed to transmit only their positions during the sked, though Bob did hear a number of colorful comments on the radio. It was obvious that *AFR Midnight Rambler* wasn't the only boat heading into what everyone knew would be white-knuckle sailing.

Almost all the boats were making great time, but some were dropping out. *ABN Amro,* a favorite to win the Tattersall's Cup, retired from the race with rudder damage and was headed for Batemans Bay. An hour later, *Sledgehammer* reported a broken steering cable and dropped out. An hour after that, *Challenge Again*—one of the best sailing yachts in Australia with two-time Hobart winner Lou Abrahams—lost a man overboard. It took the crew fifteen tense minutes, but they finally succeeded in retrieving the lost sailor alive. While the *Challenge Again* rescue effort was going on, the yacht *Sydney* reported rudder damage and pulled out of the race.

It was only the first day of the race, but the weather was taking its toll on the yachts. Some 1,100 sailors were headed to Hobart, boats were starting to retire, and this was just the beginning.

14

AFR Midnight Rambler— Hard or Squishy?

I n the south, an upper air jet stream and cold air mass were moving northward. At the same time, a low-pressure system was forming and strengthening in the Bass Strait, just below Wilsons Promontory—the southernmost point of land on the Australian continent. The front was cold enough to leave snow in its tracks, and it gave the Australian Alps an unseasonable dusting of white. The low was still in its infancy, but it was swiftly maturing. Meandering north and deepening, it would soon shift east to greet the Hobart fleet the following day.

No Retreat for the *Rambler*

The first front hit the *Midnight Rambler* at 3 a.m. on the 27th. The wind, about 40 knots, had come in with tremendous intensity. And it felt different. *It even tastes different,* Jonno thought. They were so close to land that they could smell the shore.

The Ramblers had gone from sailing with the wind at their backs— scooting down the coast with exhilarating fun—to a hard slog with the wind on their nose. They knew it would be tough, but the shifting wind direction was not a showstopper. In fact, Arthur thought the frontal system was a stroke of good fortune. It helped get the crew organized and provided a shakedown for the new boat. There were some equipment issues, but these "teething problems" got sorted out with the first blast of wind.

During the initial onslaught, Arthur saw Jonno up on the bow struggling to untangle one of the snarled lines. He ran forward to help. The job wasn't easy, and they were fighting the jumble of lines while being drenched by waves breaking over the bow. It was a tenuous situation. Partly submerged, they held onto the boat with one arm, while the other arm was dedicated to untangling the mess.

Deluged by a constant stream of waves, they were miserable yet connected by a bond of friendship and teamwork. Looking at Arthur, Jonno was struck by the irony of their situation. He shouted over the wind, yelling with a grin, "Artie, it's a strange world when yesterday morning you were in the drought-stricken outback of Australia, and now we're being drowned in the Tasman Sea."

With the wind shifting to the southwest, *AFR Midnight Rambler* was now sailing as directly into the wind as they possibly could. It wasn't a perfect course to Tasmania, but it was good enough. They were on their way to Hobart.

At 9 a.m. on Sunday, average winds of 79 knots, with gusts over 92, were observed at Wilsons Promontory Lighthouse. The lighthouse observations were made at an elevation of over 300 feet, so winds on the water may have been somewhat lower. But winds of 79 knots were rare, and they occurred only during the winter. The readings were enough to send Clouds Badham on a search of his records. In over twenty years of forecasting, he had never seen gusts over 92 knots.

At 11 a.m. the Ramblers were amazed to see Gabo Island at the entrance to the Bass Strait. It had taken them only twenty-two hours, which was extraordinary for a boat the size of theirs. The crew was excited about having made record time, and the weather was changing for the better.

Ed was relieved. *That's it, the Bureau was wrong. It's all over.* The Bureau of Meteorology was often wrong. The sun was shining, and the breeze had died. On the surface, everything looked fantastic. But Bob was uneasy.

There was something about the wind that he didn't like. Twice in his life, and in almost exactly the same spot, Bob had been caught in storms that resulted in fatalities. The wind had been the same both times. It was just like this wind. Bob had no way of knowing what was going to happen, but his sixth sense told him that there was something evil about the wind. It seemed to portend tragedy.

After plowing through 40-knot winds all night, *AFR Midnight Rambler* was now almost stalled. Arthur looked at his brother with relief. "I think we're through the worst of the front. We're going to be okay." Amazed by the light breeze, Ed called for a big headsail to get the boat going again. But ten minutes later, even before they had time to get the new sail up, the wind started to build.

The onset was sudden and it came with no apparent warning. Clouds on the horizon that had looked ominous at a distance were suddenly on top of them. The rain was coming down hard, and the storm had an extraordinary ferocity. Faced with this new front, Ed was relieved that they hadn't been able to hoist the sail. It would've been ripped to shreds. No one had ever seen anything like this before.

Arthur was in the cockpit calling out the wind speeds from the digital readout of the anemometer: "25 knots, 30 knots, 35 knots, 40 knots, 45 knots, 50 knots." As the boat was rolling onto its side, Arthur saw the digital readout go blank. He was confused. The instrument goes up to well over 100 knots, so it shouldn't just go blank.

As Arthur looked up at the top of the mast, he realized what had happened. The wind had ripped the anemometer completely off, shearing the metal fittings that secured it. Wind instruments don't just blow off the top of masts, and ten minutes earlier he had been saying that they were through the worst of it. As *AFR Midnight Rambler* was flattened by the wind, Arthur thought to himself, *No one is going to ask me for an opinion on weather forecasting ever again!*[1]

AFR Midnight Rambler was on its side and could not seem to recover. Like the loss of the anemometer, it made no sense. To qualify for the Hobart race, boats were required to have a minimum *righting angle* of 115 degrees. That meant that the boat needed to be able to rotate 25 degrees past horizontal with its mast in the water and still be able to recover.

AFR Midnight Rambler had a righting angle of 122 degrees, and it was exceptionally stable. But the boat was being held down by the sail, which still ran to the top of the mast. The crew needed to get the sail down quickly to get rid of its massive weight, and they moved with characteristic discipline. Using the routine they had practiced time and again, they sat on the side of the boat and calmly rolled up the mainsail.

AFR Midnight Rambler popped upright, solving the immediate problem, but they had other decisions to make. They could replace the main with a specialized sail called a *storm trysail,* a small sail designed for heavy weather conditions. The trysail was much smaller than the main, but it would provide stability and some forward movement and control.

Getting a storm trysail up isn't easy, even in gale force winds. The winds buffeting *AFR Midnight Rambler* were worse than gale force, and the rapid onset of the storm allowed no time for preparation. *It doesn't matter,* Ed thought. *Even the storm trysail is too much sail for these conditions.* Out of options, they raised the storm jib. It was the smallest sail they had. There was no further retreat from the wind.

Sword's Warning

The third sked of the race began at 2:05 p.m. One by one, boats reported their positions in alphabetical order until it was *Sword of Orion*'s turn. The *Sword,* about 20 miles ahead of *AFR Midnight Rambler,* had been experiencing wind speeds around 50 knots, gusting to more than 70.

Rob Kothe, *Sword*'s owner, was below deck glued to the navigation table, trying to understand what was happening with the weather. Kothe had been engaged in a running argument with Steve Kulmar, who was convinced that the boat should pull out of the race. Kulmar had been in seventeen Hobarts, and he had never seen anything like this before. Even his experience in the '93 race was different. Wind gusts had hit 75 to 80 knots, but there were breaks in the weather and the waves were nothing like this.

Kothe remained unconvinced, and the crew was divided. Dags Senogles wanted to continue, and he urged Kothe to overrule Kulmar. Kulmar was furious at the thought that the decision about whether or not to retire might be made by an owner who had done one Hobart and a relatively inexperienced crew member.

At the beginning of the sked, Kothe had hoped that he would get more clarity about the weather from the Bureau of Meteorology. He also wanted to hear from the maxis, which were already in the Bass Strait.

His hopes were not realized. Boats reported their positions, but no substantial weather information was broadcast. By the time Kothe's turn came, however, he had made a decision. Speaking on the radio with

Lew Carter, who was coordinating the skeds from the radio relay vessel, *Young Endeavor,* Kothe stated he wanted to breach protocol. Rather than simply state his position, Kothe wanted permission to report on the weather.

Carter authorized the departure from normal radio procedure. "*Sword of Orion,* I would appreciate that for ourselves and all the fleet, over."

Kothe's response was astonishing: "We have 50 to 65 knot westerlies with gusts to 78 knots, over."

Astounded, Carter asked Kothe to confirm the wind speed: "Gusts of 78 knots?"

"78 knots," Kothe answered.

Carter repeated the message to the rest of the fleet. He then issued a startling request: "I ask all skippers, before proceeding into the Bass Strait or wherever you're proceeding, to give it your utmost consideration as to what you're doing. And talk about it with your crew."

The *Rambler*—Man Down

Just as the *Sword*'s warning was being broadcast to the fleet, Chris Rockell and Mix Bencsik were below deck on the *Midnight Rambler.* They were preparing to go on watch, and Mix was sitting down, putting his trousers on. Because quarters were so cramped, Chris was standing up, trying to do the same.

As Chris balanced on one leg, the boat fell off an enormous wave. With nothing to hold him down, Chris floated through the air "with as much dignity as he could muster" and cracked his head on a bolt that was holding a fitting on the deck. Chris struck the bolt with so much force that a loud crack resonated throughout the boat.

Chris wasn't sure whether the crack was caused by the boat giving a little bit—or by his skull giving a little bit. Intent on finding which was which, he was nervous to touch his head. He had no idea if he was going to touch "hard or squishy."

There was blood everywhere. It was running down Chris' head and spilling onto the deck of the boat and into the bilges. He looked at his hands, and they were covered with something grayish white. Chris wasn't sure what it was, but his first thought was, *Bloody hell, I've cracked my skull through and I've gone through to my brain.*

Shaken, Chris turned to Mix and asked, "How bad does this look?" With blood everywhere it looked bad, but, fortunately for everyone, the grayish white substance was probably paint or fiberglass from the boat. In any case, it had nothing to do with Chris' brains.

Mix examined the injury and said calmly, "Look, if it's bleeding that much, why don't you put some pressure on it to at least stop the bleeding?" Recovered from the initial shock, Chris thought that was a reasonable suggestion. They found a first aid kit and applied pressure to the wound. Chris began probing for "squishy bits," trying to see if there were any holes or dents in his skull. The fact that he didn't find any came as quite a relief, and he began to feel considerably better than he had just a few minutes before.[2]

Ed had heard the weather report from *Sword of Orion* and was now faced with the added concern of Chris' injury. He was seriously considering the possibility of pulling out of the race. Chris knew exactly what was going through Ed's mind, but he would have no part of it. This was the second Hobart race that Chris had started, and he hadn't finished the first one. Chris was determined to make it to Hobart.

He pleaded with Ed, arguing that the *Rambler* should not pull out on his account. "I've already done my head check," he explained, "and I'm sure I don't have any holes in it." As far as Chris was concerned, it was just a bit of blood, and the injury was survivable. His condition should not be a reason for the boat to pull out of the race. He was, after all, a frontline rugby player and—as Bob often joked—a head injury can't hurt a frontline rugby player.

Chris finally convinced Ed that the *AFR Midnight Rambler* should press on, but there was a condition. Chris would stay below while they evaluated whether he was concussed, and they would continue to monitor his condition. The last thing they needed was someone with a concussion wandering around on deck in these conditions.

Chris agreed to stay below in his bunk, but he made sure that he got in the bunk on the windward side of the boat. Even though he was injured, he thought he could still act as ballast—counteracting the force of the wind that was making the boat heel over. He would position himself where his weight would be of the greatest benefit.

There was a gap between the pipe that made up one side of his berth and the hull of the boat. Seeing the opening, Chris hooked his elbow around one section of the pipe and his knee around another. He stayed in that position for the next seven hours.

Although Chris was injured, he was still focused on making sure that he was doing everything he could to contribute to the success of the team. Hanging onto the pipe as ballast was Chris' *mental medicine.* It gave him a sense of accomplishment and helped him fight the sense of disappointment that he had failed to do his job.

15

VC Offshore Stand Aside—
A Twist of Fate

James Hallion, the skipper of *VC Offshore Stand Aside,* had assembled a hybrid racing team of veterans and rookies. Andy Mariette was one of the most experienced crew members among the twelve sailors aboard. He had done two Hobarts and had been sailing all his life. As Mariette put it, "I've been sailing since I was probably knee high to a boot."

Simon Clark had also sailed since he was a boy. Much of his experience was *blue water* ocean sailing, some of which had taken him near Antarctica. Others had shorter sailing resumes. Though Hallion had done one Hobart, it would be his first time sailing this boat. Mike Marshman, like Hallion, had done only one Hobart. And John Culley was doing the race for the first time.

At the 2:00 p.m. sked on December 27, Mariette was below deck at the nav station listening intently to the reports from other boats. When *Stand Aside*'s turn came near the end of the alphabet, Mariette wanted to be ready to report their position. Like everyone else, he was also intensely interested in any weather information that could guide their decision making.

The 41-foot *Stand Aside,* built in New Zealand, was particularly good at sailing downwind. Like *AFR Midnight Rambler, Stand Aside* had had a spectacular run down the coast. When the weather worsened on the morning of the 27th, they shifted to a small storm jib.

Even with a small sail, they were still exposed to 70-knot winds when they reached the tops of the big waves. After *Stand Aside* had been knocked flat, they tried running on bare poles using just the mast and rigging to power the boat.

With no sails, maneuvering became so difficult that Hallion, who was steering, essentially gave up, letting *Stand Aside* make up her own mind about which direction to head. Sometimes the boat would slide east toward New Zealand, and other times toward Tasmania.

Stand Aside's course was so erratic that, in an attempt to regain control, the crew decided to raise the storm jib once again. This time, the sail blew out of its tracks. By the 2 p.m. sked, *Stand Aside* had taken such a beating that no one was surprised at the high wind warning issued by *Sword of Orion.*

Aboard *Young Endeavor,* Lew Carter proceeded with his standard protocol for skeds: State the name of the boat; wait for the boat to repeat its name with latitude and longitude; record the position for later verification.

Near the end of the alphabet, Carter came to Hallion's boat: "*VC Offshore Stand Aside.*" No response. "Nothing heard," he said and then moved to the next boat on his list. After every boat had been given a chance to report in, Carter repeated the names of boats that had not responded. Once again, there was no answer from *Stand Aside.*

At some point in the interval between the *Sword of Orion's* warning and Lew Carter's initial transmission to *Stand Aside,* Mariette heard a shout on deck. "Watch out! Big wave!"

Marshman saw the wave coming, and he estimated it to be more than 60 feet high. It was an enormous wave, and it was starting to break. *Stand Aside* was pulled into the bottom of the wave and then catapulted to the top. When the boat reached the crest of the wave, *Stand Aside* was hit with the full force of the wind. Then everything turned upside down.

About 35 miles southwest of Gabo Island, the boat made a complete rotation, rolling 360 degrees. When *Stand Aside* finally came back up, Mariette was still sitting in front of the nav station. The force of the spin had been so great that it pinned him to his seat. The cabin roof had collapsed on top of him, but Mariette was in exactly the same position as before the giant wave hit—and was still holding his microphone.

The boat recovered, but Marshman was trapped underwater by the rigging. He had been harnessed to the boat and was pinned by his safety equipment. Though Marshman was drowning, he still had the presence of mind to realize that he was better off attached to the boat than letting go and drifting into the maelstrom. He fought his way to the surface and he gulped for air with a full understanding of how close he had been to death.

Eight crew members were on deck when the wave hit, all but one attached to the boat with a harness. After they recovered from the capsize, the air was filled with people shouting out names, desperate to find out who was on board and who was in the water.

John Culley, who had gone over the side without a harness, surfaced over 100 feet from the boat. *Stand Aside* was so far away that it seemed hopeless. He looked back at the boat, wondering what would happen next. Miraculously, the force of the wind and the waves drove him back to the boat. He climbed aboard, saved by a twist of fate.

The four crew members who were trapped below during the roll were now on deck, pulling their mates back onto the damaged boat. It wasn't a pretty sight. The inside of the boat was awash with seawater, the mast had broken off, the hull had several fractures, and the boom was twisted sideways.

Marshman had lost the top of his ring finger and was covered with blood. Others had lacerations, gashes, cuts, and damaged cartilage. Food, clothing, and debris were floating around the cabin, and diesel fuel gushed from the motor. A winch handle had been driven through the radio, rendering it useless. The crew was exhausted and injured, and it seemed certain that *Stand Aside* would sink.

There were two life rafts onboard, one stowed below and one on deck. The crew quickly inflated the first raft and tied it to the stern of the boat. The second stubbornly refused to inflate. In the struggle, a line broke and the second life raft was lost over the side. With only one six-man life raft remaining, the shattered *Stand Aside* was all they had to keep them alive.

The crew cut away the mast and rigging, and bailed with buckets and manual pumps. To lighten the boat and create a debris trail for rescuers, they threw everything overboard that was not critical to survival. Sorting through the lifeboat ditch bag, they found a handheld radio and began sending Mayday calls. A waterproof camera floated out of the detritus, and their subsequent ordeal was documented in a series of extraordinary photographs.

The crew used every intact piece of safety and emergency equipment they could find. *Stand Aside* was equipped with an EPIRB (Emergency Position Indicating Radio Beacon) device designed to transmit a distress signal to the satellite system run by the National Oceanic and Atmospheric Administration (NOAA). The crew activated the EPIRB and deployed a red parachute and orange smoke flares. Fearful and anxious, they waited for someone to respond.

The handheld radio had a very limited range, but a helicopter from the Australian Broadcasting Company (ABC) had been filming the race and picked up their distress signal. The pilot, Gary Ticehurst, had a reputation as one of the most skilled chopper pilots in Australia. He had flown helicopters in combat during the Vietnam War, and he attributed his skill to his previous experiences. Over a drink, he had once told a friend that "you get good at flying when some bastard is shooting at you." Fifteen minutes after *Stand Aside*'s Mayday, Ticehurst was hovering overhead, relaying transmissions and coordinating rescue efforts.

Nearby, skipper Iain Moray had been fighting the waves in an even smaller boat, the 38-foot *Siena*. *Siena* was struggling but continuing south and still racing. Moray and navigator Tim Evans—who had been monitoring the radio—heard *Stand Aside*'s distress call. When no one else responded to the Mayday, Moray felt he had no choice. *Siena* changed course in an effort to locate *Stand Aside* and render assistance.

Because of the size of the waves, no one on *Siena* could see *Stand Aside*. But Moray could see the ABC chopper hovering overhead. They steered toward the helicopter and finally spotted the dismasted yacht.

Moray radioed Ticehurst, trying to figure out what *Siena* could do to help. The conversation was short and to the point.

"ABC helicopter, this is *Siena,* over."

"*Siena* this is the ABC chopper. I have a message for you from Maritime Safety, over."

"ABC helicopter, this is *Siena*. Yes, what is the message, over?"

"Roger, from the Maritime Safety. They are wondering if you feel able to hold in the area of the *Stand Aside* here in case persons need to take on into a life raft or abandon the ship, abandon the boat prior to the rescue, over."

Moray agreed to stand by, and the crew of *Siena* did their best to assist in the rescue effort. They circled the stricken vessel, trying to hold their position. But even with the help of a 20-horsepower engine, it was an extraordinarily difficult task. Then it happened.

Siena was knocked down by a massive rogue wave. Moray was almost thrown out of the boat, and Evans was tossed across the cabin. The top of *Siena*'s mast slammed the water. Evans suffered three broken ribs and a punctured lung. Other crew members were injured, and Moray realized that *Siena*'s safety was in jeopardy. He radioed the ABC chopper, requesting permission to leave.

Ticehurst told Moray that a rescue helicopter would be on the scene shortly, and *Siena* turned and headed north. Nearly twenty-four hours later, the boat arrived in a small fishing port, and Evans was rushed to the hospital for surgery. By this time he had lost 60 percent of the use of his lung, and pneumonia had set in.[1] His recovery would take months.

16

Rescue from the Sky— Angels on Winches

As Gary Ticehurst had promised, soon after *Siena's* departure, the rescue chopper *Helimed One* arrived on the scene. Aboard the helicopter was Peter Davidson, a paramedic with the Victorian Air Ambulance Service. Davidson had served with *Helimed* for eight years and was one of their best. He had extensive experience with rescues and had practiced in lakes, in the mountains, and even in the Bass Strait. Davidson would need all of his experience and strength for the task ahead.

Looking down at *Stand Aside,* it was clear to Davidson what had to be done. Rescue swimmers can't land directly on a vessel, especially in bad conditions. Either they or the person being rescued could be seriously injured by the erratic movement of the boat. Even worse, the helicopter's winch cable could become entangled in the rigging of the boat and the helicopter itself pulled into the water. To avoid these catastrophic scenarios, the crew was instructed to put the first two men to be rescued, including the most seriously injured, into the life raft.

The waves were over 50 feet high, and the life raft was flooded with water and repeatedly rolled by the sea. Davidson went down the cable into the chaos and swam to the terrified sailors. It took a full ten minutes of bobbing up and down as "live bait" and an extraordinary amount of

energy to rescue the first man. Unbelievably, Davidson repeated this feat seven times. He ultimately pulled eight of *Stand Aside's* crew into the *Helimed* helicopter.

After his last rescue, Davidson was so exhausted that he couldn't lift his arm to signal the crew to winch him up. When he was finally retrieved and pulled into the chopper, Davidson could barely move. He had completed as many rescues in one afternoon as he had in his entire career with *Helimed*. It was a superhuman accomplishment.

Eight of the twelve stranded crew members on *Stand Aside* had been pulled from the water, but the remaining four were desperately awaiting rescue. A second helicopter, *SouthCare*—from the ACT Ambulance Service—was hovering, ready to make a rescue attempt when the *Helimed* chopper left. Aboard the *SouthCare* chopper were pilot Ray Stone, crew member Mark Delf, and two paramedics.

Unlike Davidson, the paramedics in the *SouthCare* chopper did not have extensive training in ocean rescue. Both Michelle Blewitt and Kristy McAlister were experienced paramedics, but they had been with the *SouthCare* helicopter unit for only a few months.[1]

Kristy McAlister had been an Australian national champion in rowing and had joined the ambulance service after her brother was involved in a serious farming accident. She was so impressed by the ambulance officers who came to his rescue that later, when McAlister saw an advertisement for an opening with the Ambulance Service, she applied and was accepted.

It took three years to become an intensive care paramedic, and helicopter work required further training. Kristy's water winch experience was done on Lake Burley Griffin in Canberra, a very flat lake. She had practiced three or four winches, all in calm water and in perfect conditions. Kristy had never done an emergency water rescue.

Blewitt and McAlister started their shift at 8 a.m. that day and had flown to Jervis Bay to treat a patient with a spinal injury. After dropping the patient off in Sydney, the chopper was flying back to Canberra when the crew received word to stand by for dispatch to a serious car accident.

That mission was canceled, and the crew began joking about being diverted for a Sydney to Hobart rescue. Ten minutes later they received another communication telling them to head to the base in Canberra, refuel, and pick up their wet-weather gear. There was a yacht in distress in the Sydney to Hobart Race. The joking stopped abruptly.

On the trip to Canberra, the wind buffeted the *SouthCare* helicopter

violently. By the time they landed, both Michelle and Kristy were airsick. They injected each other with shots of Maxolon, an antinausea drug, picked up their equipment, and flew on to Merimbula, where the crew did a "hot refuel."

With the rotors still turning and cameramen and refuelers gawking, Michelle and Kristy changed into their wetsuits. Wearing skimpy underwear, they worried briefly about the possibility of an unwanted television appearance. Then they quickly turned their attention to the more important issue of the rescue. By the time the *SouthCare* helicopter took off, the mission was clear: They were going to do a sea rescue for a yacht named *Stand Aside,* located about 55 miles off the coast.

The *Helimed* chopper had more favorable winds for getting to the rescue and was already in the process of winching when Kristy and Michelle arrived. The pilot of the *SouthCare* chopper, Ray Stone, flew in tight circles around *Stand Aside.* He wanted to give *Helimed* as much time as needed to get survivors off the stricken vessel.

The air was so turbulent that Michelle and Kristy got airsick again. They stood by, vomiting, while Mark Delf—the crewman on their team who would coordinate the rescue—opened the doors of the helicopter so they could see what was going on below.

The rain was pelting in, the skies were black, and the waves were enormous. As Delf watched Peter Davidson attempt to winch up the survivors, he was astounded by the enormity of the task. Worried about what Kristy and Michelle were about to undertake, Delf blurted out, "Oh, God. . . . Oh, no."

Michelle and Kristy didn't know exactly what he was responding to, but they knew that he was watching winches in progress and his commentary wasn't encouraging. Kristy finally said, "Delfy, just shut up, you know? I mean, I'm about to go out there and the last thing I need to hear you saying is these sorts of things about what's happening. I'm going to be doing that." He understood and shut up.

Delf stopped reporting on the chaos, but they then made a discovery that created even more anxiety. In the scramble to refuel and get their equipment, major pieces of safety equipment had been left behind. They were missing fins, specialized helmets, and buoyancy vests.

Paramedics always have a choice about whether to attempt a rescue, and Blewitt and McAlister now contemplated the danger. They were both missing critical safety equipment. But the situation was truly life-threatening for the crew on the sinking boat. If the rescuers left the four men on *Stand Aside,* they would almost certainly die. Kristy and Michelle weighed the options and made a decision: They would attempt a rescue in spite of the danger.

Kristy was the first to go down. As she was being lowered, she surveyed the horrifying scene. One survivor was still aboard *Stand Aside.* Two had been thrown out of the life raft and were hanging on the sides of the raft. Another was in the water, floating off into the storm. Attached to nothing, he was clearly the priority person to rescue.

Prior to the winch, Kristy had been petrified. Now she was focused. She forgot about how sick and scared she was and concentrated on the physical challenge of doing the job. It was a daunting challenge.

One minute she would be buried underneath a huge wave, and the next she'd be rocketed out at what felt like a million miles an hour. Without fins, it was extraordinarily difficult to swim to the survivors. Her energy was being drained.

At one point Kristy found herself lying on her back and looking up toward the sky. Buried under the waves, she could see nothing but water. To calm herself, she thought, *I know that they'll eventually pull me out of here. I'm underwater, but I'll be out of here soon.*

The massive waves, some close to 100 feet high, were a challenge not only for Kristy but also for Delf. He had to let out just enough slack to get her down into the water—but with no excess that could create tangles.

The troughs of the waves were so high that a lot of cable needed to be let out and it was hard to control. With the continual movement of the ocean, one minute Kristy would be under the water and the next minute she'd be dangling in the air. This chaotic motion was complicated by the unstable position of the aircraft. The autohover was inoperable in the extreme winds, and the helicopter was constantly bouncing up and down.

Except for expending an enormous amount of energy swimming to the survivor, the first rescue went well. Kristy reached the sailor drifting away from the life raft and explained what she was going to do. To be heard above the noise of the wind, the rain, and the helicopter, she had to yell. "Put your arms up in the air!" she shouted. The sailor lifted his arms, and Kristy managed to get the *rescue strop*—a strap formed by a flat foam loop—over his head and under his armpits.

Her instructions were clear. "I don't want you to try to lift your arms at all, or you'll fall out of the strop. If that happens, you could die. I'm going to hold you so that you can't do it, but please don't struggle. Just let me do what I have to do. Even if you want to lift them—don't!"

With that, Kristy gave the signal to start the winch, and they went up together. Delf pulled the sailor into the helicopter, and Kristy strapped him in so he couldn't fall out. Rescue one was complete, and Delf looked at Kristy. Knowing what she had just been through, he asked, "Are you all right to go back down?"

"Yep, no worries. I'm right to go," she responded. Realizing she could do something that she'd never done before was a huge relief and a confidence boost. Down she went again, this time swimming toward the two survivors in the life raft.

The second rescue did not go as smoothly. A huge gust of wind hit the life raft, picked it up, and wrapped it around the winch cable. Just as Kristy thought, *Oh God, what am I going to do?,* another huge gust blew the life raft free of the cable. It was an incredible stroke of good fortune.

She went after the closest man and started putting the strop over him. His panicked partner began shouting, "No, don't take him! Don't take him! Take me! I can't hang on anymore! I want to go next!"

Kristy's response was matter-of-fact: "We're not going to leave you here, but I'm taking this man, he's the one I got to first." Once again, she calmly repeated her instructions and gave Delf the thumbs-up signal. The cable pulled tight. But as it straightened, the cable hit Kristy, scraping and gouging her neck. She was exhausted and injured, but once again McAlister had flawlessly executed a water rescue. It was the second in her life.

Michelle hadn't seen much of what had happened during Kristy's rescues. Her head was buried in a vomit bowl during the first winch, and she decided she would rather not watch the second.

Michelle had seen the *Helimed* paramedic being thrown around, and she knew she was going to have to go through whatever he and Kristy had experienced. Delf looked straight at Michelle, checking to see if she was willing to go down. Michelle gave the thumbs-up. As they had previously agreed, now it was her turn to go down the wire to retrieve the last two survivors.

As Michelle hit the water, Kristy was on the floor of the helicopter, retching out the door. As she watched what was going on below, Kristy was shocked to see Delf's face at her level. This shouldn't be happening. She was lying flat, and he was supposed to be standing up, conning the aircraft and controlling the winch.

After a moment, Kristy realized what had happened. With the rain, wind, and slippery floor, Delf had fallen out of the helicopter and was hanging by his safety harness. Dangling in the air, he was still focused on only one thing: taking care of Michelle. Delf was responsible for directing the movement of the aircraft and controlling Michelle's winch, and that was the only thing that mattered.

Kristy was acutely nauseated from the combination of seawater she had swallowed during the rescues and the turbulent air. But she realized that something had to be done, and it needed to be done quickly. Delf couldn't get back in the helicopter by himself because the floor was too slippery. It was up to her.

Mobilizing her last reserves of willpower, Kristy summoned the strength to get up off the floor. She grabbed Delf by his harness and dragged him back into the aircraft. Kristy lay exhausted, amazed that he had flawlessly continued the job while hanging outside the aircraft in this tempest.

As Delf's drama unfolded above, Michelle swam to the third sailor who was hanging onto the side of the life raft. Because his life preserver was so bulky, she fought to get the strop over his head. When that didn't work, Michelle told him to float on his back and lift his legs. He complied, and Michelle threaded the strop up over his waist and under his arms.

The sailor had survived the roll and was in the strop, but it wasn't over. Panicked, he screamed that he was terrified of heights and was afraid of the winch into the helicopter. Michelle realized that in order to get him into the chopper, she would need to reassure and comfort the exhausted sailor—while in the midst of massive waves and unrelenting noise. After a brief conversation, his spirits were bolstered, and Michelle gave Delf a thumbs-up.

Delf began the winch, but as they were being lifted to the helicopter something smashed the side of Michelle's head. She saw black "starry things," then came out of her daze and asked the terrified sailor, "What the f—k happened?"

"You've just been hit in the head with a metal cylinder on the life raft," he explained.

Michelle had encountered the same problem that Kristy had experienced earlier. The waves and the wind had picked up the life raft and wrapped it around the winch cable. Only this time, the wind didn't unravel the raft.

Michelle could see that the cable was fouled with rope from the raft tangled around it. She gave Delf the "winch out" signal, a large tap on her head, and she and the survivor went back down into the water.

Michelle knew that if the snarled cable threatened the safety of the helicopter, Delf would have to cut the winch line and they would be left adrift. *What will we do if we are cut off?* she wondered. Michelle quickly decided that she could grab onto the life raft and flip it over herself and the survivor. Then she would get him into the raft so they had shelter and create some sort of beacon so they could be tracked.

Seconds later, Michelle grabbed a plastic knife out of her harness. She sawed on the rope from the life raft and prayed that her knife would cut the 1-inch-thick line. The knife sliced through the rope, and Michelle felt the pressure release as the raft blew free of the cable.

Michelle turned and looked at the sailor. He had been frightened before, but by this time he was paralyzed with fear. She tried to calm him down and explained that they were going to be winched again. Once more, she signaled to Delf who activated the winch. Together they got the terrified survivor into the helicopter. He was in a state of shock, but alive and unharmed.

Michelle sat on the edge of the helicopter, and Delf asked, "Are you all right?" Michelle looked down at the one remaining survivor, left on the sinking boat with no life raft. She was concerned that the winch cable, which was kinked, could be damaged from the entanglement. She asked Delf if the cable would hold. "In the circumstances," he responded," I think it is okay to winch." Michelle nodded. "I have to do this again," she said, and Delf lowered her into the water.

The last survivor was waiting on what was left of *Stand Aside.* As Michelle approached, he jumped into the water. The second winch was easier. She didn't try to put the strop over his head and bulky equipment; she slipped it around his feet and up under his arms. Delf started the winch, and they went up without incident. The last crew member of *Stand Aside* had been winched to safety.

On the trip back to the mainland, both Kristy and Michelle had time to think about what had just happened. They had faced the very real possibility that they might die. If the winch cable had been cut, they would have been left adrift with little hope of rescue. They had both come face-to-face with their own mortality. They had overcome their fears, and they had saved four lives.

When the helicopter returned to Mallacoota, the sailors they had rescued stepped out onto the tarmac. The police quickly ran up with blankets, which they offered to Kristy and Michelle. Kristy looked at one officer and said, "You better give them to the guys we just rescued." The officer looked at her with an incredulous stare. "You mean you're not the ones that were rescued?"

"No" she replied, "It was these gentlemen here." Asked later about the incident, Kristy smiled and said, "I think it surprised a lot of people because they thought . . . Well, I guess they assumed that because we were the girls, we were the ones that were rescued, not the ones doing the rescuing."

17

AFR Midnight Rambler— Hell on White Water

After the knockdown that tore the anemometer off the top of the mast, the Ramblers had to do some quick and serious thinking about their options. The *Sword of Orion* hadn't broadcast its warning yet, but everyone knew that conditions were dangerous and getting worse.

As Ed, Bob, and Arthur engaged in a tense discussion about whether to pull out of the race, they saw another boat heading in the opposite direction. The boat was bigger than *AFR Midnight Rambler*. In the distance it appeared to be a BH 41—a 41-foot cruiser-racer, and it was not doing well.

Steering a boat in big waves is no easy task, especially with the wind coming from behind. As the boat slides down the waves, the rudder is less responsive and the helmsman has much less control. The BH 41 seemed to be sailing erratically, and Bob was carefully following her movements. Ed shouted over, "She's carrying on a real treat, yawing and rolling all over the place!" Bob nodded in agreement.

Ed, Arthur, and Bob met again to consider their options. The port of Eden was 40 miles behind them, but that meant turning in the face of the storm and running with their back to the wind. The BH 41 had shown them what that would bring. The first safe port in Tasmania was

200 miles into the teeth of the storm. The temptation to turn around and run for shelter—only 40 miles away—was huge. They all wanted to do it, but they knew the risks.

The crew had been through big waves in '94, so they realized how seas like this could affect a boat as small as their 35-footer. Turning around would be dicey. The change in direction would increase their chances of taking a wave beam on, from the side. With the size of these waves, there was a fair chance they could be rolled 360 degrees.

The Ramblers had no way of knowing what had happened with *Stand Aside* and *Siena*. But they knew that a roll would likely mean they'd be dismasted. If that happened, there was a very good chance that someone would die.

Neither pressing ahead nor turning back felt safe. But Ed was convinced that the crew was capable and they were tough. Though Chris was in pain, he was talking clearly and coherently, and making repeated requests to come up on deck and help. Taking all that into account, Ed and the crew agreed on what they needed to do.

There was no vote, no show of hands, and no formal meeting. But after Ed had spoken with everyone, the Ramblers were in complete agreement: *AFR Midnight Rambler* would sail into the storm and make the almost 500-mile journey to Hobart. They double-checked their harnesses, emergency signaling equipment, and life rafts. Whatever happened, they would be ready. It was not easy going. Official records of the Bureau of Meteorology later showed that the maximum *average* winds in the Bass Strait reached 60 knots, with frequent gusts close of 75. These sustained winds generated massive waves more than 80 feet high.

One way of understanding what the Ramblers would encounter is to use the *Beaufort Scale* as a yardstick. The Beaufort Scale—initially designed to provide a common language to describe the effect of wind and waves on the sails of a warship—is still used as a way of understanding severe weather conditions.

Based on the official Bureau of Meteorology estimates, *AFR Midnight Rambler* was sailing into weather conditions that, on the Beaufort Scale, would be classified as a *Force 11 Violent Storm*. There were reliable reports, however, that conditions were, in fact, considerably worse than those described by the Bureau of Meteorology. According to these reports, boats in the Bass Strait would encounter a *Force 12 Hurricane.*

In a Beaufort *Force 12 Hurricane,* winds are greater than 64 knots, the air is filled with foam, waves are over 45 feet, the sea is completely white with driving spray, and visibility is greatly reduced. For a small boat, a *Force 12 Hurricane* is hell on white water.

One of the weather accounts came from Darryl Jones, pilot of the police helicopter *Polair 1* initially dispatched to the *Stand Aside* rescue operation.[1] Shortly after departing, he was diverted by Australian Search and Rescue (AusSAR) to assist with the search for another boat, *Business Post Naiad*. Then his orders changed once more, and he was redirected to rescue a crew member who had been washed overboard from the yacht *Kingurra*.

On his way to the first search location, Jones encountered winds over 85 knots. These were the strongest winds he had ever experienced in twelve years with the Police Air Wing. The helicopter normally cruised at 120 knots, but the strong tailwinds increased his airspeed to 205 knots.[2]

When Jones began the search for the missing *Kingurra* sailor, the sea was—as he described it—in a "wild and horrendous state." There were rain showers and continuous sea spray with a cloud base extending from 600 to 2,000 feet. The wind was blowing about 75 knots, and the waves were 80 to 90 feet high.

The police crew finally located the missing man, John Campbell, who was drifting some 300 yards from the boat. Constable David Key was winched into the water, and Jones held a 100-foot hover above him. When Jones looked up and saw a wall of water coming toward the chopper, he realized he would need to gain altitude quickly to avoid being swamped. Jones climbed 50 feet, and the wave missed the helicopter by about 10 feet as measured by the radio altimeter. It had to be well over 100 feet high.

No two storms are ever exactly alike, but these conditions were much like the extreme weather encountered by sailors off the coast of Nova Scotia in 1991. In that Halloween nor'easter—described in Sebastian Junger's book, *The Perfect Storm*—waves over 100 feet and sustained winds of 60 knots were recorded. This "meteorological hell" led to the deaths of the six fishermen on the *Andrea Gail,* six other fatalities, and millions of dollars in damage. In many ways, the '91 Nova Scotia storm and the '98 Australian weather bomb were proving to be eerily similar.

Both storms were destructive, and both created extraordinarily high waves. But the waves of the Bass Strait were uniquely dangerous. Sailors call the Bass Strait *the washing machine,* and with good reason. Waves in the Strait are confused, and they can churn in from any direction. The turmoil created by these waves makes them even more daunting than waves in the open ocean.

Not only were the *Rambler* and her crew in a confused sea of extremely high waves, they were also fighting something else. Bass Strait waves are high—and they are "sharp," too. Because the Strait is so shallow, waves form like surf hitting the beach on a shoreline. In this weather bomb, the wind drove the waves to tremendous heights with menacingly steep faces.

From the deck of a boat, or even from a helicopter, the waves looked like gigantic moving walls of green seawater. Like waves on a beach, they would curl and break, spewing clouds of white foam at the top. The trailing edges of the waves were even steeper than the faces. Successfully maneuvering a boat through these cliffs of water took extraordinary skill.

If the *Rambler* tried to steer directly up the face of one of these waves, the bow of the boat could be thrust up violently, upending the boat until it capsized. And steering down the sharp waves could end in *pitchpoling,* with the stern pitching forward over the bow and sinking the boat.

As the most experienced helmsman, Ed Psaltis took responsibility for steering the *AFR Midnight Rambler* through the waves. Memories of the 1994 race were very much on his mind. When *Nuzulu* capsized, Ed was trapped underwater. If the boat hadn't righted itself, he would have drowned.

That experience had scared the hell out of him. Ed knew that turning 90 degrees to the face of a wave meant that they might get rolled. Even more anxiety-provoking, the waves in '94 were only 30 to 40 feet. Now they were more than twice as high. Especially on a small boat, the helmsman can't afford to be sideways in the waves. Ed had learned that the hard way.

Ed was also thinking about the things that Australian sailing legend James Hardy had said about the disastrous 1979 Fastnet Race. Hardy had been one of Ed's idols since he was a boy, and Ed had read about his experiences. Hardy was the helmsman on a well-known boat named *Impetuous,* and he successfully steered *Impetuous* through a Force 10 storm in the '79 race.

Ed remembered the strategy Hardy used in that deadly race. *Take the waves at about 60 degrees, don't go straight into them. Go up into the wave as it approaches you, and pull over the top to avoid going into thin air. Then steer down the other side and back onto your course.*

What Hardy had done in the Fastnet worked for him, and what the Ramblers had tried in '94 didn't. They had been rolled. Ed's bad experience and Hardy's advice converged, and Ed developed a plan. He would steer up into the waves until he hit white water at the top, then slide down the backside. For the next ten hours, Ed would repeat the mantra *"60 degrees, 60 degrees, 60 degrees."*

The wind was now blowing 60 to 70 knots, with stronger gusts of 80 knots or more. With the anemometer gone, there was no way to tell for sure. Jonno, for one, thought it was a blessing, since they couldn't quantify just how bad the conditions were. But regardless of the wind speeds, things were bad. When the strongest winds hit, they were engulfed in a whiteout and Ed was completely blinded at the helm.

The storm was unpredictable. At times the waves would drop to 20 or 30 feet, the height of a two- or three-story building. Waves like that were negotiable. Ed would start to relax, thinking, *We're getting over them okay, and we're in control.* Then, suddenly, a set of two or three or four of the 60-footers would come through and the Ramblers would be jolted into survival mode. It was a chaotic and erratic pattern: manageable waves and the feeling of relief, followed by a nasty set of green walls and white knuckles.

One of the most terrifying parts of the storm was the noise of the wind. It was like an old-fashioned teakettle, screaming with the sound of steam blasting from the spout—a high-pitched, deafening noise that never stopped. The only way the crew could communicate on deck was to stand next to each other, cup their hands, and shout until their voices were hoarse.

The Ramblers were not only frightened. They were freezing, wet, and some of the crew were seasick. They would throw up wherever they happened to be at the time. It wasn't a conscious act; it just happened. Normal bodily functions became unimportant. The only thing that mattered was survival.

Spray from the waves and the rain hit their faces like gravel pellets. Even with goggles, it was nearly impossible for Ed to face into the storm. But he had to know when the big waves were coming, so the Ramblers worked as a team and developed a system.

They agreed that two people would be on deck at any one time. The others would be below, protected from the storm. One person on deck would steer the boat as the helmsman, and the other would act as a *wave spotter.* The wave spotter had two responsibilities. One grueling job was to face into the storm, scanning the horizon for threatening waves. The second role was to act as a human shield, blocking the helmsman from the painful impact of the spray. With the wave spotter as his shield, the helmsman could crouch behind, ready to react when the time came.

The spotter's cry of "Bad wave!" would give the helmsman five to ten seconds to face into the storm, assess the danger, and make sure they had enough speed to maneuver over the wave. With the noise of the wind and the chaos of the storm, sometimes the spotter could shout only a single word—"big," "bad," or "wide." But that was enough. The system worked.

People below deck were living in another world. Cut off from the struggle above, they were isolated and terrified. But they found a way to stay connected. After shouting his warning to the helmsman, the wave spotter would bang on the cabin to alert those below. As primitive as the signal was, it was comforting to have this human connection—for those below to know that their mates on deck were still there, doing their jobs, and watching out for their safety.

Even with Ed's extraordinary skill, it was impossible to maneuver flawlessly over each wave. When the boat reached the top of a big wave, Ed was blinded by 10 to 15 feet of white foam, and sometimes he would pull away too late. *AFR Midnight Rambler* would launch off the wave and fly into space, hanging in the air until it hit the trough ahead of the next wave.

There were no backs to the sharp waves, so the boat would drop vertically, 30 feet or more. When it hit bottom, a shock wave would resonate throughout the boat. The mast, supported by the wire rigging, was already under extreme pressure. Everyone knew it could turn into a pile driver, and they waited to see what would happen.

It was especially frightening for those below deck. As the boat rocketed into the air, there would be nothing but silence, then a deafening noise as the boat hit the water. Arthur thought, *This is like being inside of a metal drum with someone bashing on the outside.* It was a terrifying experience, as they waited to see if the rigging would drive the mast through the bottom of the boat and water would start gushing in.

When Ed pulled away too late, the boat would fly off the back of the wave. But if he pulled away too early, the knockdowns were even worse. When the *Rambler* was at the top of the wave and got caught on the lip, the boat would slide back down the face of the wave. Anyone on deck would be engulfed by a solid mountain of water.

During one particularly bad knockdown, Ed grabbed onto his harness as a wave swept through the cockpit. The harness was attached to a strong point on the boat, but with the force of the wave, Ed couldn't hang on. He was thrown to the back of the boat until he hit the stainless steel life rail.

Ed reached the end of his 6-foot harness and was jerked back, just as his ribs crashed into metal. The pain was intense, and he thought his ribs were broken. They were just badly bruised, not broken, and luckily the railing didn't break from the impact. Because of his harness, Ed was still inside the boat—more or less.

As the boat slid down the wave, everything that was horizontal suddenly went vertical. Everyone, whether on deck or down below, hung on for their lives. Chris, his arm still wrapped around the pipe next to his berth, was glued to his bunk, trying to make sure he didn't fall out and injure himself further.

Ed was still attached to the boat, but the *Rambler* was lying on its side and the cockpit was filled with water. The boat had completely lost momentum, and Ed could see another set of big waves coming at them. If the boat didn't get moving, they would be trapped. The next waves could hit the vulnerable, flattened boat, causing it to capsize and roll.

Floating helplessly in the water, Ed thought, *This is it. This time we've gone too far.* Desperate to avoid catastrophe, he clawed his way back into the cockpit and grabbed the tiller. Ed got the *Rambler* pointed in the right direction, and the sail filled with wind. He needed to get enough forward speed before the next wave hit, or it would be over.

Just in time, the boat started to move. Not fast, but enough to make it over the top. *AFR Midnight Rambler* had survived the knockdown and continued to sail into the storm.

18

AFR Midnight Rambler—
Sharing the Helm

Ed continued to steer, but he was very, very tired. He was mentally and physically exhausted, but he kept going. *I'm the best guy to steer this boat. I'm the guy in charge, and these are my six friends. If I can't get the boat through these waves, people will die.* Feeling the full weight of his responsibility, Ed fought back fatigue and focused on getting the boat through the brutal storm.

Under normal conditions, Ed was good at thinking about managing the crew and assessing who should go below for rest. But these conditions were anything but normal, and he had lost track of everything except fighting the waves and keeping everyone alive.

While Ed was consumed with his job at the helm, Gordon Livingstone was glued to the rail as his wave spotter. Chris had been getting ready to relieve Gordo when he cracked his head open. Now Chris was immobilized below, and Gordo stayed in position.

Gordo took it for granted that he would fill in for his injured mate. There weren't a lot of alternatives, and in his view it was just a matter of getting the job done. *In some ways*, he thought, *it's better to be up sitting on the rail than trapped down below.* Gordo had a spectacular view of the extraordinary weather phenomenon that surrounded them.

The wind kept building, and the waves kept getting higher. Each time Gordo thought it couldn't blow any harder, it did. It was as if the ocean had lost its mind. The air was saturated with water, and the crests of the enormous waves were being blown apart by the wind and hurled into the air.

The drops of water hitting Gordo's exposed skin stung with surprising and excruciating pain. In an attempt to protect his face, Gordo put his hand up in front of his face to shield himself and realized he could barely see his glove through the rain and spew.

Even though sitting on the rail was agonizing, Gordo thought that going down below would be even worse. Not only was it claustrophobic, but being stuck below deck meant losing any sense of what was going on. It was like riding a roller coaster in the dark and blindfolded. At least on the rail, Gordo had some idea of what was coming. There weren't as many surprises. Bad things were happening, but he had some sense of when and how to brace himself.

With Ed completely preoccupied with steering, Gordo had been forgotten in the confusion of Chris' injury and the storm. Arthur was the first one to realize what had happened. *Jesus, Gordo has been on the rail for almost four hours!* Even an hour would have been too much. Gordo needed a break, and Arthur decided to speak up.

Ed and Arthur had a special relationship. They had sailed together since they were young boys. They were best mates and rivals at the same time. They were close but connected with the prickly competitiveness of brothers. Arthur understood that Ed could push too hard, and he often "had a go" at Ed on this sensitive issue.

Ed realized he was a lot like Sly Stallone in the Rocky movies. His default mode was a boxer who was flat-out determined even when faced with impossible odds. Arthur thought more about conserving strength. It wasn't that Arthur was soft—he wasn't. But Arthur was always thinking like a marathon runner. Ed saw life as a sprint. In many ways, they complemented each other.

It was clear to Arthur that they were not going to survive the storm by sprinting. There was no way of knowing how long it would last. Looking at Gordo on the rail, he realized there was a reason Ed had lost track of him. Ed was exhausted after hours at the helm, and he was completely focused on steering.

Yelling over the noise of the wind, Arthur shouted into Ed's ear.

"Dammit, Ed, Gordo's still on deck! We've got to get a grip, we can't go on like this. The crew isn't being managed. It's not your fault, I know you've got to steer, but let me take over and manage the watch."

Ed came out of his hyperfocused state. He didn't hesitate. "Yes, just do it!" he screamed back. "I can't even think about it!"

To the relief of everyone, Arthur dedicated himself to looking after the welfare of the crew, leaving Ed at the helm to do what he did best. Gordo went below and took shelter from the maelstrom, and Mix came on deck to replace him as wave spotter. Gordo felt a sense of relief, but he was also shocked by what he saw below.

Everyone was visibly shaking, not just from the cold but also from fear. Gordo was battered from his time on the rail. He had been sliding back and forth between two deck fittings, and their shapes were clearly outlined by the dark bruises on his legs. Like everyone else, he was trembling. To warm himself, Gordo crawled into a bunk with Arthur. Arthur tossed a sea blanket over him, but Gordo's quivering continued.

Arthur was shaking, too. At first he thought he was just cold. *That'll go away when we warm up a bit,* he said to himself. But an hour later he realized it was more than being cold. He was gripped with terror about what the next wave would bring. And in the back of his mind, he knew he would have to get up on deck again and face the storm. The deep physical and psychological pain of the experience was immense, and it couldn't be fixed with a blanket. Surviving the storm was the only remedy.

Everyone, whether up on deck or below, confronted the very real possibility of death. There was a point at which Arthur came close to despair. *We've done everything we possibly can do to survive in these conditions; I can't see a way out, and it's actually getting worse.*

He thought about his fourteen-month-old daughter. At this really low point, he couldn't help but think, *I just didn't have a chance to have an impact on her life.* It was a waste, and he felt angry. *If only he had a chance.*

Mix didn't know if it was fear or because he was completely drenched and cold after spending hours wave spotting. Maybe it was the aftermath of having waves constantly breaking over him, washing him down the deck against the safety railing. Or maybe it was the horror of watching the storm intensify around him. But Mix just couldn't stop shaking. In the background, the radio was blaring with distress calls. It all added to his feelings of isolation and terror in the middle of the Bass Strait.

Mix kept thinking about his family. His wife, Annabel, was expecting their first child. He wondered if he would ever see her again or get to meet his unborn child. *What is Tink seeing on the news? What does she know about our condition? Does she know we're in trouble? Does she know we are still okay?* The questions raced through his head, unanswered.

Everyone thought about their loved ones. Ed thought about Sue and their two boys, Ben and Matthew. He reflected on how he could have been a better husband, all the things he didn't do that he could have done, and how he could have been a less grumpy father and spent more time with his family.

None of this was spoken aloud. Ed felt that keeping these dark thoughts to himself was important. As the skipper, he couldn't let the others know he thought there was a chance they might not make it. But he knew they were in serious trouble, and he was the leader. He would do what he thought was right.

The airwaves were filled with distress calls. The men below could hear radios broadcasting the plight of boats just a few miles away. They were surrounded by disaster.

Gordon listened in horror. He kept thinking, *We can't go into that water because there's no way we can survive. The boat can't turn around and come back and get us; it's physically impossible.* Then at 5:21 p.m., a Mayday call from the *Winston Churchill* made his blood run cold:

WINSTON CHURCHILL: Mayday. Mayday. Mayday. Here is *Winston Churchill, Winston Churchill.*

ABC HELICOPTER: *Winston Churchill. Winston Churchill. Winston Churchill.* [This is] ABC chopper. Go ahead with your position. Over.

WINSTON CHURCHILL: Twenty miles southeast of Twofold Bay. Over.

ABC HELICOPTER: *Winston Churchill.* Two zero miles southeast of Twofold Bay. Nature of your Mayday? Over.

WINSTON CHURCHILL: Affirmative. We are getting the life rafts on deck, ABC chopper. We are holed. We are taking water rapidly. We can't get the motor started to start the pumps.

ABC HELICOPTER: Roger. How many onboard?

WINSTON CHURCHILL: Niner. Niner.

The content of the Mayday was terrifying enough, but the despair coming through the voice of the skipper, Richard Winning, made it worse. Gordo started to shake even more. He knew the crew of the *Winston Churchill* was in very serious trouble.

Everyone dealt with their anxiety in different ways. Arthur was angry and fearful, but he realized that this emotional state was not where he wanted to be. It wasn't effective. There was no sense in thinking about *if only.* He needed to focus on what they were going to do to get out of this mess. Arthur had descended into a state of despair, but then—by force of will—he brought himself out.

Like the rest of the crew, Mix had private thoughts about whether they were going to get out alive. But he still felt completely confident in the team, and in their ability to fight the storm. Buoyed by this sense of connection with his mates, he pushed his doubts into the back of his mind. He decided to focus only on the present, about the things he could influence, one moment at a time.

Jonno didn't allow himself to think that they might not make it. To some extent, he felt that their fate was in the hands of the gods. He thought, *If the boat gets knocked down, we'll just have to hang on and see what happens. Then we'll deal with it.*

Each time *AFR Midnight Rambler* recovered from a knockdown and righted itself, Jonno gained more confidence in the boat. His only concern was that if conditions continued at the current intensity into the night, there could be gear damage. But until it happened, there was no need to focus on the unknown.

Jonno marked progress by doing a rough calculation of the amount of time they were "in control." When the boat was knocked down on its side, they were completely out of control. But even when the boat wasn't sideways in the water, the winds were so strong that they were rolling all over the place. They were still not in control of the boat.

A sense of control is the most important thing, Jonno thought. *If we have some control, we will have some way of predicting the outcome.* Intent on measuring their power over the storm, Jonno developed a metric.

His scale was simple. If they were in control less than 50 percent of the time, that was bad, demoralizing. Being in control half of the time—exactly 50 percent—was a good thing. If they were half in control, then they were doing all right. Being in control more than 50 percent of the time was really good.

There were long periods when Jonno calculated they were in control less than half the time. Every ten to fifteen minutes, he would gauge their situation. Tracking the degree of control became an engaging distraction. It provided a way of marking progress and, paradoxically, a device for feeling in control—even when they were out of control.

In spite of the scare that came with his injury, Chris found his own way of dealing with the uncertainty. He framed their situation quite clearly. *We, as a crew, are pretty good at what we do. We've all been doing it for a while. We're all doing what we all agree is the best thing we can do right now, to make sure we get through this. If we still lose, then we've given it our best shot, and there were no lost opportunities.*

In Chris' mind, there was nothing else that they could do. That freed him to be philosophical about the danger and to get on with doing what could actually help them. *The alternative*, he thought, *was running around in a blind panic or curling deep in the corner of the boat and crying out, "We're all going to be killed!"* It was a liberating way of thinking about their uncertain and dangerous condition.

Though each person found a personal strategy for dealing with fear, they also found ways to support one another. They were all conscious of visibly showing each other that they were doing the best they could under the circumstances.

The crew focused on short-term goals, making sure the equipment on the boat was working as well as it could be. They kept the boat "tidy," helping to impose a feeling of order on their chaotic state.

They monitored watch changes to make sure that people on watch were relieved and rotating on time. They made sure that the helmsman steering the boat had water. They did everything they could to make sure that they were taking care of the boat and that they were taking care of each other.

Those coming off watch would get a pat on the back with a congratulatory "well done." Everyone below knew what it was like up there, and anyone who stuck it out on deck had given it their all.

On deck, they made sure that the mainsail was tightly rolled up and lashed to the deck with the boom. They wanted to be certain that everything was properly secured so that if they did capsize, no one would be hit by loose equipment, adding injury to the mayhem.

Everyone was scared, but negative thoughts went unspoken. No one said, "Be positive." But they all concluded, privately, that they shouldn't be talking about doomsday when doomsday could come at any time. Catastrophic possibilities were imagined, but spoken comments were optimistic.

Some of the positive banter was transparently artificial. Arthur would say, "The clouds up there are clearing, the skies coming through are blue," or "The seas aren't quite as big now, I think we're getting through it."

Half the time, Ed thought, *This is a load of BS.* But then he thought again and concluded, *That's beside the point. It's reassuring to hear him say that we're going to be okay. It helps.*

Everyone had their peaks and troughs—moments when they utterly excelled and moments when they couldn't push themselves any harder. The crew was acutely sensitive to this ebb and flow of ability, and they all were willing to step into the breach and pick up the slack when somebody else had reached his limit.

Gordo had done this for Chris when he did a double watch without complaint. Chris was inspired by the thought of Gordo staying up there and simply doing what had to be done. The team also took notice when Arthur stepped in to take over crew management from Ed.

Establishing a watch system with people on deck for only an hour at a time and below deck for two hours, was critical to sharing the burden. There were three ways in which the system helped them maintain stamina.

One hour on deck meant that they could physically deal with the exhausting task of fighting the cold, rain, wind, and waves. In addition, the psychological impact of this system was equally important. They were much more resilient knowing that their time in hell would end after sixty minutes. Finally, Arthur's intervention was also symbolic. It demonstrated in a tangible, concrete way that they were aware of each other's needs—and that they would find a way to take care of each other.

In spite of everything they were doing to help each other, by the end of the day on Sunday the storm had taken an enormous toll. Ed had been steering for most of the afternoon. Bob had done his share to relieve Ed, and he had been washed off the helm twice by the gigantic breaking waves. Bob was willing to do whatever needed to be done, but Ed was the best driver and everyone knew it.

Ed was doing a truly extraordinary job, but even he had limits. Dusk was coming on and he began thinking, *I'm at the end of my tether. I'm not telling the crew, but if this continues, I can't keep going like this, and there's no one else that can steer this damn boat, so we're in serious trouble.*

Arthur sensed what his brother was feeling. And the thing that struck him about their situation was that the storm was getting worse—and it was still daytime. *What would happen when it got dark? This is not good,* Arthur thought. *Our best helmsman is Ed, and we've got to get him to rest before it gets dark. The last thing we need is to have him exhausted and fatigued at night.*

Arthur huddled with Bob and agreed on a plan. It was critical that they get Ed down below for a couple hours before it got dark, and that would mean they needed three helmsmen. The only way that could happen was if Arthur took a turn steering.

Climbing up on deck into the storm, Arthur shouted at Ed: "You've got to get off the bloody helm and get some sleep. If this thing keeps going through the night, it's going to get much harder—we might not see daylight! Get off the bloody helm and get down below!"

Ed shot back, "No, no, don't be stupid! This is tough, tough right now. I'm okay, let me go."

Arthur didn't flinch. "You're not okay. You're already knackered. You've got to let me have a go at steering this boat. I think I can do it. You're tired. Dusk is only an hour away, and we need our best man in the dark if we're to going to survive this. Get the hell down below and get some rest!"

Ed looked at his brother. He realized that Arthur was right. He had been pushing, pushing, and pushing, but he was struggling to keep going. He had to rest before dark. Exhausted, Ed went below and collapsed.

Arthur sailed superbly. Sprawled on a berth below, Ed began to understand what had happened. If Arthur hadn't stepped in, he would have been steering at night, physically and emotionally drained, with ragged reflexes. The thought of that was too horrifying to think about. Ed drifted into a half sleep. He was thankful that his brother had given him such a hard dose of reality. Then everything went fuzzy.

19

Sword of Orion— Out of Control

Tension had been building all day on *Sword of Orion*. Some time before 12 noon on Sunday, December 27, Steve Kulmar confronted owner-skipper Rob Kothe and said in no uncertain terms that conditions were unlike anything he had ever seen in all his sailing experience. Gusts of over 80 knots were hitting them on a regular basis, and Kulmar was concerned about the safety of the crew. He was convinced they should retire.[1] In fact, Kulmar thought they should have turned around much earlier—at 9 a.m. But Kothe resisted, saying "We need to wait until the twelve o'clock official radio broadcast." Kulmar wasn't happy, but he agreed that they would hang on and try to get a fix on the exact position of the low-pressure system. When the twelve o'clock forecast came, it wasn't much help. The broadcast said only that the low-pressure system was in the Eastern Bass Strait.

Leaving aside the question of where in the Eastern Bass Strait the center of the low-pressure system was located, the forecast was clear about the *storm warning.* Kothe believed that he had better knowledge of meteorology than anybody else on *Sword,* and Kulmar, like many others in the race, did not fully understand the implications of the forecast.

Based on the storm warning, Kothe believed that they should be prepared for winds of 40 to 50 knots, with gusts up to 60 or 65. The extreme weather they were experiencing was far beyond his expectations. It was a puzzle that Kothe wanted to unravel. He was intensely focused on the radio, hoping for any weather information that would help him make sense of the mess they were in.

The roles and decision-making structure on the *Sword of Orion* were as confusing as the weather. Rob Kothe was the owner, the skipper, the navigator, and the resident meteorologist. Steve Kulmar was the most experienced Hobart veteran and the principal helmsman. Glyn Charles was a sailing rock star who had done the Fastnet and was considered a senior helmsman. But his experience was largely in small boats, and he had never sailed in weather remotely close to this. Added to the mix was Adam Brown, the third member of the crew qualified to drive the boat as a senior helmsman.

There are conflicting accounts of exactly what happened on *Sword of Orion,* but there is consensus about the confusion and lack of alignment. Brown had been steering *Sword of Orion* since 8 a.m., and conditions were so unmanageable that he often needed help turning the wheel. Glyn Charles had been below since 10 a.m., incapacitated by seasickness. Kulmar continued to lobby Brown and other crew members to turn around, while Kothe stayed below at the nav station trying to decipher the mystery of the storm from radio transmissions. He hadn't been on deck in hours.

Brown had been on the wheel for five hours when he was finally relieved by Kulmar. Trembling and shaking with exhaustion, Brown went below. He was sitting "like jelly" on the bottom of the stairwell. Seeing his condition, Kothe said, "He's going into shock, for God's sake, give him something to drink."

Glyn Charles emerged from below deck around 1 p.m. and spoke with Kulmar. Charles had joined the increasingly loud chorus of voices arguing that they should retire from the race, and he asked Kulmar to try to get Kothe to pull out. Kulmar agreed, and Charles took over the helm while Kulmar went below to, once again, confront Kothe.

Even with the added weight of Glyn Charles' opinion, Kothe wasn't convinced. Kothe hadn't had a direct conversation with Charles about the weather, and he felt that Charles was being "lent on" by the others. So in spite of growing resistance, *Sword of Orion* continued onward with Glyn Charles at the helm.

Charles was not in good shape. Before he had gone on deck, Kothe suggested that Charles take another seasick tablet. He refused, thinking that the pill would never stay down. Just before climbing topside to take the helm, he had vomited on the shoulder of another crewman.

Charles was not in top form, but he felt guilty about not doing his part. He was, after all, a rock star and a paid helmsman, and he needed to be earning his keep. In spite of his nausea and weakened condition, Charles was determined to do what he had been paid to do.

With Charles driving the boat, Kulmar approached the exhausted Brown and continued his lobbying efforts to get *Sword* out of the race. Kothe finally agreed that the decision about whether to continue should be made by the three helmsmen, and Brown had one vote. Brown wanted out, but, exhausted, he crawled into his sleeping bag and focused on recovering from his ordeal at the helm. A formal vote was never taken.

After the 2 p.m. sked—when *Sword* broadcast the weather warning to the fleet—Kothe had intended to go on deck and speak with Charles about the weather. But he became preoccupied with a new assignment: acting as a radio relay for boats whose broadcasts weren't getting through to *Young Endeavor.*

It wasn't his choice, Kothe thought, *to spend time passing messages back and forth.* He just happened to notice that some transmissions weren't getting through and thought that his interventions were important. One boat, *Ausmaid,* had been out of touch for two skeds, and he relayed their status to *Young Endeavor.* Kothe believed that he may have prevented a needless search-and-rescue effort. Whether or not he was right, the transmissions required his full attention.

Finally, around 3:45 p.m. the weather shifted. Blue sky appeared over *Sword,* and the winds dropped to about 15 knots. The crew thought that this was the center of the storm, but it is more likely that *Sword* had simply entered a corridor of lighter winds. Still uncertain about what was happening with the storm, Kothe finally made an announcement: "If the wind goes back above 65 knots, we're going to go home." Kothe never did speak to Charles about the weather.

Soon after Kothe's declaration, the winds did increase, and he made good on his commitment to turn around. In Kothe's mind, *Sword* was not "retiring,"—that is, pulling out of the race for good. They were simply turning back for shelter, hoping to continue the race after the storm. For the crew, there was a significant emotional component to the decision. Safety aside, it was a huge relief to be headed back toward land.

Sword was now only 90 miles from a safe haven, but steering toward Eden would put the waves almost directly behind them. This was the dangerous scenario rejected by *AFR Midnight Rambler. Sword* would now be running ahead of the monstrous waves, and the potential for losing control greatly increased. Aware of the danger, Kothe suggested going west. They could then take the waves at an angle and be less vulnerable to a knockdown.

Kothe broadcast their decision to seek shelter at 4:44 p.m. He knew that the announcement would be heard by other skippers, and he hoped that they might follow suit. If *Sword* was later able to get back in the race, it would improve their competitive position if other boats had dropped out as well.

Turning *Sword* around was not easy. It required a sailing maneuver known as a *jibe,* which involves turning the stern of the boat into the wind. In the process, the boom could swing around quickly and violently, sweeping across the cockpit. *Sword* jibed, but without a hitch. Charles may have been seasick, but he executed the about-face flawlessly.

Sword was now on a new course, but not the westerly track they had agreed on. Instead, Charles was heading north, directly toward Eden. Darren Senogles—Dags—who had just congratulated Charles for his brilliant work in turning *Sword* around, was now concerned. He asked if Charles was okay. Charles brushed aside his worries and seemed concerned only about the time he had spent below. Feeling guilty about having let the team down, Charles continued to steer the northerly course. The waves continued to pound *Sword* from behind.

Dags became increasingly concerned about Charles, and anxiety intensified as he watched him hunkering down inside his foul-weather gear. Charles could barely see past the hood of his jacket. Shouting over the deafening noise of the wind, Dags volunteered to steer. But Charles refused the offer. He seemed fixated on the instruments, almost in a trancelike state. Dags continued to insist that they needed to change course to avoid surfing uncontrollably as waves hit them from the rear.

Charles seemed oblivious to Dags' advice, instead focusing on the miserable conditions and his leaking wet-weather gear. Dags thought that Charles needed to be relieved at the helm, but the only one with that power was Kothe, and Kothe was down below at the nav station, where he had been all day.

Other crew members felt the boat sliding down the waves and were worried enough to confront Charles. Carl Watson decided to brave the weather on deck, and he made his way to the rear of the boat to complain about the dangerous course Charles was steering. It was no use. Charles insisted that he had experience with the Fastnet, and he knew what he was doing.

Down below, Brown felt the boat spinning out of control. He yelled to Kothe that they had to change course or get Charles off the helm. But Kothe, believing that Brown was still recovering from exhaustion, insisted that Charles be left alone.

Brown felt otherwise. He stuck his head out of the hatch and shouted to Charles and Dags. With the noise of the wind, neither could hear what he was saying. Dags moved closer to Brown, who again shouted that they needed to change course. Then it happened.

It was the catastrophe that the crew had been trying to avoid. An enormous wave, its face a vertical wall of water, picked up the stern of the boat. Traveling almost 35 knots, the wave turned the boat sideways, covered the deck with foam, and tossed *Sword* on its side.

The boat tumbled down the face of the wave and hit the bottom of the trough with tremendous force. Dags saw the top of the mast hit the water, then submerge as *Sword* lay on its side. Dags panicked as he realized that he was underwater and was still attached to the boat by his safety harness. He thought he would drown. He tried desperately to unhook his tether, but failed. A few seconds later *Sword* was hit by another wave and flipped back up, having been rolled 360 degrees.

Dags was now above the surface of the water and still connected to the boat. Had he been able to unhook the safety harness, Dags would have been carried away by the waves and almost certainly drowned. Thankfully, he was still attached, and Dags dragged himself back into the cockpit.

As with *Stand Aside,* the 360-degree roll nearly destroyed *Sword of Orion.* The deck and cabin top were damaged, and the cockpit had been compressed into the hull. The mast was broken and lying in the water, and the spokes from the boat's wheel were buckled. The boom, which normally would be used to secure the bottom of the mainsail, had been lashed to the side of the boat. But it broke free and swept across the deck, smashing the wheel and everything in the cockpit.

Below deck, Kothe was trapped, with an injured knee, under a pile of sail bags. Looking around, he saw smoke and sparks coming from the long-range high-frequency (HF) radio. Fearing an electrical fire, he managed to turn off the radio and pull the cables from the computer. This left only their shorter-range VHF radio operational.

The cabin was flooded to the crew's knees, and the hatchway stairs had broken away. The housing to the motor had collapsed. With the broken stairs, debris, and sails floating around, it was difficult to get on deck.

In the cockpit, Dags recovered from his brush with death and looked desperately for Glyn Charles. He saw only the bright orange strap of Charles' safety tether, with one end attached to the yacht and the other draped over the side. Dags ran to the lanyard, grabbed it, and pulled it in. There was nothing on the other end except broken stitching where the lanyard had been attached to Charles' harness.

Dags frantically scanned the water and saw Charles floating about 100 feet behind the boat. He screamed at Charles to swim back, but *Sword* was being driven away by the water and the wind. Charles tried to swim. He did all of six strokes, but he could barely lift his arm out of the water. He appeared to be injured, and he couldn't swim as fast as the boat was moving.

Dags called out for the others to get on deck. Oblivious to the fact that there were injured crew down below, he couldn't understand why only a few people responded. Desperate to rescue Charles, Dags shouted for a rope. He thought that if he could swim toward Charles, and Charles toward him, they could meet somewhere in the middle and both would be dragged back into the boat.

It took a few precious minutes to find a rope long enough to give them any chance of reaching Charles. When they finally found one, Dags climbed outside the lifelines, preparing to jump into the water. Before he could launch himself, *Sword* was hit by another bad wave. The boat was pushed more than 300 feet farther away from Charles. The situation now looked hopeless.

Even if Dags had jumped into the water, he wouldn't have been able to see Charles. And by this time, the distance was too great to swim. They watched Charles bobbing in the distance, ever farther away. It was only when *Sword* reached the top of a wave that they could see him treading water, fighting the waves and losing the battle.

Charles would struggle and start to go underwater, then disappear, and then bob back to the surface. The third time Charles went under, he never came back up. Helpless to intervene, Dags and another crew member kept a lookout for a while, scanning the spot where he had last been sighted. He never reappeared.

With Charles gone, Dags and others began cutting away the wreck-age with hacksaws. The mast was broken into pieces, but it was still attached to the yacht. The tangle of wires and metal had folded around the boat, and the snarled rigging was holding *Sword* with its side exposed to the waves. It was the most vulnerable position, and it invited another roll.

Those on deck worked to get rid of the remnants of the mast, while the crew below tried to bail. The switches needed to start the motor were gone, and the engine had shifted in its mounting so the bilge pumps were worthless. Water kept pouring in, and the crew needed to do some-thing quickly. They could find only one bucket, but someone found a drawer. They bailed with whatever they could find, trying to keep *Sword* afloat.

After activating the boat's EPIRB, they broadcast Mayday transmis-sions. Then they sat on what remained of *Sword of Orion,* waiting for rescue. About an hour and a half after the capsize, Steve Kulmar sighted something in the distance, about a thousand yards away. Another boat, the *Margaret Rintoul II,* was sailing almost directly toward them.

A call for signals went up, and the flare container was passed to Nigel Russell. Russell had been designated as the *Minister in Charge of Flares* in more lighthearted times. Russell and Kulmar grabbed the first set of flares and fired them so that the trajectory would take the signal toward the passing vessel.

Kulmar thought they could see three people on the boat. The weather had abated considerably, and the wind had dropped to around 40 knots, but it was drizzling and they couldn't be sure they saw three people. But there was someone on deck, they knew that.

Aboard the *Margaret Rintoul II,* skipper Richard Purcell saw the dis-masted yacht. He could see men on *Sword*'s deck, and he definitely saw a flare. He told his navigator, Colin Betts, to advise *Young Endeavor* that they had sighted the flare. The question was what to do next.

In a similar situation, *Siena* had stood by *Stand Aside.* But they sus-tained injuries in the process, and *Siena* had a motor. *Margaret Rintoul II* didn't have a functioning motor, and it was dangerous to make an attempt to turn the boat in those circumstances without power.

Purcell didn't know the condition of *Sword,* but he decided to continue without stopping. He looked to his navigator, Colin Betts—an experienced sailor who had done thirty-five Hobarts—for confirmation that he had made the right decision. He thought he heard Betts say, "You are making the right call."

Betts radioed Lew Carter on *Young Endeavor,* identifying himself with a message: "Lew, it's Colin Betts on *Margaret Rintoul II.* We have just sighted one flare; it's bearing 090 from our position, approximately half a mile." Betts recalls giving Carter the latitude and longitude of their position, and saying that the yacht was dismasted. He heard only a response of "Thanks for that."

The radio log on *Young Endeavor* records a transmission from *Margaret Rintoul II* saying that a red flare had been sighted at 6:45 p.m., but the words "dismasted yacht" were not recorded. Betts was sure he said the words, and Carter was sure he did not hear them. The *Margaret Rintoul II* continued on its course and sailed by the *Sword of Orion.* As they passed by, Steve Kulmar estimated that the two boats were less than 300 yards away.

Responding to *Sword*'s distress signals, Navy helicopter *Shark 05* was dispatched by Australian Search and Rescue. The chopper reached the stricken yacht at 10:45 p.m.—about six hours after the boat had been rolled. *Shark 05* confirmed that one man had been lost overboard and that the rest of the crew was in no immediate danger. Running low on fuel, with a 100-mile return trip to Merimbula, the helicopter returned to shore.

Shark 05 was replaced by a second chopper, *Shark 20.* The weather was so bad that the spiral search pattern *Shark 20* was flying kept taking them over the same yacht—not the *Sword of Orion,* but another vessel. *Shark 20* flew over the boat so many times that the yacht finally radioed to ask if the helicopter needed assistance. The misunderstanding provided a rare humorous moment during an extraordinarily difficult and tense search.

Shark 20 ultimately found *Sword of Orion* and rescued three crew members, including Darren Senogles and Steve Kulmar. With a low fuel state, the chopper had no choice but to return to shore, leaving six men aboard.

A third helicopter, *Tiger 70,* took off from Merimbula in the very early morning of December 28. Because of the dangers of a night operation, the chopper hovered until daylight to execute the rescue. Rob Kothe smashed his head during the winching, but all six remaining *Sword of Orion* crew members were safely extracted from the wreckage.

A search for Glyn Charles continued until 9:30 p.m. that night. An entry in the Australia Search and Rescue Briefing Notes stated simply: "Target—Man in water wearing yellow suit and harness. No buoyancy aids." Glyn Charles was never seen again.

Ed and Arthur Psaltis
near their home on the
Parramatta River.

Bill Psaltis, veteran of twenty-three Hobart races.

Nuzulu in the 1994 Hobart with a jury-rigged sail.

AFR Midnight Rambler leaving the CYCA dock before the start of the 1998 Hobart.

The start of the 1998 Sydney to Hobart Race.

The *Winston Churchill* sailed in the first Hobart in 1945
and circled the world twice.

Sayonara and *Brindabella* leading the fleet
at the start of the race.

AFR Midnight Rambler sails into the storm
to become the overall race winner—
the smallest boat in ten years
to win the Tattersall's trophy.

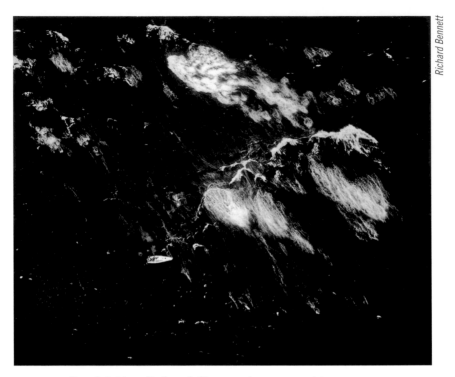

Stand Aside rolled and dismasted; crew awaiting rescue.

SouthCare helicopter comes to the rescue of *Stand Aside* crew.

The crew of *AFR Midnight Rambler*
with Sue Psaltis at Constitution Dock in Hobart.

John Whitfeld, Ed Psaltis (holding the Tattersall's Cup),
Bob Thomas, and Chris Rockell.

Ed Psaltis and Bob Thomas, 2006–2007 Ocean Racers of the Year.

AFR Midnight Rambler passing the Organ Pipes
on the coast of Tasmania in the 2001 Hobart.

20

General Mayday—
An Official Catastrophe

The strong winds and waves were nothing that superb sailors couldn't manage. Southerly busters had prepared them for big seas. But there was no way of preparing for the worst of what this storm would bring: the destructive force of the rogue waves. The kings. The freaks.

Winston Churchill

About 4:30 p.m. on Sunday, December 27, the *Winston Churchill* was sailing quite well. The winds were strong, around 55 knots, and the waves were sizeable but not particularly frightening. Two crew members were on watch: Richard Winning, the owner and skipper, and John Dean. Winning was an accomplished sailor, and he was comfortable at the helm. True, the weather was rough, but there seemed to be no cause for alarm.

Suddenly, one of the deadly freak waves appeared. Winning never considered himself very good at judging the height of waves, but he saw this one coming. He wasn't sure about the size, but it was higher than the boat's 60-foot mast. The wave was a deadly vertical cliff of green water.

Winning knew what to do. He wanted to get up the mammoth wave and over the top as quickly as possible. They started to climb, but *Winston*

Churchill didn't have the momentum, and without enough speed it was impossible to get over the massive wave. The wave picked up the boat and threw the yacht down on its side.

Winston Churchill didn't roll, but it hit the wave like a brick wall and was knocked down so severely that it suffered serious damage. Winning and Dean were instantly swept over the side. Three windows near the navigation station were smashed, and 6 feet of the boat had been ripped away. The damage above the water was significant, but it wasn't the biggest problem. *Winston Churchill* was shattered below the waterline as well.

Winning and Dean made it back aboard, and Bruce Gould took over the helm. He asked Stanley to check below and see what was going on. Whatever was happening, it wasn't good. It was obvious they were taking on a lot of water, and the boat was sinking lower and lower in the water. The crew got the two life rafts on deck, and everyone put on life jackets and waited to see what would happen. Gould had a gut feeling they weren't going to be there for long.

As Winning got ready to send a Mayday, he discovered that their long-range HF radio was out of commission, and the main GPS, which would establish their exact position, had been saturated and was also not working. Their portable GPS was not functioning properly either, so Winning had to estimate their position. Believing that they were about 20 miles southeast of Twofold Bay, Winning used their shorter-range VHF radio to transmit the chilling *Mayday* message that echoed below deck on the *AFR Midnight Rambler.*

Approximately 5:30 p.m.—about an hour after they had been knocked down—the crew abandoned *Winston Churchill.* There were two life rafts on deck: an oblong life raft designated Raft A, intended to hold six people, and a circular life raft designated Raft B, designed for four. John Stanley, John Gibson, John Dean, and Michael Bannister climbed into Raft A. They were joined by Bill Psaltis' friend Jim Lawler. Richard Winning, Bruce Gould, Michael Ryan, and Paul Lumtin climbed into Raft B.

Initially, the two rafts were roped together, but the line quickly broke, separating the two groups. Raft A stayed upright until just after midnight on the 27th, when it was hit by a large wave. The raft flipped upside down, and the five men found themselves standing on the canopy that had previously been the roof. They were surprised to find that the raft was as stable upside down as it was right side up, if not more so. In their inverted position, they weren't thrown around as much by the waves. But there was a problem: They were running out of air in the confined space.

Faced with a critical shortage of oxygen, the survivors decided to cut a small hole in the floor—now the roof—of the raft, hoping that oxygen would enter through the incision. It worked, and they were able to push the top up and down like a bellows, pumping air into the raft. But ten minutes later, there was a large explosion of water. The raft was thrown a considerable distance, spinning the men around inside. They were tossed violently, but at least Raft A was now flipped upright.

A series of large waves slammed into the raft, and each time the men were thrown around inside. The section of the floor that they had cut continued to tear, and the canopy was disintegrating. They clung to the raft for a long time until they were hit by one wave that Gibson described as appearing "without any warning at all, without even a sound, at terrific speed into what became tumbling white water. It was an extraordinary experience. I was traveling at very fast speeds. It was as if I'd cracked the biggest wave of my whole life. And I continued on in this manner. It was just a rushing, tumbling, noise deafening experience."[1]

When the wild ride came to an end, only John Gibson and John Stanley were still clinging to the inflatable tubing of the raft. They could see two figures in the distance, and one—believed to be Jim Lawler—activated a strobe light. What was left of the raft was buffeted by the wind and waves, and Gibson and Stanley clung tightly as the men who had been thrown out of the raft disappeared from view.

Gibson and Stanley held on to the raft throughout the remainder of the night and till dawn on Monday the 28th. Rescue aircraft flew by, and the two men tried frantically to get their attention by waving a yellow life jacket. Finally, at 8 p.m. that night, they heard planes overhead. Gibson flashed his personal strobe light, and Stanley signaled with a handheld flashlight. Between the two of them, they got the attention of the aircraft and were eventually rescued by helicopter.

Like Raft A, Raft B floated upright for a while, then capsized in the heavy seas, ejecting the survivors. But the crew in Raft B attempted to flip the life raft upright again. It was a dangerous operation that required one person to remove his life preserver and swim under the raft. Richard Winning volunteered to undertake the mission. As the skipper of the *Winston Churchill,* he considered it his duty to take the chance.

Winning swam down to the entrance of the canopy, which was now submerged, got through the opening, and then made his way to the raft's upturned bottom. Using a strap attached to the raft's bottom, he managed to get Raft B right side up. The other three crew members then reentered the raft.

Sometime in the night, Raft B was again flipped by a wave. Once more, Richard Winning took off his life vest, swam outside the overturned raft, and righted it. On each occasion, if Winning had lost his grip, he would have been swept away by the waves, with no life preserver. His chances of survival would have been virtually nonexistent.

No one was sure how it happened, but Life Raft B also developed a slit in its floor. The lower tube of the raft started to leak. With part of the pump missing, the men had no way of inflating the tubing. They eventually found themselves jammed together in a standing position as the floor of the raft took on a V shape. Realizing they had to do something, the men improvised a way to connect the pump to the lower inflatable tube. Then they pumped and bailed until they were able to restore the raft to a semblance of its former shape.

In the afternoon of Monday the 28th—nearly a day after abandoning ship—the survivors in Life Raft B sighted a fixed-wing aircraft. Using flares, they were able to attract the attention of the pilot, and some thirty minutes later they were all rescued by helicopter.

Business Post Naiad

At 5 p.m., faced with an onslaught of emergencies, the Australian Maritime Safety Administration (AMSA) declared a Mayday for the general area southeast of Eden. It was now an official catastrophe.

Twenty minutes after the AMSA declaration, *Business Post Naiad* was hit by a large wave beam-on, directly from the side. Four crew members were on deck, and *Naiad* went straight over, rolling 360 degrees in about ten seconds. When the boat came back up, the scene was a familiar one. The mast was broken, the cabin roof was damaged, windows were smashed, and everything below deck was in disarray.

The crew members on deck had been saved by their safety harnesses. Though thoroughly soaked, they managed to climb back on board. Navigator Peter Keats sent a Mayday, and they started the engine. They agreed to set a course for Gabo Island and to take shelter from the storm.

Everyone had survived, but the men who had been washed overboard started to have difficulty moving their limbs. About two hours after the roll, *Business Post Naiad* requested a rescue helicopter to winch three crew members who were suffering from seasickness and hypothermia.

Four hours later, they were struck again. This time, the boat did not immediately recover. Two crew members were on deck, Robert Matthews and Philip Skeggs. Matthews was trapped in the back of the cockpit but found an air pocket. He was able to breathe long enough to unclip his safety harness from its tether and swim to the surface. Matthews sat on a piece of the rigging—either the boom or the broken mast—for a couple of minutes until *Naiad* was struck again. Miraculously, the wave righted *Naiad* and threw Matthews back onto the deck.

Recovering from the ordeal and simultaneously trying to steer *Naiad,* Matthews saw Skeggs pinned down under a pile of ropes, about 6 feet from his original position. Matthews shouted for help, not realizing that the rest of the crew was trapped below.

The capsized yacht had filled with water, and everything below had become dislodged. The freezer had emptied its contents, and the engine, operational at the time of the capsize, had covered everything with diesel fuel. Debris blocked the hatch leading to the deck.

The crew below tried to kick out the hatch to get on deck. Bruce Guy, the skipper, and crewman Stephen Walker were trying to push out the life rafts onto the deck. Suddenly Guy arched his back, as though there was a severe pain in his chest. His eyes rolled back, and Walker grabbed him. He knew instantly that Guy was having a heart attack. Walker sat down with Guy's head in his lap. Guy was breathing when they sat down, and Walker continued to hold his head, unsure if the skipper was still alive.

The crew below heard Matthews calling out to Skeggs, and they scrambled to help. They were able to get him out from under the heavy ropes, but he was unresponsive. Shayne Hansen and Matthew Sherriff attempted CPR, but he was still unresponsive.

Philip Skeggs was gone. Bruce Guy had died in Walker's arms. The engine and all of the electronics aboard *Naiad* had failed. The crew had no radio and no means of communicating. Two life rafts were placed over the side of the boat, but a large wave carried them away. The survivors were left in a desperate situation.

The seven remaining crew members of *Business Post Naiad* were located and rescued by helicopter early on the morning of December 28. Bruce Guy and Philip Skeggs were left on board, and the boat was eventually towed to shore by the police launch *Nemesis.*

Kristy McAlister and Michelle Blewitt flew over the *Naiad* later that day. They had been assigned to search the area, which was the focal point of emergency signals. As they flew over the boat they saw a body on the deck.

Unaware that people had already been winched off the boat, the pilot radioed Australian Search and Rescue to inform them of their discovery: "We've come across the *Business Post Naiad,* there is a person lying on the deck."

The response was stark: "No, negative, that boat has already had people winched off it. The person on it is dead. Disregard, keep going on your search."

21

AFR Midnight Rambler—
Listen to That

The airwaves were filled with sounds of anguish and desperation. Aboard *AFR Midnight Rambler,* the crew listened to the frightening Maydays and man overboard alerts. They heard helicopters coming to the rescue of stricken boats, searching for people lost in the water.

These were men they knew. Friends they had shared time with and sailed with, not just competitors. Some, like Jim Lawler, they knew personally. It was sobering, and everyone on board the *Rambler* knew the danger. A wave that had knocked down and dismasted another boat could have just as easily crushed them.

Ed, Arthur, and Bob were steering magnificently, and the members of the crew were supporting each other with exceptional teamwork. But it was impossible to ignore the tragedies unfolding around them. *VC Offshore Stand Aside* had been hit to the north, less than 20 miles away. *Winston Churchill,* close behind them, had sunk. *Sword of Orion* had met its fate about 20 miles to the south. And *Business Post Naiad* had rolled about 10 miles to the east. It was excruciatingly apparent that *AFR Midnight Rambler* was in the bull's-eye of a deadly target. (See illustration on p. 120.)

Bob Thomas was steering the boat as straight as he could. With Mix blocking the waves, he hung on, ducked as low as he could, and let the water break over him. Three times the waves ripped Bob from the helm

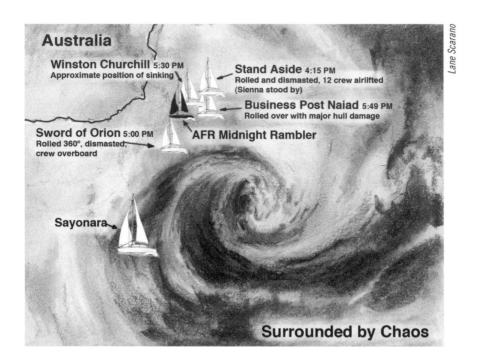

Lane Scarano

and slammed him down into the cockpit. Each time he would lunge toward the tiller, push it over hard, and focus on getting over the next one.

Bob was a disciplined master mariner, trained in lifeboat drills and sea safety. He had faith in his boat, and he believed the little *Rambler* would survive. But with the mayhem surrounding them, he needed to prepare the crew for the worst.

Abandoning ship is always a last resort, but sometimes it has to be done. The crew of *Winston Churchill* had no choice but to take to their life rafts. If the *Rambler* reached that point, Bob wanted to make sure that they would leave the boat in the right way. They would not throw the life raft over the side of the boat, inflate it, and expect everything to work out. It would be a planned, methodical operation.

With Ed at the helm, Bob went down below to brief the off-watch crew on everything they would need to do if the boat went down. He calmly explained the process and assigned tasks to each member of the crew. Some were to get the life raft on deck. Others were to grab the *ditch bag,* which they dubbed the *panic pack.* The panic pack held flares, the EPIRB, and other essentials for survival. They discussed other things, including water bottles and flashlights. The irony was that no one—especially Bob—exhibited any display of panic when talking about the panic pack.

"If we have to go to a life raft, it's got to be a very controlled procedure so that we all get into the life raft," Bob said. He was emphatic in saying that the process of leaving the *Midnight Rambler* had to be precise. Otherwise, two or three men could jump into the raft and be blown away, leaving the rest of them alone on a sinking boat.

After briefing the crew down below, Bob climbed on deck and told Ed about what had just happened. Ed understood and agreed: They needed to be ready for anything. Then, while Arthur steered and Mix spotted waves, Bob repeated the instructions he had given below.

It was an intense moment. As bad as conditions were, they knew things were going to get worse. The fact that Bob was now talking matter-of-factly about the life raft meant that they were headed into further trouble.

The winds were blowing around 65 knots, and waves continued to crash over the boat. The wind, screaming through the rigging, made conversation almost impossible. But Bob talked calmly, speaking right next to their ears.

"A lot of boats are in trouble," he explained, "and conditions ahead are as serious as those behind." Bob repeated his instructions about the panic pack, the spare EPIRB, the flares, the location of the lifeboats, and how they should be deployed. Finally, he reiterated the cardinal rule for abandoning ship: "Always step up into a life raft, never down." The meaning was clear: *AFR Midnight Rambler* needed to be unquestionably sinking before they would even consider getting into a life raft.

Though Bob went through the whole process very deliberately, it hit Mix squarely just how serious conditions were. If bigger boats ahead and behind them were sinking, what chance did a 35-foot boat have? They could only beat this storm with a combination of teamwork, skill, and luck. They had no control over luck, but they were skilled sailors. And they continued to work together with extraordinary cohesion.

At the helm, Arthur thought that the faces of the waves were about the length of a football field. They were big, steep stretches of water, and the only advantage the small *Rambler* had was its maneuverability. Arthur would move across the face of the wave, and, if he didn't like what he saw to his left, he would go right.

In the troughs, the breeze would drop and the *Rambler* was protected by the face of the waves. Arthur would get a brief relief, but it wasn't much. He was still surrounded by deafening noise and spew. It was just that the boat was a little bit more in control. But soon the *Rambler* would be sucked into the next wave.

Arthur would feel the boat being pulled ahead, and the *Rambler* would rise up the face of the wave. As they reached the top, the boat would be hit by the full intensity of the wind, and the *Rambler* would tilt dramatically. With rain and spew hitting him in the face, Arthur would contemplate his next move. He had to find a path through the next wave.

Steering a boat in these conditions required total concentration. It was exhausting. Ed's ability at the helm was unsurpassed—there was no question about that—and he would bear the heaviest burden. But *AFR Midnight Rambler* had two others who could drive and give him relief from the arduous task of steering. And they also had a system so that fresh people would be on deck every hour.

In these conditions, there were going to be mistakes, but minimizing errors and recovering quickly were critical. The Ramblers' ability to share the helm meant that there were far fewer blunders than if one person had been steering without relief. And their reflexes were far better when they needed to react.

Even with the watch system, the Ramblers were at their limits. The crew had been fighting the weather since eleven o'clock that morning. By 7 p.m. the storm's ferocity was still building. Arthur looked at his watch and thought, *It's still getting worse. Eight hours is a long time when you know the next wave may kill you.*

As he tried to comprehend what they'd gotten themselves into, another disaster metaphor popped into his head. This wasn't like a car accident, where things happen and it's over. In a car accident, if you live and you're okay, you can say, "That was close." This seemed like it was never going to be over. It was ever present and it was getting worse. It was a hard, frightening feeling.

About 8 p.m., Bob relieved Arthur at the helm. Arthur and Ed were in bunks below, trying to rest. The *Rambler* was a racing boat. The bunks were tight and uncomfortable. Ed kept thinking, *It's like lying in a coffin.* It wasn't a good way to think about it, he realized, but *coffin* was the word that kept coming to mind. The brothers were about 6 inches apart, their heads almost touching. They weren't sleeping; it was impossible. They just lay in their bunks, exhausted.

Suddenly, Arthur spoke. "Listen to that," he said. Ed's first reaction was that something had broken. *He's heard something come apart,* Ed thought. Gear failure in these conditions could mean fatalities. Ed's mind raced: *Oh, no, here we go. It's about to happen.* Then he said aloud, "No, I can't hear it. What are you talking about? Listen to what?"

"Ed," said Arthur. Arthur was very emotional, choked up, close to tears. "You can hear Bob," he said. "You can hear Bob in the cockpit. You can hear him talk."

Ed listened, and he could hear Bob talking to Mix and Jonno on deck saying, "The wind's dropping." The screaming kettle had stopped. Minutes before, you could be right next to someone and you couldn't hear him. Now you could hear people in the cockpit giving orders. You could hear the world again.

In the space of a half hour, the wind had gone from 80 knots to 40. The wind was still gale force, but Arthur was elated. A gale was survivable. He was going to see his family again. He was going to do whatever he needed to make it home. *No matter what happens,* Arthur thought, *I'm going to fight harder to get through whatever it throws at us. We're going to keep going.*

Ed became emotional as well, tearing up with the realization of what his brother had just said to him. Arthur was telling Ed that they had survived something ghastly. They had made it through the worst of the horrible storm.

The two brothers were lying there together, feelings of relief flooding through them. The connection was unspoken. Arthur had communicated everything with one choked-up sentence: *Listen to that.* When Ed realized what Arthur was saying, he had responded with one word: "Yes." Nothing more needed to be said. They had gotten through the storm together, and they knew they were going back to the land of the living. Together.

At that instant, there was a dramatic shift in the race. But it was not over, and they had not reached safety yet. Everything below deck was soaked. There was water everywhere, and their electronics were a disaster. The main GPS had failed, the portable GPS wasn't working, the radio was coming in and out, and they had nothing to navigate with.

Their wind instruments had been blown off the mast, and all they had left was a compass fixed to the cockpit on deck. Ed thought it was like Captain Cook when he came to Australia. They were in the middle of the Bass Strait with only a compass, sailing by the seat of their pants.

There were no lighthouses to get a bearing from, and they couldn't use the sextant. The sextant, though antiquated, was a reliable navigational instrument—but only if they could see the stars. And there was no chance of that.

The Ramblers were not out of danger, but Ed had faith in Bob. Together, they had done eight Hobarts, and Ed had come to know Bob's sixth sense as a navigator. Ed trusted Bob's ability to dead reckon—to estimate their position with nothing but a chart, a compass, and a pencil.

For the next fourteen hours Bob plotted their course south, estimating their direction, speed, and leeway—the sideways movement caused by the force of the wind and waves. The chart was sopping wet from floating in the seawater and was pretty much unreadable. It was scary not knowing exactly where they were. All they knew was that they were somewhere in the Bass Strait. But they knew where they were going, and, with Bob's navigational skills and a compass, that might be enough.

They had enough for primitive navigation, but without a radio they had no way of knowing what was happening around them. They didn't know the fate of the sailors who had been on the damaged boats. And they didn't know about the other boats that were hit after *Business Post Naiad*. The plight of another boat would compound the fears of their loved ones.

At the time of the 2 p.m. sked, *Midnight Special* had been within a mile of *AFR Midnight Rambler*. *Midnight Special* was doing exceptionally well—but with the wind increasing and boats with experienced sailors turning around, they decided to run for shelter. Their plan was to steer north to Gabo Island, only 38 miles away.

Turning around may have felt like the safest course, but *Midnight Special* was hit by large waves again and again. The boat was knocked down repeatedly. Crew members were injured, but the boat seemed to be holding together.

Around 8 p.m.—almost exactly the same time as the "Listen to that" moment on *Midnight Rambler*—Peter Carter was at the helm of *Midnight Special*. Carter had sustained several broken ribs earlier, but was taking his turn on deck when the boat was hit by an enormous wave.

Midnight Special was rolled 360 degrees and dismasted. The roll wrapped the mast around the boat, but the *Midnight Special* came back up, half-filled with water. The wave had hit the side of the boat with such force that it smashed the cabin siding, buckled the fiberglass deck, and smashed out all the windows on the port side. It tore a large hole in the top of the cabin where the mast had been.

Carter, broken ribs and all, operated the bilge pump while others bailed. With a combined effort, the crew managed to get enough water out so that the boat was stable and afloat.

They drifted some 40 or 50 miles during the night, and early in the morning were able to signal a search aircraft. As the rescue helicopters came on the scene, two crew members were on deck. Carter and five others were down below. Another huge wave came and rolled *Midnight Special* for a second time, trapping Carter and his mates in the upside-down vessel.

One person tried to dive through the upside-down hatch but couldn't make it. He was wedged below the surface of the water, drowning. As Carter wondered if this would be the end, another wave flipped the boat upright. All nine members of the crew were eventually rescued. *Midnight Special* sank just as the last sailor was lifted off.

Back in Sydney, Ed's wife, Sue, was desperate for news. Her husband, brother, and brother-in-law were all at risk, and the news reports were frightening. When reports of the *Midnight Special* disaster got out, the phone started ringing. There were frantic calls from confused friends who thought that the *Midnight Rambler* had been rolled. It was almost too much to bear. Sue thought of her children, and the same words kept running through her mind: *Just please get there. Please get there, please be safe.*

22

Sayonara—Tack the Boat

By Sunday evening *Sayonara* was far ahead of *AFR Midnight Rambler*.[1] It was a fast boat. Not only was the big maxi 48 feet longer than the *Rambler,* but Ellison had every technological advantage imaginable on his side. *Sayonara's* hull had been constructed with sheets of lightweight carbon fiber fabric. Its carbon mast, much lighter than aluminum, alone cost more than two *AFR Midnight Ramblers. Sayonara* was designed for speed, and it was flying across the Bass Strait.

Sayonara, like the other maxis, escaped the worst of the storm. But the boat was still hitting huge waves and strong winds. During one maneuver, as Chris Dickson was turning the boat, Oracle's Phil Kiely was washed across the deck. He landed on one foot and broke his leg.

In an attempt to get their torn mainsail down, another crewman, Joey Allen, was hit in the head by a sail fitting that flew out of his hand. The impact gouged his head and nearly knocked him unconscious. And another, T.A. McCann, sliced his thumb so badly he thought it had been cut off.

Ellison watched the crew struggle, amazed with the impressive display of tenacity and skill. After the sail had been secured, Kiely was carried below by two crew members who had been trained as medics. They cut off his boot, gave him a dose of morphine, and strapped him into his bunk. Then Ellison came over and knelt down to speak with Kiely.

Like Chris Rockell on *AFR Midnight Rambler,* Kiely did not want *Sayonara* to pull out of the race on his account. He insisted that he was okay and that they should continue racing in spite of his injury. Ellison agreed, but then reminded him—as if Kiely could forget—that it was his idea to come on the race to begin with.

Throughout the night and early morning, *Sayonara* continued to suffer casualties. A mainsail trimmer, Bob Wylie, cracked his ribs when he fell against a winch. And Mark "Tugboat" Turner, the chief engineer, sprained his ankle while moving around the boat looking for signs of delamination. The high-tech carbon fiber layers were separating. Little by little, *Sayonara* was coming apart.

The weather on Monday was even worse than on Sunday. The waves were steeper, and Ellison, along with many of the crew, was seasick. By Monday night he was glued to his bunk, incapacitated. Ellison hadn't eaten anything for twenty-four hours, and any swagger that he had once had about the race being cool had been washed away. He had made up his mind—this would be his last Hobart.

Ellison's ordeal continued throughout the night and into Tuesday. He had thrown up so frequently that he was dehydrated. With nothing left in his stomach, every time he tried to vomit he felt like his insides were being ripped out. Totally exhausted, Ellison wedged himself into his bunk and tried to sleep. But it was hopeless. There was absolutely no way he could fall asleep in this nightmare.

Earlier, when Ellison was on deck, he had seen waves of 40 to 50 feet. Now he heard crew members talking about bigger waves—waves higher than *Sayonara's* 105-foot mast. It's doubtful that they encountered anything of that size, as they were far south of the weather bomb. The maxi's speed had enabled them to beat the worst of the storm, but the waves were still enormous.

Because of her size, *Sayonara* didn't have the ability to maneuver like *AFR Midnight Rambler.* The boat would bury its bow into the steep cliffs of water, then be catapulted straight up to the crest. Ellison felt it was like going up the elevator of a five-story office building, then being pushed off the top floor—every twenty seconds.

While Ellison stayed below, other members of the crew were on deck in the maelstrom, steering and running the boat. Even Lachlan Murdoch, though seasick and worried that the boat might capsize, was on deck during his watches. Murdoch was at the edge, but he would not be beaten by the Hobart. In spite of his fear and nausea, Murdoch resolved to do his job to the best of his ability. Trying to be positive, he was happy that the rain would rinse the vomit off his foul-weather gear.

For Ellison, riding out the storm in his bunk was "no picnic, either."[2] Every time *Sayonara* would go airborne, he would feel weightless for a moment, then crunch back into the bunk when the boat hit the trough of the wave.

The constant pounding took its toll. At one point Ellison watched crewman Zan Drejes pump water from the hull. Noting his bloodshot eyes, Ellison said, "What a bunch of dumb s—ts we are to call this fun." Drejes responded, "You'll look back on this race with pride, and you'll be out here again someday."[3] Ellison said nothing, but he knew that Drejes was wrong.

Early Tuesday morning, Tugboat was tapping on the hull, trying to determine the extent of *Sayonara's* delamination problems. There was no doubt that the boat was coming apart. Tugboat was simply trying to assess how quickly it was happening.

Bill Erkelens watched the engineer tapping near the bow and became alarmed. He asked Tugboat how serious the problem was, and the answer was clear. It was very serious. Erkelens went to find Chris Dickson and make the case that they needed to slow down.

Dickson was not sympathetic. They were on the rhumb line—the most direct course to Hobart—and he wanted *Sayonara* to be the first boat across the line. They didn't know where *Brindabella* was, and he didn't want to be beaten by George Snow's maxi.

Another crew member expressed his concerns about the delamination problem with navigator Mark Rudiger. Rudiger's response was the same as Dickson's: They needed to hold their current course. It was the most direct route and the quickest way home. Though Rudiger was not persuaded, he agreed to raise the issue with Dickson and Ellison.

That conversation never happened. Below in his bunk, Ellison watched Tugboat drawing circles on the inside of the hull with a red marker. When Ellison asked "Tugsy" what he was doing, Tugboat explained that he was marking the spots where the bow was delaminating.

Ellison was incredulous. There was Tugboat, calmly marking the spots where *Sayonara's* bow was coming apart. Ellison climbed out of his bunk and made his way back to the navigation station. He asked Rudiger where they were on the chart, and the navigator showed him their position.

They were about 75 miles off the coast of Tasmania, with the wind coming out of the southwest. It was hitting them on the starboard side, and *Sayonara* was taking a beating. But on their current course, Rudiger explained, they were headed straight to the finish line.

Ellison had seen enough. He was sick, he was afraid, and he was done with this race. He had been done with the race for a long time. He was no longer trying to prove himself. He wanted out. It was clear to him that the only sensible move was to change their course and head west. If they could reach the protection of the Tasmanian coast, they could escape these terrible waves—waves that he was convinced were trying to kill him.

Rudiger pushed back. They didn't know where *Brindabella* was. If they changed course, *Sayonara* could lose the race. Ellison didn't care. He was angry, and he was the owner of the boat. "We won't win the race if we sink," Ellison said. "Tack the f—ing boat."[4]

Ellison's order ended the debate. *Sayonara* turned and headed west, and the new angle eased the strain on the boat. Soon after, the weather began to improve, and everything looked brighter.

They had made it through the storm, and the worst was over. For the crew of *Sayonara,* and for Australian Search and Rescue, it was a blessing. If *Sayonara* had been caught in the center of the storm like the smaller boats, it could have been much, much worse. With its size and limited maneuverability, the maxi might well have broken apart, leaving more than twenty people adrift in the Bass Strait.

Feeling good, Ellison congratulated himself on his decision. He believed not only that he had saved *Sayonara* but that he had made a smart tactical decision: "Tacking the boat turned out to be the right thing to do for the race, too. God was smiling on us."[5]

There is no way of knowing what would have happened if *Sayonara* had continued on its direct course to Hobart. But Ellison had asserted his power, confident that he had made the right decision. God and Larry Ellison were happy. Chris Dickson and Mark Rudiger had done what they were ordered to do. They had tacked the boat.

23

AFR Midnight Rambler— A Commanding Position

At 8 p.m. on Sunday, the crew of *AFR Midnight Rambler* could actually talk to each other on deck without shouting. It was astonishing to go so quickly from the hell they had been trapped in to this moment of relative tranquility. One by one, the crew below climbed up on deck to see what had happened.

The Ramblers took in their surroundings and looked up into a clearing sky. It was surreal. They talked about stripping off their wet-weather gear, even joking about changing into shorts. Then it dawned on them. This was just the eye of the storm. As the rolling cloud formation from the other side of the storm closed in, they realized they had made it only halfway. They weren't going to be in the sanctuary for long.

Soon they were back in the fight, though this second round wasn't quite as punishing as the first. The wind had dropped to speeds of 45 knots, and the waves were now only as tall as five-story buildings. But the crew was still in survival mode.

Most of the Ramblers were still seasick and vomiting. Eating was out of the question. And because their eyes had been pounded by the saltwater spray and spew, their vision was blurry. In spite of it all, however, there was a sense of relief. With the drop in wind and the easing of the storm, these horrible conditions seemed almost normal.

At midnight, *AFR Midnight Rambler* was sailing in pitch-black darkness. Except for the compass located at the forward end of the cockpit, they had no navigational equipment. Mix and Chris took turns squinting at the tiny compass light and relaying the boat's course to Ed, who was back at the helm.

At 2 a.m. Monday, they still had no way of plotting their exact position. Fearful that the boat may have been blown too far east to have any chance of winning the race, Ed and Arthur took stock of their situation. As they talked in the darkness, a clear picture emerged. It finally began to sink in that they really were through the worst of it. And the boat was still in good shape. It was time to switch gears—to move from survival back to racing.

The transition back to racing was remarkably smooth. Gordo thought they were all so bloody relieved to be out of the storm that everyone needed to focus on something else, anything, to occupy their minds. And the faster they went, the faster they would get to Hobart. This time, getting to Hobart would mean more than having a "quiet little drink." It would mean that they had made it through this ordeal together and beaten the storm.

The crew started racing again and taking more chances. They raised the mainsail part way, and the *Rambler* began to pick up speed. By 3 a.m., they were in the middle of the Bass Strait and sailing well. It was just starting to feel right, when they began to hear reports of what had happened to the rest of the fleet. The news was hard to comprehend: Boats dismasted, boats rolled, sailors overboard. The realization that people in front of them and behind them had died was overwhelming.

By first light they could see that the storm was truly abating. The sun came up with a spectacular display of spreading light, and, for Arthur, the bright sunshine was an undeniable sign. They had really survived the storm—they were going to live.

By noon, conditions had improved so much that they could fully raise the mainsail. They were racing flat-out, and, as a celebratory lunch, the crew feasted on Greek meatballs made by Ed and Arthur's mother, Margaret. It was the first time that anyone had eaten in at least thirty hours.

The meal, as delicious as it was, was followed by something even better. Bob had finally gotten the small handheld GPS working and determined their position. Remarkably, after sailing 200 miles, *AFR Midnight Rambler* was only a few miles from where Bob thought they would be. With his dead-reckoning skills and a compass, Bob's estimate was spot-on. Captain Cook could hardly have done better.

The Ramblers were elated. They were farther west than they thought they would be, almost on the rhumb line leading directly to Hobart. Depending on what had happened to the other boats, the *Rambler* could actually be in a position to win the race. Their plan may have worked.

Early on, Ed and Bob had decided to aim high into the wind rather than easing off toward New Zealand. Sailing west meant giving up the additional speed advantage of the East Australian Current, but it had two huge benefits.

First, based purely on the direction of the waves, it was the right choice. Steering away from the waves would have increased the risk of taking a hit beam-on and being rolled. So they tried to attack the waves as directly as they possibly could. It wasn't a racing decision, it was a survival decision. If their chances of surviving had been improved by another move—even turning north—they would have taken that option.

There was a second reason for their decision to aim high. Storms of this power have a predictable pattern. In the northern hemisphere, hurricanes rotate in a counterclockwise direction. In the southern hemisphere, the spiral is clockwise.

The highest wind velocities occur when the direction of the spiral is combined with the direction in which the storm is moving. In the southern hemisphere, this deadly combination occurs in the left-hand semicircle—the most dangerous part of the storm.

Bob knew what the Ramblers needed to do to get through the storm as quickly as possible. The storm was moving southeast, so they had to go as far west as they could, as fast as they could. The *Midnight Rambler* aimed high and pointed as directly into the wind as the boat could sail.

This was a decision made with survival in mind, but it kept them as close to the rhumb line as they could possibly be. The move also improved their chances of winning the race. But what had the other boats done?

By the 2 p.m. sked on Monday, the *Rambler* had made it to the northern coast of Tasmania. Bob got the position of every boat he could, racing or not. Plotting their coordinates, it was clear that the balance of the fleet had sailed east toward New Zealand, going with the gale. As a consequence, they were in the storm longer—some, for as long as thirty-six hours—and they had been blown away from the rhumb line.

What this meant, Bob realized, was that during the night the Ramblers had gained a huge amount of ground over their competitors. Not only had they beaten the storm, but the decision they made to minimize risk turned out to be the best racing strategy as well.

The boats that had gone east included a number of bigger and more favored yachts. *Ragamuffin, Quest,* and *Ausmaid* were world-class opponents. *Ragamuffin* was known and respected in ocean racing circles around the globe. They were superb boats, and the *Rambler* was beating them all.

Even though the bigger boats were farther south, they were also much farther out to sea. To get back to the Tasmanian coast they would have to tack, zigzagging into the wind. That would cost them huge amounts of time as they sailed the extra miles to Hobart.

It was exciting. After listening to the sked, Bob was sure that they had a real chance to win the race. And to cap it off, he realized that they were actually leading in the handicap standings—the ranking that would determine which boat got the Tattersall's Cup. *AFR Midnight Rambler* was, by a very large margin, winning the race. This was fantastic news.

Bob scrambled up onto the deck to share the news. He had one thing on his mind: *We can't screw up now.* Bob looked at the mainsail and thought, *If we can just stay in one piece, we can win this race.* Showing more emotion than he had in the worst of the storm, Ed heard Bob shouting, "We're winning! Just don't break the bloody boat! Reef the main!"

The news lifted everyone's spirits. It jolted them out of the shock of the last twenty hours. They were now in a commanding position. All their hard work could actually pay off. They had done better than the major boats that had survived the storm; they just had to hang in there. The adrenaline was pumping, and they were on their way to the finish line, only 160 miles away.

The journey down the Tasmanian coast was a blur. The Ramblers were exhausted from the storm, but completely absorbed with capitalizing on their position. With the wind from behind, they raised the spinnaker, something they had not done since the first day of the race. They sailed as hard as they dared, intent on not "breaking the boat."

AFR Midnight Rambler was seventh in the race, with only *Sayonara* and five other large boats ahead of them. The small boats were far behind, and it wasn't until they got to Tasman Island on the evening of the 29th that they saw other competitors and helicopters. They were getting closer to civilization. Boats were coming in from all directions, but they were much bigger than the *Rambler.*

They made a hard right turn into Storm Bay, the same stretch of water where *Nuzulu* had persevered with a makeshift sail just four years before. Within striking distance of the finish line, and with the wind "on the nose," they zigzagged 45 miles to the Derwent River. They could taste victory. All they had to do was sail the last stretch into Hobart.

The crew was at the edge, both mentally and physically. Everyone was exhausted, sleep deprived, cold, wet, and hungry. The wind began to get "fluky," and they were facing a strong outgoing tide that was pushing them in the wrong direction.

The Ramblers were struggling to get up the river. They knew precisely how much time they had left to become the overall winners of the race. The clock was ticking.

To compound matters, they still had no navigational instruments other than the handheld GPS, everything below was drenched, and Bob had no nav table for his chart. He probably should have thrown it away, but he was so tired—and so fixated on the chart—that he spread it out on the wet cabin deck.

Bob was focused on trying to locate the Battery Point landmark in Hobart. This led to a fatigued conversation with Ed and "a bit of a stand-up." Finally, they both admitted that it didn't really matter where Battery Point was. They knew where the finish line was, and that's all that mattered.

The wind was dying, and the pressure to win kept building. The breeze kept coming and going. It would be 20 knots, then nothing. Then 20 knots, then disappear.

The wind was intermittent, and it was shifting directions as well. Had their electronic instruments been intact, at least they would have some understanding of exactly what the wind was doing. Then Jonno suggested another jury-rigged innovation: They broke apart a music cassette and tied a piece of tape to the rigging. The *telltale* wasn't perfect, but they would have some way to gauge the wind's direction.

Ed was getting frantic. Each time the wind shifted, he would call for a sail change. They had to get the most out of each puff of air. It was maddening, Ed thought: *After all we've done and all we've gone through, it's entirely possible that we could lose this race through lack of wind!*

Ed was technically right about the sail changes. But practically, by the time the new sail was up, the breeze would be different. With the exhaustion of the crew, it simply wasn't worth the effort.

Up in the bow, Jonno had borne the brunt of the work to change the sails. He looked at Ed with a grimace and said, "Listen, mate. That's enough. If you want another sail change, you can bloody well do it your-self." It was the sort of smart-aleck remark that they often made to each other, but this time Jonno was only half joking.

Ed didn't like being told he was wrong. But he also realized that he was so focused on winning the race that he had lost touch with reality. He was changing sails too much, and it wasn't working. The crew was spent.

Tension had reached a breaking point. Watching the exchange, Gordo picked up the last winch handle that they had on the boat. The winch handle is a critical piece of equipment, and without one it would be nearly impossible to adjust the sails. They had started the race with several handles, but all but one had been lost over the side. The second to last winch handle had been dropped by Mix, as his job as pitman relied heavily on cranking the winches.

Gordo moved across the cockpit and looked at Mix. He held out the last remaining winch handle. With a tone both serious and nonchalant, Gordo said, "Just chuck this one over the side, will you, Mix?"

Everyone burst into laughter. It was obviously the worst possible thing that Mix could have done. They would have been reduced to turning the winch with their fingers—clearly, a hopeless task. Gordo the comedian had broken the tension. They could almost see the finish line, and they would work together to get there.

24

Sayonara—A Thousand Years

A
t 8:03 on Tuesday morning, *AFR Midnight Rambler* was still scooting down the coast when Larry Ellison and the Big Yank Tank crossed the finish line in Hobart. It was not the victory that Ellison had expected.

Sayonara was first across the line, about three hours ahead of its closest competitor, *Brindabella*. Hundreds of people were waiting at the docks, and Ellison had achieved his goal of winning line honors. But unlike the usual victory celebration, the mood in Hobart was different.

As Ellison crossed the finish line, he was met by the plaintive sounds of a bagpiper. The melancholy notes intensified what was already a somber atmosphere in Hobart. Australian flags were flying at half-staff in honor of the six sailors who had died. The traditional welcoming fireworks had been canceled.

The media throng was eager to hear Ellison speak, and an emotional Ellison wanted to talk. His remarks were tearful. After crediting the inspirational work of the crew, he went on to make a statement that would forever connect Larry Ellison and the Sydney to Hobart Race:

> Never again. Not if I live to be 1000 years old will I do a Hobart race. This is not what it's supposed to be about. Difficult, yes. Dangerous, no. Life-threatening—definitely not.

Ellison went on to describe the race "nightmare," and to offer prayers for the search crews and the people still in the water. And he gave himself credit for making the decision to tack *Sayonara,* telling the media, "We got in under the lee of Tasmania, otherwise I'm not sure the boat would have lasted."

Ellison's assertion that he had saved *Sayonara* by tacking the boat may have rankled some of the crew. But it was his statement about avoiding the race for a millennium that resonated throughout Hobart.

Lachlan Murdoch, who had stood almost all of his watches in spite of his sickness and amateur status, agreed that the experience was like watching a disaster movie. But he was steadfast in his commitment to continue racing. The race had simply reinforced the importance of preparation and the critical role played by skilled sailors.

When *Brindabella* arrived, the crew's comments about the storm contrasted with Ellison's. After George Snow was asked about Ellison's vow to avoid the Hobart for a thousand years, Snow responded with a terse "His call."[2]

Scott Gilbert, a crew member on *Wild Thing,* was more vocal:

What I really don't like is when someone gets to Hobart and says, "This is the worst bloody race I've ever been in, I'm never coming back." That guy should be seriously kicked up the a—. . . . Regardless of what he thinks about it, it's not up to him to tell the world that the race is no good . . . and that he'd never do it again.[3]

Gilbert did not speak for everyone, but his view was consistent with that of many veterans of the race. After his unequivocal statement, Ellison was not a popular figure among many Australian sailors.

Not that it mattered. Less than an hour after he stepped off *Sayonara,* Ellison was on a private plane headed to Antigua, where his 250-foot motor yacht, *Katana,* was waiting. *Katana* was fully equipped with a two-story apartment, giant movie screen, basketball court, and wraparound glass balconies. Ellison was done with the Sydney to Hobart Race and ready for some relaxation.

His rapid departure further annoyed many who stayed in Hobart to reflect on the race and to wait for the results of the search and rescue. Geoff Cropley, an unofficial crew spokesman for *Brindabella,* acknowledged that the professionals like the crew of *Sayonara* were good for competition, but he found it difficult to understand how professionals:

... can just fly in, get to Hobart, grab their kitbag and get on the next plane out without hanging around for lunch or a few drinks and reflect on the race. . . . On *Brindabella* we're all mates, a bunch of guys who are good sailors. We pay our own way and have a good time.

Cropley's remarks underscored the reality that there are very different worlds of ocean racing. One is a rock star world with wealthy sailors who can hire professionals to crew their expensive boats. Another is a world of talented amateurs who want to experience a challenge with their mates and have a good time.

Nothing precludes a sailor with money from entering the second world of talented amateurs. But sailing alongside friends is far different than hiring rock stars and ensuring their loyalty with lavish retainers. Both worlds come together in the Sydney to Hobart Race.

After the 1998 race, there was no doubt in anyone's mind about Ellison's resolve to avoid future Hobarts. There was also little doubt that he had been shaken by the experience. In *Softwar*—an "intimate portrait" of Ellison—Matthew Symonds wrote that Ellison "was traumatized by the experience" and "has sworn never to enter the race again."

In an unusual agreement for a biography, Larry Ellison was given an opportunity to comment on everything in the book and to counter anything that he thought was wrong. In his rejoinder, Ellison insisted he "wasn't 'traumatized' by the race." When he wasn't in his bunk trying to sleep, Ellison wrote, he was "busy in fight mode." According to Ellison, he simply didn't have time to think about being scared.

With respect to his thousand-year retirement, Ellison remembers making the statement but then recalls a follow-up:

I remember saying, "No, not if I live to be 1000." Then I thought about it for a moment and said, "Hold it, wait a second, if I live to be 1000, I'll come back. . . . Mark this down, 1000 years from now we'll be back."[4]

Perhaps that's what he said, or what he would like to have said. Since 1998, however, Ellison has limited his sailing to the America's Cup. In the America's Cup "you just go out for a few hours, race around the buoys, and come back for a nice seafood and pasta dinner." It's all "very civilized."[5]

25

Go the *Rambler*!

Bill Psaltis and his wife, Margaret, knew the storm was coming. But Bill had learned over many years that storms come and go. It's all part of sailing. *The* Midnight Rambler *would be fine.* When they started to hear the news of other boats getting into trouble, though, they began to worry about their two sons. And when *Winston Churchill* went down, everything changed.

Bill believed that Jim Lawler was one of the finest sailors in the world. He was also a very good friend. They had done the Aegean Rally together the year before, and if Jim had asked Bill to sail on the *Winston Churchill*, he wouldn't have hesitated.

It was shocking that such a seaworthy boat with exceptionally capable sailors aboard had been lost. Bill started to think, *Well, maybe the old man is wrong. Maybe these new boats with their new technology are as good as the old ones that break up anyway.* Everything that Bill knew about sailing was suddenly being challenged.

When the situation deteriorated further—with boats in trouble and sailors washed overboard—there wasn't much sleeping in the Psaltis home. Bill tried to reassure Margaret that Ed and Arthur would be okay, that things like this had happened before. But he knew that, in fact, nothing like this had ever happened before—not since the first race in 1945.

It wasn't good, and Margaret knew that Bill was deeply troubled. They both agonized, wondering whether they would ever see their two boys again. They thought about their grandchildren, and worried even more.

Then all of a sudden, news came on the radio that *AFR Midnight Rambler* had stayed farther west than the rest of the fleet. The boys had done exactly what Bill would have. The boat was zipping down the coast of Tasmania. The Ramblers had made it through the storm, and they were sailing hard.

Sue Psaltis had been in close contact with Bill and Margaret since the beginning of the race. When the storm hit, they urged her to get down to Hobart and, God willing, greet the *Midnight Rambler* when it arrived. They volunteered to watch the children, and Sue booked her flight. On Tuesday, December 29, she flew down to Tasmania.

Sue found a room in a hotel right on Constitution Dock, where the smaller boats tie up after they cross the finish line. She immediately ran down to the dock, hoping to get some news. She was hungry for any scrap of information about what was happening at sea.

Making her way through the crowd, Sue stopped a crew member from a big maxi that had just arrived. He knew nothing about the smaller boats. Sue was astonished to discover that he didn't even know the names of other sailors on his boat. He had flown in to do the race and was off to the next event.

Sue called the Tasmania Yacht Club and learned that not only was the *AFR Midnight Rambler* safe, they were leading the fleet on handicap. It was so exciting to think that they might actually win the race after all this time. But it was also a conflicted set of emotions. People had died in the race. She was filled with pride, but respectful and restrained because of the tragic losses.

Shortly before 5 a.m. on Wednesday the 30th, the Ramblers began to grasp the possibility that they could actually win the race. About 2 miles from the finish, Arthur became convinced that they were going to make it. He said to anyone within hearing distance, "I think Huey is going to let us through."

Ed had a superstitious feeling about Huey. Huey was temperamental. He brought them good luck and he brought them bad luck. In the last few days he had given them an incredible test and had been fickle when they finally reached the Derwent.

In spite of their ordeal, they had kept at it. Now they could see the finish line. Arthur looked at his brother and said, "You know, Ed, our father's sailed in this race for years, and we've tried for years. I think we're going to make it. I think we're going to do it." Arthur was close to tears. It was such an incredible achievement, such a relief to be alive.

It was an emotional moment for Arthur, but Ed was quiet. He just continued steering the boat. Somewhat taken aback by Ed's silence, Arthur started trimming the sails. About forty-five seconds later, Arthur felt a big hand on his shoulder. He turned around and looked at Ed. His hand had said it all.

Ed was deep in thought. *This is going to happen. We're going to do what our father tried to accomplish eighteen times without success. We're not doing it for him, but we can be proud of the fact that he has left us a legacy. He taught us how to sail. Now we can, in our own way, repay him with the glory of winning the race.*[1]

AFR Midnight Rambler sailed across the finish line at 5:04 a.m. There was no kilt-clad bagpiper, not even the traditional sound of "Midnight Rambler" playing on their tape player. Because of the tragedy, the Stones were silent.

The *Rambler* was the smallest boat in ten years to win the Tattersall's Cup. And she was the tenth boat to cross the finish line, close on the heels of many of the much larger maxis.

As the Ramblers took down their sails, they saw a number of big maxis docked off to the side of the river. Because of their size, the boats were much too long to fit at Constitution Dock, where the smaller boats tied up.

The sailors on the maxis stood up when they saw the Ramblers. Bob was surprised. He couldn't imagine that the *maxi boys* even knew that they were alive, much less took notice of the little boat. But it was much more than that. The maxi crews came to the bows of their towering boats and began clapping. They gave the crew of *AFR Midnight Rambler* a standing ovation.

The maxi boys waved to the Ramblers, shouting, "Tie up with us!" Bob thought it would be fun to see their 35-foot boat tied up with an 80-foot boat on either side. But Bill Psaltis had always ended the race inside Constitution Dock, and the Ramblers would follow that tradition.

As unexpected as the standing ovation was from the maxis, something even more surprising was in store. Sue had gotten the news about the *Rambler* some ten minutes after they crossed the finish line. By the time they were headed to their mooring, she was waiting at the edge of the dock.

The sun wasn't yet up, and the light was dim. Sue was bouncing and jumping frantically, shouting, "Go the *Rambler!* Go the *Rambler!*" Ed peered through the darkness, trying to figure out just who was making all the commotion. Perplexed, he turned to his brother and said, "Who the hell is that?"

Arthur looked back amused and said, "Ed, you'd better start thinking about what you're going to say to that woman, because that's your wife." Ed looked closer and saw that it was, indeed, Sue Psaltis. It was the perfect capstone to the victory. His wife was there in Hobart to greet him, standing next to a case of Cascade Lager—their favorite beer.

The crew was still groggy and dazed. There was some leftover tension from their arguments in the Derwent. Sue's cheers cut through the stress, and everyone started to smile. As they pulled alongside the dock, she jumped on board and gave everyone a hug. She put her arms around Ed and gave him a kiss. Then she went up to her brother, Jonno, and gave him a kiss—followed by a punch in the stomach.

"What did you do that for?" asked Jonno. "The kiss and the punch were both from your wife," explained Sue. "That punch was in exchange for all the stress that you put her through."

In the midst of the commotion, Arthur handed Ed a cell phone, saying, "Listen, Dad wants to talk to you, quick. Talk to Dad." Ed took the phone. He was taken aback to hear his father sobbing. Ed could hear him crying on the other end of the phone, something he had never heard before in his life.

Bill Psaltis came from an era when men didn't cry, and Ed was always taught that crying was soft. It was so strange for him to hear his father being so emotional. Between tears, Bill said, "Thank God, you're both alive. You survived the storm, and you're safe. Thank God, thank God. I'm glad you made it, Ed."

Ed wanted to say, "Dad, calm down, it's okay." But before he could get the words out, his father said, "And you've actually won this bloody race that we tried to win for so many years." It was uplifting for Ed to hear those words and to hear the elation and relief in his father's voice.

Then Bill said, "Before the reporters start talking to you, you must understand that Jim Lawler has died. There are people missing, and they aren't going to find them. Please be humble and take that into account when you talk about the race."

The conversation was a jumble of emotions—the elation that Bill felt about his sons surviving the lethal storm and winning the race, mixed with the devastation of losing such a close friend. It was a conversation that neither Ed nor Bill will ever forget.

It was an extraordinary moment. Against all odds, the Ramblers had won the race. But because people had died, they couldn't rejoice and show obvious pride in their accomplishment. They were proud, but they were quiet because of the tragedy of the last few days.

For the media, the extraordinary accomplishment of this small boat was completely eclipsed by the disaster. The fact that *AFR Midnight Rambler* had won the race was almost insignificant. The scene of their tiny boat alone at Constitution Dock—a dock that, in previous years, would have been crowded with dozens of other boats—went unnoticed. The press were focused on death and destruction and had little interest in the teamwork and triumph of the Ramblers.

The press may not have cared, but there were people in Hobart who understood exactly what the Ramblers had accomplished. Many of those who got it were at the Shipwright's Arms Pub, off Battery Point.

Ed had been going to the Shipwright's Arms ever since his first race when he was 18. All the greats had gone there for a drink—the *heroes of the Hobart,* as Ed thought of them. He had followed the tradition of going to the pub after every race, and this night would be no exception.

All the Ramblers walked in together, ready for a drink. Because people had died, they were in a somber mood. But they were inwardly elated. They had won the race, and it was a huge achievement.

As the crew walked in, everyone at the packed bar looked up and saw their *Midnight Rambler* shirts. Roger Hickman, a tough competitor and a good friend, started the applause. Soon everyone in the pub was standing up and clapping. It was their second standing ovation, but this one—in a pub filled with people who were Ed's heroes—meant the most to the crew. People who had been doing the race for years—ever since he was a kid—were clapping for them.

Seeing the recognition directed at Ed, her brother, and all the Ramblers was a magical moment for Sue. She remembers, "People knew that they had won. It was an acknowledgment, and they were beaming."

It was a moment that none of the Ramblers will ever forget. For Ed, having sailors he respected stand up and say, "Guys, you've done it" was better than any trophy he could have possibly imagined.

26

Wake of the Storm

Six sailors perished in the race. Aboard *Business Post Naiad,* Bruce
Guy died of natural causes from a heart attack and Philip Skeggs
became entangled in his equipment and drowned when the boat
capsized. On *Sword of Orion,* Glyn Charles died after being washed overboard when his harness failed. And from *Winston Churchill,* John Dean,
Jim Lawler, and Michael Bannister drowned when their life raft was
struck by a wave and they were washed away.

On New Year's Day, a memorial service was held in Hobart to honor
the six sailors who had been lost. More than 2,000 people attended, and
four planes flew overhead in a "missing man" formation. Friends and
relatives of the six who had died had an opportunity to speak. For each
lost sailor, a wreath of white daisies and a single red rose was set adrift in
the harbor.

Richard Winning, who heroically risked his life as the skipper of the
Winston Churchill, offered these words of solace: "May their loved ones
find some comfort in the knowledge that these men died doing something that they loved."

The Commodore of the Cruising Yacht Club, Hugo Van Kretschmar,
spoke as well. "We will miss you. We will remember you always. We will
learn from the tragic circumstances of your passing. May the everlasting
voyage that you have now embarked on be blessed with calm seas and

gentle breezes. May you never have to reef or change a headsail in the night. May your bunk always be warm and dry."

Not surprising after a tragedy of this magnitude, the memorial service ended neither the mourning for lost comrades nor the remaining questions about the race. The Cruising Yacht Club of Australia launched its own investigation and, after six months, released a 180-page report with recommendations intended to improve race safety.

The report found that "no one cause can be identified as responsible" for the multiple incidents that occurred during the storm. Acknowledging that no one measure could by itself be significant, the report went on to suggest a series of incremental changes. Taken together, the investigators argued, these changes could have a substantive impact on the safety of the race.

Changes recommended in the CYCA report included specific measures such as compulsory reporting on strong winds above 40 knots (the "*Sword of Orion* protocol"); compulsory safety equipment including EPIRBs and personal strobes; increases in required experience of crew; and compulsory attendance at prerace weather, safety, and search-and-rescue briefings by at least 30 percent of each crew.

Though the events of the 1998 race were tragic, the CYCA report concluded that the dismastings and rollovers were caused by extraordinarily large waves. Whether one of these "rogue waves" struck a particular boat was, ultimately, a "matter of chance."

A second investigation was conducted by New South Wales Coroner John Abernethy. The coroner's inquest was initiated because five of the deaths did not occur from natural causes, and Abernethy felt that an incident involving five or more people should be considered a "disaster." Thus, the 1998 Sydney to Hobart Race was a disaster that warranted further investigation.

This coronial inquest produced a document with evidence and findings more than 350 pages long, not including hundreds of additional pages of appendices. Acknowledging that "the window of hindsight is the clearest window of all," the coroner's report made a number of additional recommendations about safety and equipment.

Abernethy recognized that implementing these recommendations would create extra work and expense. One specific requirement, for example, was that at least half of the crew complete a safety and survival course every three years. Abernethy explained that, from the evidence of the survivors of *Winston Churchill,* it was "indisputable that trained crew have a greater likelihood of survival than untrained crew."

After hearing testimony from two expert witnesses, Abernethy concluded that the missing caulking "Mega" Bascombe had reported before the race was not a factor in *Winston Churchill's* sinking. Damage from the wave that hit the boat created problems so severe that the yacht foundered. Any small amounts of putty that may have come loose would have had no impact on the *Churchill's* fate.

The investigation did reveal some specific shortcomings in the screening process for qualifying boats. For example, the *limit of positive stability* (LPS) for *Business Post Naiad* was inadequate. The LPS is a measure of how far a boat can tip over and still recover.

The minimum requirement for the race was 115 degrees, or 110 degrees for boats that had been "grandfathered in." *Business Post Naiad* had a limit of positive stability of 104.7, which would have made it ineligible to race. Whether that would have made a difference is unknown. A number of other boats with qualifying stability metrics met disaster when hit by the enormous waves of the storm.

The coroner's inquiry also probed deeply into the communication between the Bureau of Meteorology and the Race Management Team (RMT). The report was especially critical of the RMT's lack of understanding about the significance of weather forecasts—in particular, predictions about wind speed and wave height.

Abernethy had harsh words about some aspects of race management. But by the end of the inquest he was satisfied that the CYCA had, on its own initiative, achieved radical changes in time for the 1999 race. A number of the club's recommended changes were, in fact, incorporated into the coroner's report. One specific measure was that Bureau of Meteorology personnel would be more involved with the Race Management Team throughout the race.

Newspaper and magazine reporters had a field day with the disaster, and their investigations ran parallel with official inquiries. Looking for scapegoats, the press pointed fingers at anybody and everybody who could be blamed for the deaths of six sailors.

The rescue effort was expensive and lives were put at risk, but fascination with the race seemed to be about more than the number of fatalities and the cost of the rescue. The end of the year is historically a news drought in Australia, but in 1998 reporters had everything they needed to write vivid, shocking stories. The reporter's expression "If it bleeds, it leads" seemed to fit perfectly. It was a target-rich environment for anyone who wanted to find a villain.

Scathing words were spoken about "the captains who went out in the storm when it was blowing a gale," and "their recklessness that cost lives." Though the sailors weren't the only ones to blame, critics argued, "they had the final responsibility about the decision to launch or not."

For many sailors who had started the race prior to the storm warning, and who were expecting only the usual "southerly buster," these statements seemed odd. They were trapped in a situation that ultimately became a race for survival. Their view was that "you can call off the race, but not the storm."

All this controversy and scorn came as a surprise to the Ramblers. They had made a series of decisions, each of which they believed to be reasonable at the time. They had faced everything that nature threw at them with courage and equanimity. And there were no cowboys, hotshots, or rock stars aboard *AFR Midnight Rambler*.

The Ramblers' view of the storm was very different from that of the derisive public critics and many in the media. As Ed Psaltis saw it, "In the end, only the storm is to blame. There was a very volatile low forming, and it could have moderated or it could have intensified. Well, it intensified—but that's ocean racing."

With all the debate, analysis, and investigation surrounding the 1998 Sydney to Hobart Race, the story of the smallest boat in ten years to win the Tattersall's Cup went largely unnoticed. Many newspaper articles were satisfied to write that "*Sayonara* won the race," with no mention of *AFR Midnight Rambler* as the overall winner of the Tattersall's trophy.

Though the victory of the Ramblers was largely overshadowed, their story provides an extraordinary metaphor for understanding *Teamwork at The Edge*. And it is a story that has continued long after 1998.

Larry Ellison declared that if he lived to be a thousand he would never do another Hobart. But for the crew of the *Rambler*, it's always "next year." *AFR Midnight Rambler* has sailed in the Sydney to Hobart Race every year since 1998, with many of the original crew members aboard.

Their passion for sailing, and for each other, keeps bringing them back. Ed Psaltis put it this way: "To my mind the Sydney to Hobart is a chance to maintain the spirit of adventure—of 'having a go,' which is part of the average Aussie. I'll certainly keep doing it. It's part of my life, and I'm still aiming for that second victory."

27

Blue Water, Short Ocean— The Ramblers' Record of Sustained Success

A fter their triumph in the '98 Sydney to Hobart Race, the Ramblers continued to win tough races against the best competitors. These victories have been achieved not only in individual races but also in competitions that require consistent performance in a series of demanding events.

The year after taking home the Tattersall's trophy, the Ramblers took on another hard challenge: the Lord Howe Island Race. Like the Sydney to Hobart Race, the Lord Howe is a *Category 1* race that takes the fleet well offshore. Lord Howe Island is 450 miles northeast of Sydney, and there is nowhere to hide if the weather gets nasty. The Lord Howe can be a three-and-a-half-day race, and as tough as the Hobart.

Weather conditions in the '99 Lord Howe were reminiscent of the '98 Hobart. The fleet was hit by another East Coast low and 45-knot winds pounded the fleet. *AFR Midnight Rambler* won the race by a substantial margin. Coming on the heels of their Hobart win, the Lord Howe victory added to their momentum.

In 2001, *AFR Midnight Rambler* scored again in the Bird Island Race.

They knew the course well. The 100-mile sail to Bird Island had been their qualifying race for the '98 Hobart. The Ramblers took first, with a double win on two handicap systems. Buoyed by these successes, *AFR Midnight Rambler* continued to excel. By 2009 they had won every East Coast ocean race in Australia, except one: the Sydney Gold Coast Yacht Race.

Promoted as the "great winter escape," the Gold Coast race was second only to the Sydney to Hobart in its reputation as a tough, tactically challenging ocean race. Like the Hobart, the race begins in Sydney, but then the fleet heads north to Queensland. The 384-mile race is not only demanding—the competition is tough, too. All the hot boats turn up for the Gold Coast.

After another hard slog in 2011, *AFR Midnight Rambler* was declared the overall winner. It was the most grueling race that the Ramblers had done since the 1998 Hobart. But the boat held up, the teamwork was superb, and the *Rambler* was forty-six seconds ahead of her closest competition on handicap. With that victory, the Ramblers had won every major Australian race that they had set their sights on.

Perhaps even more impressive than these individual victories, the *Rambler* has succeeded in races that require consistent performance in an extended series of sailing competitions. The two most prestigious awards are the *Blue Water Point Score* and the *Short Ocean Point Score,* given each year by the Cruising Yacht Club of Australia.

The *Blue Water Point Score (BWPS)* incorporates the big two of Australian yacht racing—the Sydney Gold Coast and the Sydney to Hobart—along with four other long-distance races. The names are exotic: Cabbage Tree Island, Flinders Island, Bird Island, and the Lion Island–Botany Bay races.

Winning the *BWPS* is a tremendous challenge. It demands consistent performance in an arduous series of long races—not unlike running six marathons over hilly terrain. By 2005, the Ramblers had taken second in the *BWPS,* but the title of *Blue Water Champions* remained elusive.

In the 2006–2007 *BWPS* competition, the Ramblers were on their way to victory when they encountered a setback in the Flinders Island Race. They had won the race twice before, but in 2007 the weather was particularly harsh. Racers were confronted with 40-knot southerly winds, big seas, and cold, rainy conditions. When one powerful gust hit the *Rambler,* her mainsail exploded. The sail was Kevlar, and Kevlar doesn't tear—it just goes "Bang!"

They still had 40 miles to go before reaching Flinders Island, the point at which they could turn around and head home. The Ramblers had two options. They could retire from the race and admit defeat, taking them out of contention for the *BWPS*. Or they could continue with a much smaller storm sail, but at a slower pace in miserable weather. The Ramblers had been in this jam before.

No one in the crew even considered the first option. The word *retire* didn't come up, and there was no discussion. Almost instantaneously, the mainsail was down, the storm sail was up, and they were back in the race, plugging away.

It was slow going with their little "handkerchief" of a sail. The mainsail acts like a second rudder for the boat. Without it, the Ramblers were struggling to sail high enough into the wind. Ed Psaltis remembers, "We were going too slow and sailing too low. Boats were passing us. We could see lights behind, overtaking us and passing us. It was very depressing, but we didn't give up."

They reached Flinders Island and were faced with another decision. Headed home, the wind would be behind them. Under normal conditions, when they rounded Flinders, they would raise a spinnaker. But with the "handkerchief" trysail and spinnaker combination, the boat would be so unbalanced it would roll erratically. Steering downwind in these big seas would be extremely difficult.

They had previously decided against the spinnaker, electing instead to use a smaller headsail. But when the *Rambler* began its homeward run, Ed had second thoughts. He proposed trying the spinnaker to see what would happen, and everyone agreed. Confident that it was a risk worth taking, the Ramblers raised the kite in the dark of night.

Had it been daylight, the sight of the *Rambler* pitching and yawing with a tiny trysail and huge spinnaker would have been a rather terrifying sight. But in the dark, only the Ramblers knew about their roller coaster ride.

AFR Midnight Rambler was difficult to control, and, as expected, the crew did experience some "wipeouts." But they stayed on course through big waves, hit some top speeds, and got home in reasonable shape.

When the race was over, the Ramblers found that a number of other boats had encountered similar problems, with torn mainsails and broken rigging. Many of those boats retired and went home, but the Ramblers had persevered. Even with the storm sail, they finished third in the race, upholding their reputation as a crew impervious to brutal weather.

The final race of the 2006–2007 *BWPS* series was the Gold Coast race from Sydney to Southport. Five of the crew that had sailed *AFR Midnight Rambler* in the '98 Hobart were on board. To win the *BWPS,* the Ramblers had to do well, beating tough international competitors. Their experience working together as a team in '98 would prove to be invaluable.

Ed recalls, "The sea was horrible. It was a bloody hard race." They had traded in their old Hick 35 for a faster boat called a Farr 40. Still named *AFR Midnight Rambler,* the new boat was lighter and faster. But sailing downwind in the boat was hard work. Because it was relatively light, they were tossed around in the heavy seas. They ripped the main and two spinnakers, but—with the help of Bob Thomas' navigational skills—they excelled.

After years of trying to win the prestigious *Blue Water Point Score, AFR Midnight Rambler* finally cemented a victory. They won the point score series by two points—a slim margin, but enough for a victory. Had the Ramblers turned around in the Flinders Island Race, they would have lost the series. Because they persisted, the six-race series ended in a spectacular finish and a *Blue Water Championship.*

The *Short Ocean Point Score (SOPS)* is the second prestigious award for a series of sailing competitions. The *SOPS* consists of twelve 30-mile races off Sydney Heads, each of which lasts about three hours. It's different than the *BWPS,* and it calls for a somewhat different set of sailing skills. These shorter races are less about heavy seas and endurance, and more about being quick around the buoys with just the right sails and trim.

Though the demands of the *SOPS* are different than the Hobart and the *BWPS,* the Ramblers have been successful in these shorter races as well. And in the 2006–2007 season, *AFR Midnight Rambler* was victorious in both the *Blue Water Point Score* and *Short Ocean Point Score* competitions. It was an extraordinary accomplishment—one that few boats have achieved in a single season.

Within a decade of their triumph in the '98 Hobart, the Ramblers had won every major race on the East Coast of Australia, along with the two most prestigious series competitions of the Cruising Yacht Club. And capping off a banner season in 2006–2007, the CYC broke tradition with a joint award. Both Ed Psaltis and Bob Thomas were honored for the second time as *Ocean Racers of the Year.*

The Ramblers' sustained record of success reflects an extraordinary breadth of seamanship, tenacity, and teamwork. As impressive as these victories have been, however, one of their most important achievements had nothing to do with the past. It involves the future of *AFR Midnight Rambler.*

Though the Ramblers continued to sail well, it became clear to everyone that—if they wanted to sustain their winning record—younger sailors would be needed. And not only did they need to bring in new talent, but these talented rookies had to be successfully integrated into a crew of veterans who had sailed together for years.

The process of finding fresh talent has taken time, but the Ramblers have demonstrated an unusual ability to recruit new members—and to create a unified crew of rookies and veterans. This was brought home to me when I went to a crew dinner for the Ramblers before the 2006 Hobart.

When I arrived at the CYCA, I was somewhat surprised to meet a young woman who had been asked to join the crew. Samantha Byron, an energetic Scottish sailor, had met Ed Psaltis at a work function. Ed encouraged her to come along on a couple of weekends for some inshore sailing, and "Sammy" did a few Saturday sails with the Ramblers. That led to the Bird Island Race, and eventually to the Sydney to Hobart.

Sammy was the first woman to do the Hobart on *AFR Midnight Rambler.* I saw her with the crew at the Shipwright's Arms after the 2006 race and was struck by the realization that Ed and the team truly understood the importance of diversity. They realized that continuing to win meant changes not only in technology and technique, but also in the talent they brought to the team.

Ed recruited another new member, Tom Barker, from the CYCA's Youth Academy. Tom, who had sailed since he was two months old, had done match racing and had a great resume. Ed had done his homework, and he was confident that Tom would be a tremendous asset to the crew. He left a message on Tom's voice mail with a very specific request: Ed asked Tom to sail with the crew for the offshore season, including the Sydney to Hobart Race.

Tom joined the crew in 2004 at the age of 18. With a combination of his ebullient personality and exceptional sailing skills, Tom quickly won the respect of the "old guys." He was savvy enough to come on board in an understated way, seldom speaking and learning how the crew worked together. Eventually his superb sailing skills and pleasantly "cheeky" personality emerged. And his relationship with Ed evolved as well.

Ed had long realized that he often tried to do too much. He had his mind on everything, including steering, trimming sails, and giving orders. Doing all that effectively was an impossible task. With the help of Tom's technical skills, however, Ed shifted focus to steering. He can now maximize his extraordinary skill at the helm, letting Tom worry about sail changes and planning the next leg of the race.

AFR Midnight Rambler has compiled a truly extraordinary record of team successes. And individual crew members have received awards as well. Ed Psaltis and Bob Thomas have been cited as *Ocean Racers of the Year,* and both Michael Bencsik and Tom Barker have won recognition as *Ocean Racing Crew Person of the Year.*

A new chapter in the Ramblers' story began in 2012, as Ed, Bob, and Mix purchased a new boat—the fifth bearing the name *Midnight Rambler.* Still passionate about ocean racing, the Ramblers have continued their impressive record, winning the *Short Ocean Point Score* for the 2011–2012 season.

The *AFR Midnight Rambler* story is inspiring. But what are the lessons that can be extracted from their success at *The Edge*? What, specifically, are the factors that underlie their victories? And what are the takeaways that can be used by teams in any organization faced with big challenges? Part Two of the book provides answers to those questions.

PART TWO

Critical Strategies for *Teamwork at The Edge*

28

Introduction
to the Strategies

A lot of things need to go right for a boat to win the Tattersall's Cup. The vessel itself has to be structurally sound, and technology makes a difference. The sport is constantly innovating and—even though each boat is given a handicap—it's unlikely that a boat in poor condition held together with duct tape will be victorious.

The sailing skill of the crew is fundamental. These seamanship skills can be related to specific competencies, such as the ability to steer in heavy weather or navigational savvy. And they can also be more general capabilities developed through experience in ocean racing—particularly in tough races such as the Hobart or the Fastnet.

Winning boats often rely on a support team that extends beyond the crew sailing in the race. Meteorologists can interpret and relay weather information to boats that have the right information technology. This was an advantage of enormous benefit to *Sayonara* in the 1998 Hobart. Ellison and his crew were making decisions based on the advice of "Clouds" Badham, while following the storm on a computer screen. Lacking that level of support, *AFR Midnight Rambler* relied on intermittent and somewhat confusing forecasts from the Bureau of Meteorology.

The skipper of a boat can also be critical. The leader sets the tone and can have a direct influence on the outcome of a race. A volatile personality or a disorganized leader will put the team at a significant disadvantage. And an experienced skipper, one that people enjoy sailing with, can have the opposite effect.

And, of course, there is *Huey*—the weather god. For me, Huey has become an icon for a more general collection of things that could be called luck or chance. In the '98 Hobart race, the big maxis were fortunate because they missed the worst of the storm. In other races, Huey might smile on a boat of a different size. And there are the rogue waves, with their unpredictable patterns. Any crew hit by a huge wave in hurricane force winds could fall victim to bad luck.

Chance plays a role in any victory. But Roger Hickman, a veteran of thirty-four Hobarts, observed:

> With an event like the Sydney to Hobart Race, luck plays a part. But if you're not smart enough or good enough or professional enough to be in the right place at the right time, you won't get lucky either. If you work very, very hard and have a good team around you, you will get luckier. The harder you work, the luckier you get.[1]

As Hicko notes, teamwork is a critical ingredient in the record of successful boats. A well-built boat with the best technology and skilled sailors can win if they are lucky enough. A good skipper can help create a good team. But if there are fundamental problems of teamwork, it will be extremely hard to win races. And it will be difficult to get people to return to the boat for future races and to maintain a record of success.

It's clear that teamwork is important, but efforts to understand the characteristics of effective teams can be confusing. We are immersed in a constant stream of articles, books, and webcasts—each one purporting to provide authoritative advice. Yet the prescriptions are frequently different. And sometimes the same expert seems to say different things at different times.

These variations or inconsistencies can be troubling. How can we really know that findings are fully grounded in reliable evidence? How can we know when the theories we are reading about are valid? And how can we be sure that insights about teamwork are both well thought out and helpful?

Neither academic credentials nor persuasive writing can guarantee the validity of anyone's perspective. But there are some questions worth considering before reaching conclusions about effective teamwork. There are some challenges that need to be understood.

29

The Research Challenge

I n his provocative book *The Halo Effect,*[1] Phil Rosenzweig lists nine "delusions"—errors in logic or judgment—that can lead to a distorted understanding of organizational performance. In my experience, three of these are particularly problematic.

Was It Just Luck?

The first barrier that gets in the way of drawing conclusions concerns the role of *luck.* We all want to learn from success, so we look at the victors and draw conclusions. We do it with organizations, with successful executives, and with winners of ocean races. We all want to be winners. But a lingering question concerns the role of luck in winning performance.

Michael Raynor and his colleagues with Deloitte Research use an interesting example to make the point. They describe how a professor at MIT, Rebecca Henderson, illustrates the role of luck to her class in strategic management.[2]

At the beginning of the class, she asks all the students to stand up and flip a coin. After the coin toss, only those whose coins came up heads are told to remain standing. After six or seven rounds, only one student is still standing—the winner!

Professor Henderson runs up to congratulate the successful student, offering to write a case study about him or her or do an interview in *Fortune* magazine. The student is a hero, a winner. But in this instance, of course, it's clear that there was nothing about the student that contributed to his or her success. The student benefited from what we would call *luck*.

This theme has been echoed by others. In *Fooled by Randomness*, Nassim Taleb[3] argues that we often mistake luck for skill. This tendency occurs in all areas of life but is especially apparent in the world of markets. Frequently, according to Taleb, we mistakenly believe that a particular investment strategy works, an entrepreneur has vision, or a trader is talented when, in fact, the successful performance is almost entirely attributable to chance alone.

I understand the problem, and I know that there is a degree of luck involved in any successful endeavor. But when I look at boats that successfully complete the Sydney to Hobart Race—and particularly those that take home the coveted Tattersall's Cup awarded to the overall winner of the race—I am confident that there is much more than luck involved. I've tracked the performance of the *Midnight Rambler* for more than a decade after the 1998 race, and her success involves much more than flipping a coin.

To win the Sydney to Hobart Race in a hurricane, the team would have to flip those coins for 628 miles in *Force 12 Hurricane* conditions. And they would have to keep winning the coin toss for a decade. In any particular race, of course, there is an element of chance, and other boats were close competitors of the *Rambler*. But it is this sustained record of success in different racing conditions and different time periods that gives me confidence that they are doing much more than capitalizing on chance.

Correlation vs. Causality

In a classic experiment, renowned behavioral psychologist B.F. Skinner designed a box to drop food pellets to hungry pigeons. The food was presented at regular intervals, and the reward had nothing at all to do with the behavior of the bird.[4]

What Skinner found was that the birds became conditioned to perform a specific response that—at least from the perspective of the pigeons—was connected to what the birds happened to be doing at the time they were rewarded. Skinner's observations were very telling and somewhat comical. One bird was conditioned to turn counterclockwise around the cage. Another repeatedly put its head into one of the upper corners of the cage. A third developed a "tossing" response. Two birds developed a pendulum motion of the head and body. And yet another bird made incomplete pecking movements directed toward—but not touching—the floor.

Apparently, Skinner's birds tended to repeat whatever they were doing when the food hopper appeared. In a sense, what Skinner had discovered was delusional or superstitious behavior on the part of the birds. They behaved as if there were a cause-and-effect relationship between a particular response and food, when, in fact, there was none.

To really understand organizational performance—in this case, effective teamwork—we need to make sure that the elements we identify as ingredients really are causes and not just accompaniments. We need to tell a coherent story, and we need to be able to separate the causes from the effects.

Knowing What to Look For

The third challenge in examining the characteristics of effective teams is sorting out all the different factors that can contribute to high performance. Suppose you find the team that you're confident is good and not just lucky. How do you know what the really important ingredients are—the things that make a difference? Here's an example of the problem.

A *Wall Street Journal* article described a twelve-year study of 361,000 middle-aged American men.[5] The research showed that among nonsmokers there were 1.09 suicides per 100,000 person-years. The rate increased steadily with the number of cigarettes smoked, reaching 3.78 suicides per 100,000 person-years for people who smoked three packs of cigarettes a day. And there was more.

Not only did the risk of suicide increase steadily with the number of cigarettes smoked, but the relative risk of murder also rose with smoking. Two-pack-a-day smokers were twice as likely to be murdered as nonsmokers.

It was hard to conceive of a way that smoking could cause people to commit suicide, and it was even harder to understand why murderers would be intent on hunting down smokers—preferring them to non-smoking victims. This appeared to be another case of confusion between cause and effect. It seems much more likely that smoking, suicide, and murder were all part of a much bigger picture. All three increased together, but the research gave no hint about the underlying cause of all three.

If the researchers in the study had spent time living in areas with a high concentration of smokers who were likely to be murdered or commit suicide, they might have reached plausible explanations for the bigger picture of underlying causes. Lacking that firsthand experience, there was little that could be gleaned from statistics alone.

The problem of knowing very specifically what causes what has plagued books about organizational performance. When people are asked about the things that contribute to success, their memories are often biased and incomplete. It's hard to be objective, and we tend to remember the things we want to remember. And if we try to understand underlying causes based on analyzing more "objective" information—for example, financial statements, newspaper articles, and so forth—there is another problem. How do we know that—as distant observers—we're not identifying things that may be related but are relatively unimportant?

My Approach

The reality is that there is no feasible scientific method that will completely resolve all of these problems. If I were a medical researcher, I could randomly assign some patients to receive a dosage of the special teamwork formula—that is, the strategies I believe are important. I could use a control group of teams that employs strategies I don't think are important. I could even assign another group of teams to get a dosage of other randomly generated strategies. I would then see if my teams did better in the experiment, and I would confirm my results within a certain range of probabilities.

I can do laboratory experiments within certain limited situations to learn more about teams. But my ability to understand the dynamics and successes of teams that are really at *The Edge* is limited. Nonetheless, even if "scientific truth" about successful teamwork is elusive, it is possible to gather significant insights about teams. It is possible to draw reasonable conclusions that will help people and organizations struggling with significant problems.

My approach is based on two primary strategies. First, in an effort to rule out success being the result of luck—of chance alone—I looked at sustained performance over a period of years. Second, I reach my conclusions by getting firsthand experience with the research topic.

I immersed myself in the world of teamwork—particularly teamwork in ocean racing—and even more specifically, the Sydney to Hobart Race. I watched the competitors and interviewed successful ocean racers. And I've sailed with the team of the *AFR Midnight Rambler*. This immersion has extended over a period of eight years since I first contacted the skipper of the *Rambler,* Ed Psaltis.

That background gave me a context for understanding the race and a perspective about the ingredients of effective teamwork in ocean racing. But as I began to draw lessons from the race and to write about teamwork, something seemed to be missing. What was missing, I concluded, was that I had never done the Hobart. What I was missing was experience—up close and personal—with the Everest of ocean racing. With some trepidation, I decided to find a way to enter the Sydney to Hobart Race.

30

My Hobart

I am not an accomplished ocean racer. In fact, in comparison with most of the skilled sailors described in this book, I'm clearly an amateur. At the same time, I believe I know enough about sailing to be able to look past the headlines and dig deeper into what makes a great team. To put this in perspective, here is a brief background on my adventures at sea.

I first climbed aboard a sailboat at the United States Naval Academy, where I learned something about *marlinspike seamanship*—essentially, how to tie knots—as well as intramural racing. I learned the names of ropes and lines, and the difference between the two. I learned a little about sails, and that when they were flapping and making a big noise it was called *luffing* and not flapping. And I learned what it was like to cling to a boat that had turned upside down in the Severn River when a storm came up, unexpectedly capsizing a fleet of midshipmen.

Unlike the majority of my classmates, I had little to do with the Navy after graduation—and I had nothing to do with sailing. As an officer in the Marine Corps, my thoughts were far removed from the graceful white sails I had seen on the Chesapeake Bay. In Vietnam, I was much more concerned with securing defensive perimeters, creating fields of fire for automatic weapons, and registering artillery concentrations.

The Navy was still a part of my life, and I have vivid memories of a dark night when my Naval Academy roommate—John Beardsley, the gunnery officer on a destroyer—fired illumination rounds that prevented my company from being overrun. Fortunately for me, the Navy was close by, but I had left the world of recreational sailing far behind.

After returning to civilian life, I got reacquainted with sailing and learned more about the sport than I had absorbed at Annapolis. I crewed on boats that sailed from the Chesapeake up to Connecticut. And I learned more about the tools of navigation—current at the time, but primitive by today's standards. Lacking a GPS, I struggled to master the sextant, radio direction finders, charts, and techniques for estimating my position with *dead reckoning.*

I continued to cruise after moving to Connecticut, accompanying the charming Victor Vroom—a fellow faculty member at Yale—on excursions to the Newport Jazz Festival. We took more extended voyages down the East Coast, but this was all "cruising" sailing. It was far different than racing, but it was sure fun. Nobody cared how fast we went, only that we knew where we were and where we were going.

I finally gave in and bought my own boat, and I enjoyed cruising on Long Island Sound. On occasions I ventured farther, sailing the waters of Nantucket and Martha's Vineyard, but I hadn't been in a sailboat race since the Naval Academy. Then I met Edgar Smith.

Edgar—sometimes known as "Eddo" for reasons I will explain—is an expert racer from a family of expert sailors. Edgar learned to sail from his father, Gaddis; and his son, Emmet, has represented the United States in international competitions. Edgar owned a boat called *Wasabi,* a popular racing boat known as the J/29. Although the J/29 has been around since the early 1980s, it's a relatively fast boat and perfect for the "around the buoys" races popular in New England.

As a crew member on *Wasabi* I learned a little bit about racing. But my knowledge of ocean racing was developed largely through reading and from conversations with those who had a passion for more serious sailing.

As I began to develop the narrative for this book, I spent time in the Australian racing community. And in talking with the crew of the *Midnight Rambler,* I became more and more intrigued with the sport of offshore ocean racing. I began to comprehend the enormous differences between my sailing experiences—sailing small boats in the Severn, cruising to the Newport Jazz Festival, and racing in Long Island Sound—and the far more demanding sport of offshore racing competition.

My interest in the sport was further heightened by the experience of sailing with the crew of the *Midnight Rambler* in a Sydney race. The event was held in Sydney Harbour, and in many ways it was like one of the local races I had enjoyed in Connecticut. But there was something else.

Sailing aboard the *Midnight Rambler,* I was struck by the seamless interaction I saw among members of the crew. Everything that happened aboard the *AFR Midnight Rambler* seemed to be done quietly, with few words spoken aloud. Unlike the shouting that accompanied a lot of the sailing I had done, crew members seemed to be reading each other's minds. Sailing with the Ramblers, I saw what it was like to have a team that could move into a zone of seemingly effortless coordination.

Absorbing all this, I decided that I needed to find a way to do the Hobart myself. Part of my decision was based on the simple reality that there was a lot I didn't know about ocean racing—in particular, the Sydney to Hobart Race. To write a book that would do justice to the *Midnight Rambler* story, I had to understand the race and I needed to understand the Australian culture.

The country of "Oz," a slang term often used by Australians, is far different than the United States. I had served with some Aussies ("Ozzies") in Vietnam, but we didn't have much time to chat about cultural differences. Because the Sydney to Hobart Race seemed so rooted in the Australian culture, however, I wanted to learn more.

There are superficial differences in slang. I discovered, for example, that feeling "crook" had nothing to do with dishonesty. It meant that someone was sick. I also learned why someone could be working so hard that they were going "flat-out like a lizard drinking." (This is, apparently, the only way lizards can reach the water.) But there were other cultural differences that ran much deeper.

I was intrigued by the way in which rugged Australian individualism seemed to be combined with the ability to collaborate. I wanted to understand how these cultural norms would play out in a demanding ocean race, and I was especially interested in the leadership structure of the team.

The skipper of a racing boat is the ultimate decider, but it's hardly like the Marine Corps. The sailors are civilians, and there are no punitive sanctions for disobedience. How does this work in practice, I wondered? And what is it like to see the structure operate under conditions not unlike combat: high stress, little or no sleep, no time to eat, and real danger?

So, for all these reasons—and because, I confess, the race sounded like a really big adventure—I looked for a boat that would take me aboard. After some searching and networking, I finally found a spot on a 60-foot racing boat. The skipper, Peter Goldsworthy, understood my limitations, but he made it clear that there were no *jewel positions* on his boat. I would be expected to pull my weight as best I could.

With the prospect of the race looming, I did everything I could to be ready. I remembered that, at one point during my trip to Antarctica, I was crossing South Georgia Island. The belated thought occurred to me: *I really should have been in better shape for this.*

It was too late for Antarctica, but I resolved that next time I would be in better physical condition. Consequently, I did my best to prepare physically for the Sydney to Hobart Race, and I was as disciplined as I could be in my training.

As a result of my research, I also knew that this was a serious undertaking. People had died in this race. So I spent as much time as I could possibly spare getting the array of clothing and technology I thought would improve my chances of survival.

I talked with Zach Leonard, then coach of the Yale sailing team (and more recently a member of the U.S. Olympic Coaching squad), about sleep deprivation. I found hydrostatic life jackets that would deploy even if I went over the side unconscious. I found a personal EPIRB—a small battery-powered emergency transmitting device—that would fit under my wet-weather gear. Finally, to prepare for potentially harsh weather conditions, my daughter Holly and I sailed my own boat during the Connecticut winter. Though the Sydney to Hobart Race occurs during their summer, the boats are sailing south toward Antarctica, so it can get cold. Really cold.

When I arrived in Sydney and met the other crew members on my boat, I realized just how much of a rookie I was. My friend Edgar, who accompanied me, had never done the Hobart, but he was a skilled racer. A number of others had done the Hobart, other Australian races, or similar races in other parts of the world. Although not everyone had sailed on the relatively advanced boat we were crewing, clearly everyone knew more than I did.

The situation I found myself in was unfamiliar: I was neither in a formal leadership role nor was I advising leaders. I was a team member with no formal authority, and I was a novice at ocean racing. It was not a comfortable position for me, and I had lots of opportunities to practice one of my dictums: "Cultivate poised incompetence." I did my best to swallow my pride, work hard, follow orders, and learn about ocean racing. And learn about racing I did, as I tried to absorb every part of the experience.

I learned about the painstaking preparation that goes into an event like the Sydney to Hobart Race. I learned about the austerity of a racing boat and about fundamental safety measures. For example, never put your hand somewhere that a finger could be ripped off by a huge sail attached to an 85-foot mast. And I learned that everybody on the boat seemed to have a nickname.

There was Goldy, the skipper. Then Scotty, Fairweather, Beeks, and Frenchy, who was, of course, British. With all these exotic nicknames, I felt like I was enrolled in the Navy's Top Gun school. I started calling my friend Edgar "Eddo," and by the time it was all over I became Perk—at least to Jungle, so named for his ability to climb a rope like it was a tropical vine.

Some of my experiences were tedious and routine: sitting on the side of the boat as ballast—a position often derisively referred to as *rail meat*. Some were exciting: plowing into massive waves with the wind tearing the sails apart. But in all these situations I played the role of a student trying to understand the technical complexities of this kind of ocean race. This was far different than anything I had experienced in my own sailing history.

When it was over, I had learned something about ocean racing, and I had learned a lot about the Sydney to Hobart Race. Most of my learning came through sailing, but, as a dedicated researcher, I also spent some time conversing with other sailors in off-duty hours. I learned to enjoy *Cascade Lager,* and I began to understand how ocean racers thought about the world.

At the end of my adventure, I walked into the Shipwright's Arms pub in Tasmania after finishing the Sydney to Hobart Race and bought a round of drinks for my mates on the *AFR Midnight Rambler.* I couldn't claim to be an ocean racer, but I felt ready to write a book.

The *Teamwork at The Edge* strategies that follow reflect the sum total of my learning from observation, interviews, and personal experience. These strategies have helped me and my team, and I believe they can help your team as well.

31

Team Unity

Strategy #1
Make the team the rock star.

There are many ways to assemble a team to compete for the Tattersall's trophy. Someone with the financial resources of Larry Ellison can search for the best sailors in the world and put them on retainer. Those who are not billionaires, but whose finances are still substantial, can hire individual superstars who will carry the team with brilliant sailing. Or, like the Ramblers, you can make the team itself a *rock star*.

There is no single right or wrong way to construct a competitive ocean racing team, and there are boats with some exceptionally talented and acclaimed sailors that still place a premium on teamwork. But the culture of *AFR Midnight Rambler,* and a number of other winning boats I studied, is grounded in the belief that there is only one rock star, and that superstar is the team. As Ed Psaltis puts it:

> Before the race even started, all the crew felt like they had a say in what was happening. All seven crew members were made to feel that they were part of the team, that they had a role to play, and that they could speak up if they wanted to express their views.[1]

There were no heavies on board. Everyone had to do the whole season as part of the team, and that created a close sense of camaraderie even before the race. *Flat management* is a term that could be used to describe the system. Everyone had a say, regardless of whether they were the skipper or navigator, or had another job in the crew.

The *No Rock Star* policy was put to the test when the crew had to decide whether to sail into the '98 storm and slog to Hobart or turn around and run for the safety of Eden on the Australian mainland. Because of the severity of the conditions and the urgency of the situation, there was no formal team meeting. But the decision initially proposed by Ed and Bob—to take the waves on the bow rather than the stern—was supported by everyone on the boat.

This level of alignment can be hard to achieve even under normal sailing conditions. And when the seas are rough and adrenaline is pumping, it is extraordinarily difficult to maintain. But the concept of a *Rock Star Team* is fundamental to *AFR Midnight Rambler* and to a number of other boats that perform consistently well with a committed crew.

Tactics for *Teamwork at The Edge*

Find committed team members who want to go to Hobart

The Ramblers have rejected a number of very talented sailors who were eager to do the Hobart but were unwilling to put in the hard miles leading up to the race. They've also rejected people who were willing to put in the time but didn't have the stomach for the Hobart.

It's one thing to sail around the buoys in the harbor, but—as I discovered—quite another to be on the rail in the middle of the Bass Strait. In fact, at one point I thought to myself that a lot of the race experience could be replicated in three steps: First, buy a lot of expensive sailing gear; second, find a commercial laundromat; and third, climb into a large washing machine set on cold and stay there for three or four days. It's not for everyone.

A business team that aspires to excellence may not have the same physical challenges as an ocean racing crew, but lofty goals require sacrifice, dedication, and the ability to persevere. Selecting people with the right levels of confidence and motivation is fundamental, and it would be disingenuous to suggest that—by applying the right teamwork strategies—a crew with incompetent or unmotivated individuals will perform at the highest levels. I know from personal experience that there is no magic *Teamwork at The Edge* formula that will compensate for racing with the wrong crew.

Realistic job previews are important. It's unlikely that people will join the Marine Corps or the Navy SEALs with the expectation that the job will be easy. But enlistment efforts that paint a rosy picture will attract candidates eager to step into that appealing recruiting poster. If the work is going to be tough, it's better to recognize that from the outset.

Sailing teams have a built-in assessment center that can be used to evaluate an individual's commitment and skill. A few rough days on the water will quickly reveal motivation and ability—and the fainthearted are often eager to remove themselves from the team.

Teams in more traditional organizations may not have such a straightforward testing mechanism, but a systematic assessment process can be extremely valuable. I have successfully used targeted approaches such as those proposed in *Who: The A Method for Hiring*, by Geoff Smart and Randy Street. The authors argue that mistakes happen when managers:

- Are unclear about what is needed in the job
- Have a weak flow of candidates
- Have trouble discriminating the right candidates from a group of similar-looking applicants
- Lose candidates they really want to join the team[2]

These seem like obvious factors to consider. But I once naïvely assumed that sound leadership and teamwork principles could make any group of individuals successful. After a few humbling failures, I realized that my early experience in the Marine Corps had led me to believe that anyone on my team would have the desire and ability to accomplish tough assignments.

This assumption was demonstrably wrong. I finally recognized the importance of following a systematic selection process. It was only then that I was able to assemble a *Rock Star Team* capable of competing in our metaphorical Sydney to Hobart Race. Careful selection takes time, energy, and focus, but the outcome is well worth the effort.

Look for diversity and get the right person in the right job

A sailboat is a great example of an organization with a highly differentiated set of skill requirements. The forward hand needs to be nimble and willing to endure lots of cold water. The helmsman needs to have an ability to steer a straight course regardless of the weather conditions and to adjust to a constantly changing environment. The navigator needs to understand the weather and to come up with a winning set of maneuvers in a changing environment. And there are some jobs that simply require brute strength.

The Ramblers understood the formula, and they got it right. Jonno was perfect on the bow, Mix organized the lines in the pit, Ed was great at steering, and Bob was an expert navigator. Arthur, Chris, and Gordo all had unique individual skills. But there is more to creating a *Rock Star Team* than just having the right skill set. Personalities need to mesh as well, and teams need to find balance.

Mix, for example, is not only good at organization, but he is also patient—something that Ed is not. Ed candidly admits:

> When the breeze is light and the boat is not going very fast, I get impatient very quickly. That rubs off on the whole crew. I've realized over the years that this is my problem, and I'm trying to get better at it. But I'm just not a great light air sailor.
>
> Mix, on the other hand, is fantastic. The guy just hangs on to the wheel with absolute concentration. He doesn't let the slow speed faze him, and he has time and again got the boat out of depressing situations. The rule is, if the breeze is under 5 knots, get Mix on the helm and get Ed off. And I gladly give it up, because I know that Mix can get the boat going faster than I ever could.[3]

Each member of the *Rambler* crew might have failed in the wrong job. And the misfit could have arisen from lack of technical skill or from temperament. Over time, however, the Ramblers created a *Rock Star Team* by fitting the sailors together like puzzle pieces. There was absolute clarity about strengths and weaknesses—both in sailing skills and in personality—and that clarity has resulted in exceptional success.

AFR Midnight Rambler is not the only team to solve the puzzle. When Bill Koch set out to win the 1992 America's Cup on *America,* he specifically organized the team to minimize each person's individual weakness.

He evaluated each person on a scale of 1 to 10 on the dimensions of talent, teamwork, and attitude. Not everyone on the final team was good at everything, but they had to be exceptional at one thing. "Each one gave everything he had to his individually designed role," said Koch, "and each role was designed to maximize particular skills."[4]

The American team crossed the finish line in first place, beating their Italian competitors—favored by 100-to-1 odds—by 44 seconds. Koch's formula was identical to that of the Ramblers. Find a diverse team of people who are committed to the goal and committed to teamwork, then get them playing the right position.

Minimize hierarchy and status differences

Sailors who join a crew as rock stars are highly paid, and they often get something else as well: special privileges. Celebrated helmsmen, for example, might be hired to just steer the boat and, therefore, get more sleep. They can get better meals than the other crew. They're "looked after."

In many ways this makes sense. They're very good sailors, they have special skills, and they need to be fresh so that they can sail to the best of their ability. If the boat isn't being steered properly, then it can't possibly sail as fast as its potential.

But there is a downside. Other crew members who are tired, cold, and stressed can't help but notice the special treatment given to people in so-called *jewel positions.* Intellectually, they may understand the logic of special privilege. But emotionally, there is a different level of connectedness when everyone is expected to bear the same hardships.

Minimizing hierarchy and status differences doesn't mean that everyone has an equal say in decision making. But it is a fundamental shift in the way people think about their individual value and about the ethos of the team.

Bob Thomas, for example, has a special position as a navigator. But when there's a cup of coffee to be made and others aren't up to it or are seasick, Bob makes coffee. And when there's something to be pumped or sponged out of the bilge, Bob happily does the job no one else wants to do.

As the boat's co-owner, with a special set of skills, Bob could avoid these unpleasant jobs. But his willingness to pitch in has earned him the nickname of "the janitor"—a role that is clearly the opposite of a *jewel position.* This kind of willingness to sacrifice for the team is contagious, and others volunteer to do more than their share. The egalitarian spirit contributes to the building of a *Rock Star Team,* and it helps ensure that the fundamental bonds remain strong in the face of adversity.

Strive for mateship

Not every team can create—nor should it aspire to create—the level of close personal friendships that exists among members of the *AFR Midnight Rambler* crew. But I believe close relationships can be developed among team members that extend beyond the level of connectedness that exists in many formal business environments. That kind of connection is different than a personal friendship and professional relationship. I think of it as *mateship.*

The concept was brought home to me a number of times during my sailing adventures in Australia. One particularly vivid example occurred on a dark night when I was helping *Jungle*—aka James Craddock—drag a giant sail onto the deck at night. Nicknamed the "Anaconda," the sail was so long that it wound around the cramped spaces below like a giant snake. It was also extremely heavy, so it took a tremendous amount of tugging, pulling, and pushing to get the sail on deck and ready to be hoisted.

Jungle was the powerhouse of the operation, but I put everything I had into getting the Anaconda in position as quickly as possible. When the task was complete, Jungle looked at me with a slight grin and said quietly, "Cheers, mate."

The impact of those two words was quite astonishing. Given my relative lack of experience, I wasn't contributing to the team in the way I wanted. But I had given it my best effort, and I knew that Jungle was saying, in his own way, "Well done."

Even more important, he and I were mates on that race. Jungle helped me figure out how to get into the "coffin bunk," which was so tight I could hardly squeeze into it—and I could never turn sideways. He helped me negotiate the confusing process of stumbling around in the dark while the boat was pounding into heavy waves. And he cared enough to take the time while facing his own challenges.

Although I have corresponded with Jungle by e-mail, we are not close personal friends who stay in touch. But Jungle helped me understand the concept of *mateship,* and it is something I have tried to create whenever

I'm a leader or member of a team. A simple "Cheers, mate" can go a long way in building a *Rock Star Team*.

Have a Jonno Trophy

In addition to his ability as a forward hand, John "Jonno" Whitfeld developed a reputation for his dedication to teamwork—even while taking buckets of cold water over his head without complaint. In recognition of his extraordinary contributions, the Ramblers presented Jonno with a trophy acknowledging his "Outstanding effort under adverse conditions."

Although the award began as something of a tongue-in-cheek ceremony, the John Whitfeld Trophy has evolved into an important part of the Ramblers' tradition. At the end of each sailing season, the Ramblers vote for the crew member they feel has put in the greatest effort on behalf of the team. Then at an awards dinner, the winner from the previous year passes the trophy on to the new winner.

Although the trophy is somewhat like a most valuable player award, its significance lies in the fact that crew members are voting on effort and teamwork. The winner may not be the most technically advanced sailor. It could be a less experienced person who distinguishes himself with his dedication to the team.

What started out as a bit of humor has now become an important symbol of commitment to the success of the team. Although teams in other settings may not hand out a trophy, symbolic ways of rewarding effort and commitment to the group are important to building a *Rock Star Team*.

Remember the X-Team

In their thoughtful book on teamwork, *X-Teams: How to Build Teams That Lead, Innovate, and Succeed,* Deborah Ancona and Henrik Bresman argue that the internal focus promoted by many best-selling books on teamwork can lead to failure. This inward focus can cause teams to become insular in organizational settings that require members to work in a matrix of many other teams.[5]

This is a perspective worthy of careful consideration. The metaphor in this book is one that emphasizes a crew in direct competition with a number of other boats and crews. To the extent that this model creates insular thinking with an *us-versus-them* mentality, it can detract from team effectiveness in a larger organization. But with this caveat, I believe it is possible to learn from the exceptional teamwork of boats like the *Rambler* while maintaining the ability to work outside team boundaries.

Stepping back from the events of the '98 Hobart race, it is clear that there were many X-Teams operating during the storm. With 1,000 rescuers called into action, the level of external and collaborative focus was intense. The paramedics from *SouthCare* had to coordinate with rescuers on *Helimed. Sword of Orion* broke protocol to broadcast a high wind warning. And the yacht *Siena* went to the aid of *Stand Aside* while coordinating with another team on the ABC news helicopter.

At sea, ship captains have a legal obligation to render assistance to other vessels or aircraft in distress—providing the captain's own crew will not be endangered. In a traditional organizational setting, there may be no legal obligations for collaboration. But teams that succeed in this metaphorical race need to be capable of *Janusian thinking.*

Janus, the Roman god of gates and doors, is often depicted as looking in two opposite directions simultaneously. Janus has come to symbolize the ability to hold two different thoughts in one's mind at the same time. In many settings, *Rock Star Teams* need to be able to do the same thing. On the one hand, they need to be looking inward and creating a sense of unparalleled esprit and unity. But on the other hand, they also need to maintain the ability to collaborate beyond team boundaries and build strong external ties. As paradoxical as it may seem, they need to be *Rock Star Teams* in *Rock Star Organizations.*

Navigation Points

1. Are all members of your team committed to the team goal? Are they willing to put in the time and make the effort needed to achieve that goal?
2. Do team members have a realistic understanding of the sacrifice, dedication, and perseverance it will take to achieve the goal?
3. Does your team have the diverse set of skills needed for success? Do you have the right people in the right roles?
4. Does everyone on your team pitch in to help, or do you have *rock stars* in *jewel positions*?

5. Is there a sense of *mateship* in your team? Do you have a shared personal connection that contributes to the team's effectiveness?
6. Are individual members rewarded for contributing to the success of the team? Do you have a *Jonno Trophy*?
7. When needed, are you able to look outside the boundaries of your team and work with external teams and individuals? Can you be an *X-Team* when the situation calls for it?

32

Prepare, Prepare, Prepare

Strategy #2
Remove all excuses for failure.

One of the most distinctive characteristics of the *Rambler* crew is their focus on careful preparation. Mix Bencsik captured it this way:

> I can only describe our preparation as meticulous. It's one of the key strengths of the team, and it starts with Ed's meticulous nature. The list of things to do usually runs into five or six full pages. Even if the boat is brand-new, the list is long. I think that preparation is one of the key reasons why we achieved success in the '98 race. But it is also a key element in our ongoing ability to sail well.[1]

Ed's checklist is a symbol of everything that the Ramblers do to maximize their chances of winning. They systematically review every aspect of the race—including the boat, the crew, and their strategy. Then they set about the task of ensuring that every element in this complex system is functioning to the best of its ability.

Reflecting on their careful process, Bob Thomas was reminded of the book *No Excuse to Lose: Winning Yacht Races with Dennis Conner.*[2] "When we're finished with our preparation," Bob said, "we have removed all excuses for failure."

Tactics for *Teamwork at The Edge*

Create a Team Checklist

The specifics of preparing a sailboat for the Sydney to Hobart are likely to be very different from the things your team needs to do to prepare for your race. The concept of a checklist, however, is broadly applicable.

In aviation, checklists are used extensively to minimize the possibility of pilot error. The idea originated in 1935 with a group of test pilots who had witnessed the crash of what was a complex airplane at the time—the B-99 Flying Fortress.[3]

Although the pilot of the fallen B-99 was an experienced aviator, he had forgotten to release a new locking mechanism on the controls of the airplane. As a response, the test pilots created a simple checklist with step-by-step instructions for takeoff, flight, landing, and taxi. Individually, these tasks were rudimentary, but, collectively, it was easy to miss a step.

Because fear makes it easy to overlook even the most obvious things, checklists are also used in emergency situations. While Captain Chesley B. "Sully" Sullenberger III was attempting to recover from a "double bird strike" during the *Miracle on the Hudson,* his first officer was methodically running through an *engine restart checklist.* Sully and the plane eventually wound up in the Hudson, but only after the crew had systematically done everything possible to keep US Airways Flight 1549 flying.

Hospitals and health officials also advocate using checklists for safe surgery, setting out the minimum necessary steps in a complex medical process. The benefits have been impressive, and as Atul Gawande notes in *The Checklist Manifesto: How to Get Things Right*:

> The most common obstacle to effective teams, it turns out, is not the occasional fire-breathing, scalpel-flinging, terror-inducing surgeon, though some do exist. . . . No, the more familiar and widely dangerous issue is a kind of silent disengagement, the consequence of specialized technicians sticking narrowly to their domains.[4]

Gawande argues that checklists can help bring individuals together, ensuring that nothing will fall between the cracks in an important team effort.

In *The Leader's Checklist,* Michael Useem extends the concept beyond military and hospital environments to the behavioral sciences. With an innovative approach, Useem identifies fifteen *Mission Critical Principles* distilled from his extensive research and personal experience.

The core principles specified in *The Leader's Checklist* are generally applicable to any leadership situation. But Useem goes one step further, explaining how the checklist can be tailored to account for the specific challenges faced by an individual leader.[5]

I have found that the process of creating a *Team Checklist* can, in itself, be an important tool for team development. As we prepared to write this book, our team sat down to plan the mission. We systematically outlined our goals and aspirations. Laura Gardner, our "Pit Man" made a *Countdown Calendar* and taped it to the wall of the conference room. We embellished the calendar with photos of the *Midnight Rambler* and—as a final touch—we added a picture of Indiana Jones running from a giant boulder. Laura taped Indiana right next to the deadline for the manuscript.

We then outlined team and individual responsibilities, thinking through—as thoroughly as we could—everything that needed to be done to complete the book. With an eye toward *removing all excuses for failure,* we also took into account everything that could go wrong in our planning process.

At one point, we added a simple checklist using a format borrowed from the military: the Five Paragraph Order. Using the *S-M-E-A-C* template, we reviewed the equivalents of our:

1. **Situation:** Enemy forces, friendly forces, adjacent units, and supporting units
2. **Mission:** Goal of the operation
3. **Execution:** How we will accomplish the mission
4. **Administration and Logistics:** Food, ammunition, batteries, and POWs
5. **Command and Signal:** Radio frequencies and emergency signals

Tailoring the operation order to our situation called for some creative juggling with metaphor. But we had fun and, in the process, created our own *Team Checklist.*

Keep preparing while you're racing

I recently observed a large manufacturing firm go through the process of a major organizational restructuring. The company had experienced significant financial losses, and the CEO believed that the new design would help the company become more competitive and cost-effective.

The head of human resources decided to keep the new structure a closely held secret until it was publicly announced. His reasoning was that there was no need to create unnecessary anxiety. But the secrecy policy meant that a number of significant players in the organization would be given no warning. They would simply wake up one morning to find themselves reporting to a new boss, in a completely new organizational structure.

When concerns were raised about the impact of the surprise, the HR leader had little sympathy for those affected. His view was that anyone caught off guard needed to act like a "grown-up" and get with the program. There was work to be done.

For those who had expressed concern, it came as no surprise that the preemptive change created shock waves throughout the organization. Although people were expected to calmly and logically endorse the new structure, they didn't always act like the grown-ups they were expected to be. They acted like anyone whose work life and future prospects had been unexpectedly disrupted. They reacted with anger, anxiety, and—frequently—resentment.

On a sailboat, wind shifts or other events frequently require a change in direction. Because of the potential problems that can occur when sailors are caught off guard, there is a standard protocol for making sure everyone knows what is happening. This well-established process is described in his classic sailing book, *The Annapolis Book of Seamanship,* by John Rousmaniere.[6]

Rousmaniere outlines the sequence for tacking—that is, changing course—very clearly.

It's important that the skipper and crew communicate clearly during a tack. Here are the orders and responses they should use:

STEERER: "Ready about" or "Stand by to tack."
CREW: "Ready" (when everything has been prepared for the maneuver).
STEERER: "Hard a-lee" or "Helm's a-lee" (indicating that the tiller or

wheel has been turned and that the sail will swing to the other side of the boat).

In a light breeze, the tacking maneuver might be accomplished without proper preparation. Lines might be snarled and there could be confusion, but usually no one would get hurt. In heavy weather, however, this same maneuver might well mean that an unprepared crew member could be caught off guard, smashed in the head, and knocked over the side unconscious.

The easiest way to avoid accidents, and to make sure that the boat quickly and efficiently moves to the new course, is to use the protocol—to give people a warning with the simple phrase: *Ready about*. This enables the crew to prepare physically and psychologically for the new course.

The HR team in the manufacturing organization knew that they were going to be heading on a new course. They knew exactly when the public announcements were going to occur, and they understood the implications for their jobs. But they were astonished to find that crew members on their metaphorical vessel were angry when the boat abruptly swung to a new course. They didn't understand the importance of preparing both the boat and the crew.

AFR Midnight Rambler has other systems in place for planning and preparation. While Ed Psaltis is focused on steering, others are thinking about the sea conditions and sail requirements for the next leg of the race. And their ability to look ahead was critical to their success in the '98 storm.

The *wave spotter* did much more than protect the steerer from the onslaught of the weather. He also ensured that the boat would be ready for the next big wave. At the height of a violent storm, maneuvering a boat through one monster wave after another requires incredible focus. That requirement creates a dangerous dilemma: The singular focus means that the helmsman may see only the waves directly in front of the boat, while losing sight of what lies ahead.

Teams in organizations that are navigating through a crisis run similar risks. They face the danger of solving imminent problems in ways that eliminate long-term opportunities. Successful teams master the art of *bifocal vision*: They have the ability to focus on current challenges while, at the same time, preparing for longer-term threats and opportunities.

After watching a presentation of the *AFR Midnight Rambler* story, one of our clients developed a *wave spotter* system designed to help their team focus on the next wave challenge—while never losing sight of the one behind it. They are preparing and racing at the same time.

Polish the stove

Sailors getting ready to do the Hobart understand that it makes sense to prepare for the worst. But I was somewhat surprised when the skipper of my boat, Goldy, turned to one of the watch captains and asked, "Do we have enough morphine?" The last time I had heard that question asked was in the Marine Corps.

I was also struck by the various checklists posted on the inside of the cabin: *Man down Procedure—Unconscious or Severely Injured, Helicopter Transfer,* and *Recovery from Capsize.* I first wondered if perhaps things had gone too far when I read the protocol for *Piracy Attack* (Do not fight back once they are on board). But on reflection, I couldn't see any harm in being ready for anything and everything.

What stood out for me was the extent to which crews prepare for the worst, yet also pay attention to the small things. The stove that Gordon Livingstone polished on the *Rambler* was not a critical part of equipment for either racing or survival. Yet it was important, because it symbolized the extent of their careful preparation and helped instill a sense of confidence on the part of the crew. The Ramblers knew that everything on the boat was as shipshape as it could possibly be. And the stove had another effect as well. Competitors who see the stove being polished have absolutely no doubt about the intensity of the Ramblers' desire to win.

Teams facing challenges need to prepare for every contingency, and they need to think about the big things. But they also need to be aware of the small things that symbolize careful preparation. They need to send a clear message that they intend to win and that they are willing to polish the stove.

Plan and prepare but be flexible when things change

Joe Louis, one of the greatest heavyweight boxers of all time, famously remarked, "Everyone has a plan until they've been hit." While planning and preparation are important, not everything can be anticipated—especially at *The Edge.*

This point was brought home to me by General Richard Natonski, who was Commanding General of the 1st Marine Division during Operation Iraqi Freedom II. He was responsible for leading more than 30,000 Marines, soldiers, sailors, airmen, and coalition forces in a highly stressful combat operation.[7]

In the fall of 2004, General Natonski was given the mission of preparing for a second assault on the city of Fallujah. An earlier attempt had come to a premature halt, and by September of 2004 the city had grown into a sanctuary for insurgents who launched attacks in Baghdad and elsewhere—returning to Fallujah to rest, rearm, and plan their next round of attacks.

With the Iraqi election for a transitional National Assembly scheduled for January 2005, it was imperative that the city be liberated from the insurgency. Planning for the operation was extensive. The Marines built what would later be called an *Iron Mountain* of supplies including food, fuel, ammunition, and spare parts. The mountain of supplies was designed to allow the attack on Fallujah to proceed in spite of expected enemy attacks on the Marines' supply lines.

Several days into the assault, things were not going as expected. The resistance in the eastern part of the city had been much stronger than anticipated. Despite weeks of planning, war gaming, and coordination between attack forces, the assault had been slowed. General Natonski summarized the situation with a comment reminiscent of Joe Louis: "Plans very seldom survive their first contact with the enemy. Fallujah was no different."

During the planning phase of the operation, General Natonski's Operations Officer—Lieutenant Colonel Joseph L'Etoile and his planning team—had developed an alternate contingency plan. This *Branch Plan* would have the effect of extending the boundaries into the southern portion of the city between two attacking regiments. If necessary, the responsibilities of the unit in heaviest contact with the insurgents could be adjusted. To succeed, however, this change in the attack plan would require clear communication and coordination with large numbers of troops engaged in fierce combat.

While the attack continued, all units were briefed on the new plan. At 7 p.m. on the third day of the battle, the assault shifted smoothly to the new plan. The ability of the attacking units to adjust on the fly was, as General Natonski saw it, similar to a football team's ability to change plays when the quarterback "calls an audible" at the line of scrimmage.

The shift in attack plan worked, and General Natonski's forces successfully secured Fallujah. The city was cleared of insurgents, Al Qaeda retreated, and peace and security were restored to its citizens.[8] In our discussions of leadership and teamwork, General Natonski encouraged me to keep in mind a corollary to careful preparation: "Plan and prepare, but be flexible when things change." He captures the spirit of the concept with the term *Semper Gumby.*

This tongue-in-cheek expression combines the Marine Corps motto of *Semper Fidelis, Always Faithful,* with the character Gumby—a clay figure that can be twisted in many directions. For the Marines, *Semper Gumby,* or *Always Flexible,* gained the victory on the battlefield. It is a valuable concept for any team facing challenges at *The Edge.*

Navigation Points

1. Do you use *Team Checklists* to help keep track of critical tasks and *Mission Critical Principles?*
2. Does your team keep preparing while you're racing? Are you able to prepare for the next assignment while you're completing the current one?
3. Do you *polish the stove* by ensuring that even small symbolic tasks are completed?
4. Do you have *wave spotters* on the lookout for new or unexpected challenges?
5. Are you able to shift smoothly to a new plan if the one you prepared for isn't working? Can you be flexible with a *Semper Gumby* approach to preparation?

33

Balanced Optimism

Strategy #3
Find and focus on the winning scenario.

O ver the course of a long race, sailors will inevitably encounter setbacks. In an instant, a boat can go from leading the fleet to lagging
behind. A major reversal can easily discourage the crew and, left
unchecked, can deplete the crew's energy. Worse yet, this weakened performance can quickly turn into a downward spiral. As Ed Psaltis notes:

> The issue of optimism is a critical aspect of the Hobart race. As
> in any sporting endeavor, people get tired—both physically and
> mentally. If you haven't got that spark—something to aim for, some
> good news to keep in the back of your mind—the team can get
> demoralized very quickly. When that happens we're not perform-
> ing at our best.
>
> You have to stay embedded in reality, but I try to keep a posi-
> tive outlook, because that keeps the crew going when they're cold
> and hungry and tired. We won't win every race, but if we've got a
> chance of beating our arch rival, we'll keep at it.[1]

Tactics for *Teamwork at The Edge*

Be absolutely clear about what it means to win

Every crew in the Sydney to Hobart Race would like to be declared the overall race winner—to take home the Tattersall's trophy. Any boat in the starting fleet is in direct competition with every other boat that sails out of Sydney Harbour. And because of the handicap system, every boat has a theoretical chance of winning.

In practice, not every boat is in serious competition for the Tattersall's Cup. Not every crew is willing to commit to the rigorous training, hard work, and physical rigors and discipline it takes to become a truly competitive boat. Some teams see sailing largely as a social event—albeit one that involves sailing hundreds of miles through potentially dangerous water—to enjoy "a quiet little drink" in Hobart at the end of the race.

A team that aspires to triumph at *The Edge* needs to first decide what it means to win. If the goal is winning the Hobart and taking home the Tattersall's trophy—literally or metaphorically—then the team can align around that goal. Alternatively, a team might choose to try to be first in their division—roughly equivalent to competing with teams and organizations of their own size. And if the goal is purely to enjoy the mateship of the journey, then the challenge is defined differently. The only requirement is that the crew complete the race safely and without injury.

An American boat named *Rosebud* won the Tattersall's Cup in 2007. It had been thirty years since an American entry had been declared overall winner, and it was only the third U.S. boat to win in the sixty-three-year history of the race.

Rosebud has won a number of major ocean races in addition to the Hobart—including the Newport to Bermuda and the Transpacific from Los Angeles to Hawaii. I spoke about the secret of *Rosebud's* success with Malcolm Park, a watch captain who played a key role in the boat's design. Park was filled with ideas about winning races:

> For me, the most important thing in building a winning team is that everyone has the same vision of what the team goals are. It's not enough to say I want to win. We all want to win. That doesn't cut it. The question is, what do you want to win? Do you want to win ocean races? Do you want to win buoy races? Do you want

to travel internationally? Do you want to stay locally? In our case, there is more than the result we are looking to achieve in specific ocean races like the Hobart Race. It wasn't enough simply to build a boat that would be successful. We wanted to build a class of boats that others would have an interest in.[2]

To find and focus on a winning scenario, the first step is to define winning. Only then will the team have a clear shared understanding of their race. With that awareness, the team can plan a strategy for taking home their trophy.

Find a winning scenario

I was once called in to help a senior executive team that was mired in problems. The CEO had strained relations with many members of the team, and a feedback report—consisting of anonymous verbatim comments—painted an extremely grim picture.

There were historical conflicts between key team members. The executives felt isolated from the leadership of their parent company. Some were fatigued, feeling that no matter how well they performed they would always be asked to do more. And there were numerous comments from people who did not feel like they were part of a winning team—they felt like losers.

The level of frustration and sense of hopelessness were more profound than I had ever seen with any senior team. After reading one negative comment after another, I started to get depressed myself. But the paradox was that the team members seemed to have all the ingredients needed to succeed. Individually, many were exceptional. There were some obvious problems that they knew how to solve. They had the potential to become a great team. But they weren't winning.

As part of a two-day team off-site meeting, I shared the story of the *Midnight Rambler.* I described how the crew was always able to identify a scenario by which they could be successful. The scenario didn't necessarily result in their being declared overall winners in any particular race. It could be a scenario by which they could win a bigger contest—for example, the *Blue Water Point Score* series. And it could even mean finishing the race at the end of the pack with the jury-rigged sail, as they did in the '94 Hobart.

The Ramblers' winning scenario didn't even have to be the most likely series of events. This was not about oddsmakers handicapping a horse race or about pundits predicting election results. It was not about using Bayesian statistics in a decision tree to find an option with the highest expected value. It was about giving the crew a reason to fight: a reason to believe that there was a way they could win the race on their own terms and—because of that possibility—to do everything they could to make the boat sail as quickly as possible.

The metaphor resonated with a number of team members. The idea that they needed to find some pathway to victory made sense. They realized that, absent some tangible scenario for winning, it was useless to try. But if they could see a way through the maze, then they were willing to invest time and energy in the race.

With that turning point, the team committed to a number of very specific actions. They agreed to:

- Stand behind and support the CEO
- Develop a strategy for dealing with the parent company
- Establish ground rules for operating as a team and working together
- Identify ways of more effectively running meetings, setting agendas, and avoiding dead-end conversations

Perhaps most important, they also committed to sharing the load and taking greater responsibility—rather than bringing every problem to the CEO.

This catalytic moment was a significant milestone for the team. It did not solve every difficulty with the parent company, and it didn't make all internal tensions disappear. But it did enable the team to gather the energy to get their boat upright and to turn in the right direction so that they could make it over the next wave.

Finding a winning scenario served the same purpose for this team as it had for the Ramblers. It gave the executives hope and energy so they could escape the trough of despair and start racing as a team.

Once you're committed, rely on tunnel vision

In some cases, teams can see only one path to victory. In other situations, when there are multiple options, it makes sense to deliberate. This was the circumstance that the Ramblers found themselves in during the '98 Hobart race, as they weighed the odds of sailing into the storm against turning around and running for safety.

In those moments of decision, it makes sense to debate every option, to consider the pros and cons, to express reservations, and to think of everything that can go wrong. But once the decision has been made, distracting thoughts need to be left behind. Everyone needs to focus on the winning scenario with *tunnel vision.*

On the *Midnight Rambler,* each crew member had an individual coping strategy for dealing with distracting thoughts about catastrophe. Arthur Psaltis willed himself out of a state of despair and focused on crew management. Mix Bencsik concentrated on straightening out the boat and passing water to the helmsman. John Whitfeld kept track of the relative percentage of time they had some control over the boat. And Chris Rockell took comfort in the fact they were doing everything they could do to survive the storm. They all stayed focused on what needed to be done to sail the boat and get to Hobart.

In some situations, tunnel vision can be dangerous. When Everest climbers are so focused on reaching the top of the mountain that they refuse to turn around, *summit fever* can be fatal. But in situations where there are no alternatives—as was the case with the Ramblers—tunnel vision was completely adaptive. Everything not directly involved in getting the boat through the waves was peripheral.

High-performing teams need to understand the difference between adaptive tunnel vision and dangerous summit fever. If there are choices, and if a safer option involves turning back, then teams should fight the temptation to go forward. But when a team commits to a course of action, tunnel vision becomes a valuable tool for concentrating on the goal. It is a mindset that enables the team to focus on their winning scenario and to leave distracting thoughts behind.

Consciously encourage positive, optimistic dialogue

One of the most interesting patterns to emerge from my research concerns the nature of conversation among teams that survive life-threatening situations. I've seen a similar pattern in many accounts—in teams ranging from Shackleton's *Endurance* Expedition to shipwreck survivors adrift in lifeboats, and to the Ramblers as well.

In the 1998 storm, the encouraging and optimistic banter of the Ramblers seemed to be transparently concocted. When Arthur Psaltis said, "The clouds up there are clearing," or "I think we're getting through it," his brother Ed was skeptical. Yet at the same time, he realized that

Arthur's reassurance made things better. It felt good to hear him say that they were going to be okay. It helped. But how can words that seem to be an obvious spin make a bad situation better?

I gained some additional insight about the phenomenon a few years ago at the Explorers Club in New York. Because of my previous book on Shackleton, I had been asked to do a keynote presentation at the Club's Lowell Thomas Awards Dinner. I was looking forward to the dinner and to meeting a number of the distinguished honorees, including Yvon Chouinard, the founder of Patagonia.

At a reception before the awards dinner I found myself in a room filled with explorers, a number of whom had impressive resumes. None of the faces in the room were familiar, however, and this was not my usual social circle.

Much to my surprise, my wife, Susan, began waving at a figure across the room. I was supposed to be the writer and adventurer, but Susan— who grew up in Queens and has never been camping—seemed to know one of the honorees.

We crossed the room, and Susan was soon engaged in an animated conversation with Kenneth Kamler, a doctor with whom she had studied while a medical student at Mount Sinai. It seemed somewhat ironic that Susan was more at home at the Explorers Club than I was and that she knew the distinguished adventurer who was being honored at the awards dinner. It was my good fortune, however, because the event introduced me to Ken's work.

Ken Kamler has climbed, dived, sledded, and trekked through some of the most remote regions of the world. He was the only doctor on Everest during the 1996 expedition documented by John Krakauer's book *Into Thin Air,* and he helped treat the survivors.

As a physician, Ken's life work involves understanding how people respond to extreme conditions—how they succumb and how they prevail. And in his fascinating book—*Surviving the Extremes: A Doctor's Journey to the Limits of Human Endurance*—Ken shares his experience in places ranging from the jungle to high altitudes and even outer space.[3] One story in particular caught my attention.

Ken had volunteered to accompany an expedition to study the tectonics of Mount Everest and to measure its exact height using a laser telescope. On the second day of the expedition, a Sherpa slipped and fell while crossing an aluminum ladder placed over a crevasse in the ice. He dropped 80 feet and ended up wedged headfirst between walls of ice at the bottom of the crevasse.

Pasang, the Sherpa, spent thirty minutes hanging upside down before his fellow climbers could bring him back to the surface. The climbing party then made its way down to the base camp where Ken was waiting. At first Pasang had been conscious and walking, but he began to stumble badly and collapsed, unconscious. It took hours to lower him slowly down the mountain.

This kind of head-on collision, followed by loss of consciousness, would have likely been fatal for someone brought into Ken's emergency room in New York City. And at the Everest base camp, 17,559 feet above sea level, none of this advanced equipment was available.

Pasang had made it down alive, but just barely. His respiration and pulse were slowing, and less oxygen was getting to his brain. Pasang's body was about to shut down, but something was keeping him alive.

Gathered round the injured climber were fellow Sherpas who had come to pray. They were facing toward him, and their lips were moving in a monotonous chant. Outside the tent there was more chanting—a chorus arising from tents around the camp where other Sherpas were keeping vigil. As Ken describes it, "In the stillness of the night the effect was powerful, primal, and unnerving: a quadraphonic rumble emanating from within the mountain itself."

The sound was calming and hypnotizing, engulfing both the doctor and the injured climber. Ken administered oxygen through a face mask and fluids through an IV line. He performed some of his medical tasks without conscious effort. Was it possible, Ken wondered, that the Sherpas had evolved a method for matching the pitch of their chanting with the vibration of brain waves—that they could create a harmonic that was helping reverse Pasang's brain shutdown?

There was no course in medical school that showed Ken a protocol for treating a subdural hematoma in below-zero temperatures using a combination of oxygen, IV fluids, and Tibetan chants. But there on the mountain in the dark, Ken would not dismiss the possibility that the chants were helping Pasang recover from this traumatic event.

Pasang survived the night. His pulse strengthened, the swelling in his face receded, and he opened his eyes. With the morning light, the chanting stopped. Ken felt as if he had been watching the scene from a distance, and he was certain he had witnessed a healing force—that the chanting had released an energy within Pasang, a will to live that had reversed his decline.

The recovery of Pasang the Sherpa can be explained in medical terms describing nerve impulses and chemical reactions. It can be described in religious terms as a miracle. Or it can be understood through the power of human connection—the power that comes from the strength that we draw from each other in times of crisis.

Without grasping the complexities of the human brain or the possibilities of divine intervention, one thing is certain: The power of a team to surmount adversity is extraordinary. With encouragement from others, we can overcome overwhelming odds.

Navigation Points

1. Does your team have absolute clarity about what it means to succeed? Do they know what it will mean to take home the Tattersall's trophy?
2. Do all team members see a path to victory? Can they envision a scenario by which the team will win?
3. Once the team is committed, are you able to exclude distracting thoughts and focus on the goal with *tunnel vision*?
4. Do team members speak positively and optimistically, encouraging each other? Do they support individuals who may be discouraged—helping them regain confidence and energy?

34

Relentless Learning

Strategy #4
Build a gung-ho culture of learning and innovation.

The very best teams develop the ability to learn from experience. They have the ability to innovate, and to generate and implement new ideas. In practice, however, these fundamental skills are difficult to develop and even harder to maintain.

My colleague Robert Shaw and I have invested a considerable amount of time trying to understand why learning and innovation are so problematic.[1] As we looked at everything that needed to happen for a team to learn effectively, it became easier to understand why it is so challenging to create learning-friendly teams and organizations.

At a conceptual level, the steps involved in creating a learning team are relatively straightforward. Teams need to do three essential things. They need to: take action, reflect on the outcomes of their actions, and gain insights that will help them improve future performance. In a larger organization, individual teams need to disseminate their ideas and learnings to help other teams as well.

Although the concepts are simple, we found an imposing list of things that can interrupt the learning cycle.

- The *capacity to take action* is inhibited when organizations create risk-averse cultures that penalize failure, when teams lack the resources to experiment, when team members experience the strain of too many conflicting priorities, and when people feel powerless, resigning themselves to simply following orders.
- The *capacity to reflect and gain insight* is diminished when teams deny that problems exist, when they get complacent because of previous successes, and when they lack forums to talk about team performance.
- The *capacity to share learnings* is blocked when teams become inwardly focused and when they view other teams as competitors. For a team on a sailboat racing against other competitors, this insular view makes sense. But, as Ancona and Bresman argue, when different teams in the organization need to work together to succeed, this isolation becomes counterproductive.

Although many conditions must be met in order to create a learning team, we found success stories along with the failures. Here are some tactics that will help your team innovate and learn.

Tactics for *Teamwork at The Edge*

Think gung-ho

The expression *gung-ho* often conjures up an image of someone—maybe a football player or soldier—charging ahead with unbridled enthusiasm. But the origins of the phrase are rooted in a concept quite different from that stereotypic picture. Originally an abbreviation for Chinese industrial cooperatives, the two characters in the phrase *gung-ho* came to be translated by some Americans as "work together," or "work in harmony." One of those Americans was a Marine officer named Evans Carlson.

Carlson had heard the term while serving with the Chinese resistance in 1937 and 1938. In 1942, Carlson—now a Lieutenant Colonel—was placed in command of the 2nd Marine Raider Battalion.

The 2nd Raider Battalion was specifically organized and tasked with conducting guerrilla operations against the Japanese. The idea of a specialized "commando" unit was strongly supported by President Franklin Roosevelt, who was desperate to find a way to strike back against Japan. The history of *Carlson's Raiders* is rich in drama, but one of the most interesting chapters of the *Gung-Ho Battalion* concerns Colonel Carlson's approach to training and organization.

Carlson had served in both the Army and the Marine Corps, and he had been both an officer and an enlisted man—a member of the rank and file. Carlson's experience convinced him that the sharp divide between officers and the troops was counterproductive. Consequently, in the egalitarian spirit that he had observed while serving with the Chinese resistance, Carlson decided to hold weekly gung-ho meetings.

In these gung-ho assemblies, anyone—officer or enlisted—had the right to speak without fear of reprisal. Observing the Raiders in action, one news correspondent was astounded to see a corporal disagree with his captain over a maneuver they had practiced earlier. When questioned about the exchange, Colonel Carson responded simply, "I like men who think."[2]

Some questioned Carlson's unorthodox view of hierarchy and the chain of command, but the concept of gung-ho meetings, where everyone has a right to speak up, is central to the concept of learning and innovation. The ability to talk honestly about what works, what doesn't work, and what might work is critical to effective teamwork.

Neville Crichton is the owner and skipper of the super maxi yacht *Alfa Romeo*. Crichton comes from a long line of adventurers—his grandfather accompanied Shackleton on an expedition in the Antarctic—and he himself is a distinguished sailor. Crichton has carried the New Zealand flag to victory in almost 200 races throughout the world, and he was honored by Queen Elizabeth II for his contributions to yachting and business.

Unlike many wealthy businesspeople, Crichton is a hands-on skipper who actually sails his boat. And in the spirit of gung-ho, he is also committed to learning as a team. As Crichton describes the team on *Alfa Romeo*:

> We don't have prima donnas on the boat; we just have very good sailors. We work as a team, not as prima donnas screaming at everyone else. We have a talk as a crew before the start of the race, and after the race we do a debrief and we take notes. We follow-up and we fix things that go wrong—and that applies even if I'm the skipper. If I've stuffed up the start, it's discussed and we find out why I stuffed up the start. It's not an embarrassment. We talk openly about it, we make notes on it, and we fix it for the next race.[3]

The ability to talk openly about why things get "stuffed up" is a central tenet of gung-ho, and a hallmark of winning teams.

Encourage and invest in innovation

Like *AFR Midnight Rambler, Rosebud*'s impressive record is based on teamwork, not individual rock stars. As Malcolm Park put it:

> We aren't the big names in sailing. On some boats we sail against, every single person aboard is an America's Cup helmsman or tactician. That's just not who we are. I'm not taking anything away from how those teams function—they're incredibly competitive and they are great groups to sail against. But that's not our vision.
>
> Our vision is much more oriented to offshore sailing. As a result we don't necessarily want an America's Cup tactician. We want people who can get along and have confidence in the rest of their team members to do their job.
>
> When you're down below at the end of the day and it's blowing 40 knots up on deck and is miserable, you need to be able to rest and be prepared to come back on deck again in three hours. But the only way that you can do that is if you've got absolute confidence in the team that's on deck so that you can relax.
>
> Having confidence in everyone on your team is a key to success. It's been my experience that if you have rock stars aboard, they don't necessarily function as part of the team. I'm not saying it can't happen; it just hasn't been my experience.[4]

Park's description of the *Rosebud* team reminded me of the Ramblers. The *Rosebud* crew had worked together for a significant amount of time. They were all good sailors, but there were no *rock stars* or *jewel positions*. In addition, Park noted the consistency between his leadership as a watch captain and that of Kevin Miller, another watch leader.

The commitment to teamwork aboard *Rosebud* came as no surprise, but Park went on to describe the creativity encouraged by the owner, Roger Sturgeon. Sturgeon is a mathematician who thinks about the world in a way that invites creative thinking. To encourage ingenuity, *Rosebud* has devoted 10 percent of its total budget to invest in ideas that are "outside the realm of what is normally expected or used in the marine industry."

All of the sailors in key spots were encouraged to come up with a new idea. And each of the individuals who had something they wanted to experiment with could have the satisfaction of seeing their idea being implemented.

Not every suggestion resulted in a workable idea. But as Park sees it:

If just one of the ideas out of that 10 percent of the budget succeeds, people will have an acknowledgment of their success and we will have a better boat for it. It could be a completely outrageous idea that nobody's tried before. I think it's important to allow that. It enhances creativity and allows people more involvement in the boat. People might come up with something that nobody else has thought of. And that's a huge upside.

I asked Park if he could recall any new ideas that were especially interesting. He responded: "Yup, I can think of three specific things right now." When I asked him what they were, he replied, "I can't tell you. We don't think anybody else has come up with them." I suspect he was right, and I understand why he had no interest in disseminating his innovative ideas to his competitors.

Keep learning in the heat of the battle

One dark night in Vietnam I was standing at the opening of my sand-bagged bunker, listening to radio messages that were being broadcast on a variety of tactical frequencies. Most of the messages were routine, but the urgency I heard in the voices during one exchange caught my attention.

I had a small reel-to-reel tape recorder, and, for reasons I can't fully explain, I decided to tape the radio conversation. Three radio call signs were the most active: *Klondike,* used for a Marine observation squadron equipped with armed "Huey" helicopters; *Switch,* used by the helicopters designed for troop transport; and *Duckbill,* the call sign of a ten-man reconnaissance team.

The initial exchange that I heard was as follows:

KLONDIKE: Duckbill, this is Klondike, over.
DUCKBILL: Go ahead, Klondike.
KLONDIKE: Be advised if we can get one bird in there the ceiling may
   come down again and we will be unable to get the rest of your team

out. Will this be acceptable to you? We'll stay in the area all night if we have to, but they may be left there for a period of time until we can get another straight shot in.

After a short pause, the recon team responded: "This is *Duckbill*. If you could kick some M-60 out the door we could definitely use it, over."

This short sentence told me everything I needed to know about the situation. *Klondike* was trying to execute a night extraction of a reconnaissance team. The team, *Duckbill*, was in contact with the enemy. They were so low on ammunition for their M-60 machine gun that they wanted the gunship to kick some ammunition boxes out the door. They were in danger of being overrun. All ten Marines could be killed in a matter of minutes.

Klondike responded: "I'll give it a try, if you can use the M-60 ammo. . . . We're about out of it now but . . . I'll tell you what . . . I think we can use it better than you can right now. . . . If worse comes to worst, we'll go back and get some more and bring it out for you."

The recon team responded with a terse "Roger," and the extraction helicopters maneuvered to get in position to bring out the team. The pilot in the gunship, *Klondike*, was orchestrating the whole operation. I could visualize the scene.

The recon team was using a strobe light cupped around a cap to provide a directional beam of light that would guide in the extraction helicopters. *Klondike* would lead the way in with the two extract choppers following behind. The message exchange continued.

KLONDIKE: Okay, fine. I'm heading straight in toward the strobe light . . . now on heading of about 180 from my present location. Okay, let me have hot guns, please. You got the strobe light, *Switch*?

SWITCH: Yeah.

KLONDIKE: Okay, I'll get my door gunners to shoot.

DUCKBILL: Guide on the strobe light, *Switch*. We got you coming in.

The extraction helicopter made two unsuccessful attempts to land on the hillside where the recon team was located. But it was dark, visibility was limited by the fog, and the helicopters were taking ground fire from the attacking enemy.

Klondike continued to coordinate the confusing situation and to provide encouragement: "Okay, fine, *Switch*. Third time's a charm if you want to try it."

The extraction chopper agreed to try it once again, and *Klondike* continued his narration.

KLONDIKE: I'm going to be holding a tight orbit. What I want to do this time is let you go in first and have your door gunners fire forward and down on the way in. My ammo's getting pretty low. I'd like to put a couple rounds of 2.75 [rockets] in ahead of you . . . from behind you. . . . Don't worry, I'll miss. . . . But I think that might be a little more impressive to those gents that are shooting at us.

It was now clear to me that all the helicopters were taking fire from the ground and that *Klondike* had kept his lights on so that everyone could see where he was located. But this made him a sitting duck and a clear target.

In spite of the fact that *Klondike* was taking fire and running low on ammo and fuel, he continued his relaxed and encouraging tone: "Okay, have you got a base of fire down there, *Duckbill*? I know *Switch* would appreciate it."

I was sure that the extraction helicopters would indeed appreciate suppressive fire from the recon team. I had been in a number of dangerous situations with people who were cool under fire, but *Klondike*'s calming presence was exceptional. He could have been on a golf course on Nantucket instead of a mountainside in Vietnam. Whoever *Klondike* was, he was orchestrating this dangerous and complex operation without the slightest bit of frustration or anxiety.

Once more, *Klondike* attempted to get the extraction helicopters into the recon team's landing zone.

KLONDIKE: All right, I'm going to lead you in this time. I'll have my door gunners shoot for a while. I'll bank off to the left. As I bank off, I'll give you the word and then you can use your door gunners to fire forward. I'll come around behind you for one rocket in. I'm on my way in right now. Do you have me?

Switch replied, "Affirmative," and the *Klondike* pilot continued to orchestrate the operation, directing the extraction helicopter to the strobe light. Things appeared to be going well, and *Klondike* kept up his encouragement saying, "You're looking good, you're looking good."

I then heard sounds of shouting and yelling from the recon team. I didn't know what had happened, but I knew it wasn't good. Their next transmission told the story: "*Switch*, this is *Duckbill*. *Switch* just shot right into our position."

The door gunner from the extraction chopper had accidentally fired right into the position of the recon team. Everyone wanted to know what happened, and the transmissions continued:

KLONDIKE: *Duckbill*, this is *Klondike*. Can you still talk to me?
DUCKBILL: That's affirmative, I can still talk.
KLONDIKE: Okay, how are you making out down there?
DUCKBILL: We have one man wounded from that last pass. Other than that . . . Correction . . . Two people hit.

It is impossible to exaggerate the level of tension, anger, and frustration that surrounded the mission. The extraction helicopters were taking fire and had trouble finding the recon team. The recon team was about to be overrun. The door gunner from one of the helicopters had just wounded two Marines. It was clear that this mission could end in complete disaster.

The next transmission from the recon team was terse: "*Klondike*, inform *Switch* that the strobe light is friendly, over!"

The *Klondike* pilot knew that something had to be done to straighten out this mess. Once again, he transmitted a matter-of-fact, calm message: "*Duckbill*, I'd like a little discussion on what happened that time please. . . . So we can try to remedy it this time in."

I had seen a lot of things in Vietnam, but this was one of the most unusual. It was a difficult mission to begin with, and everything had gone wrong. The recon team was taking enemy and friendly fire, and not a single member of the team had been extracted. Fuel was getting low, and some support aircraft were leaving the scene with a *bingo fuel state*—the minimum amount needed to return safely to base. Still, the pilot coordinating the mission stayed calm, simply asking for a *little discussion* about what happened *so we can try to remedy* the problem.

The faces of the Marines in my bunker were grim as we listened to the back-and-forth transmissions among *Klondike*, *Switch*, and *Duckbill*. Was it possible that after all this they could simply have a conversation about what had gone wrong, then develop a solution while continuing to engage in a firefight?

They developed a new plan. The door gunners on the extraction chopper would not fire on the way in, and the recon team would pop a parachute flare just before the *Switch* chopper touched down.

KLONDIKE: *Switch*, I've got you in sight. I'm on my way in. I'll have my door gunners shooting a bit on the way in and I'll put two rockets in ahead of you.

KLONDIKE: Okay, let's have your flare now. Flare now, *Duckbill.*

DUCKBILL: Be advised we don't have any more flares. We popped them in that last pass, over.

The *Klondike* pilot wasn't fazed by this latest problem. He contacted *Bushrose,* a C-130 flare ship that was circling overhead, and continued the mission.

KLONDIKE: *Switch*, I'm going to put one rocket in behind you. That's going to be me making noise back here. I have you in sight. No sweat. Go straight ahead now. Straight ahead. Okay, *Bushrose* your flares are good. Don't let them die out this time, though.

BUSHROSE: We won't.

KLONDIKE: Okay, straight on up, *Switch.* You're looking real good. Don't be afraid to wave it off if you get in trouble. We're right on top of you. Okay, *Duckbill*, let's have some fire out of the zone. Good, good, good. Okay, you're looking real fine, *Switch.*

DUCKBILL: Forward and to your left, *Switch.*

KLONDIKE: Left, left, left.

DUCKBILL: Little bit more, a little bit more. Put her down.

KLONDIKE: Looking real good. This is *Klondike.* How are you making out? You're shooting right underneath me now. Give me a call prior to you coming out. Call coming out, please.

SWITCH: Do we have everyone?

KLONDIKE: This is *Klondike.* You're going to have to decide that. Take a count. Still taking fire out here. And we're still taking fire.

About twenty minutes later, the final transmissions of the operation were sent.

KLONDIKE: *Bushrose,* much thanks for the flares and the lights down here. They were a big help finding holes in the clouds. We're all through. We got everybody out and thanks much for your work.

BUSHROSE: Okay, good job. You did a real fine job. Looked good from up here.

KLONDIKE: Okay, fine. We'll see you later.[5]

With that, the mission was over. Though two men had been wounded, all ten Marines in the recon patrol had been flown to safety. What could have been a tragedy ended as a successful extract.

When I got back to the States, I played the tape for a colorful Marine pilot named *Crash Kimo* who had gotten his nickname after being shot down five times. His ability to survive, combined with his never-give-up attitude, had made him something of a legend. Even after his helicopter had run out of rockets, *Crash* was known for continuing the fight by sticking his .45 pistol out of the cockpit.

As soon as *Crash* heard the tape, he knew exactly who it was. "That's John Arick, no question about it," he said. I eventually found John, who had retired from the Marine Corps as a Brigadier General. For his actions that night, he had received a gold star—in lieu of a third *Distinguished Flying Cross*—for his "superior aeronautical skill, fearless determination, and steadfast dedication to duty under extremely adverse conditions."

I spoke with John at his home in Texas, and he was as unassuming in that conversation as he had been in Vietnam. But I've never forgotten what happened that night, and how it's possible to learn—even under the most adverse circumstances. All it takes is a simple statement: *I'd like a little discussion about what happened that time, please—so we can try to remedy it this time in.*

Navigation Points

1. Does your team discuss things that go wrong as well as things that go right?
2. Do all team members feel free to speak up about problems without fear of reprisal? Do they feel free to comment on decisions and actions of the team leader?
3. Does the team extract learnings from mistakes and use them to prevent future errors?

4. Are people encouraged to come up with new ideas and new ways of thinking? Are they rewarded for innovation?
5. Does the team have a continuous learning process that enables them to have *a little discussion* about things that are going wrong—while the team is in the heat of the battle?

35

Calculated Risk

Strategy #5
Be willing to sail into the storm.

Danger lurks everywhere. At least that's a common perception, according to a *Wall Street Journal* article that describes how a fixation on risk—fed by labs, law, and media—haunts the United States, a comparatively very safe society.[1] But it's impossible to read the newspaper or listen to a news broadcast without sensing danger.

The threats are described in vivid detail. One headline, for example, reads "Furniture Tip-over Kills Two-Year-Old."[2] The article goes on to describe how a young child was crushed by a dresser when it fell over and punctured his heart. He had been trying to reach a drink when the accident happened. Each year about a dozen children die and almost 15,000 are treated for injuries caused by tipping furniture and televisions. (The problem can be prevented with a tip restraint that can be purchased at a hardware store.)

For those who don't have small children, there are other things to worry about. A *New York Times* article about a bizarre and tragic elevator accident got my attention. An executive at one of Manhattan's most prominent advertising firms stepped into an elevator. It suddenly lurched up with its doors still open, killing the trapped executive.

The article mentioned that there were about 60,000 elevators in New York City and fifty-three elevator accidents. The piece went on to say that only three of the accidents were fatal.

The article was on my mind as I stepped into an elevator in New York City during a client visit. The office building was modern, and the elevators were well maintained. At least I assumed they were well maintained. But the phrase *three of them were fatal* kept running through my mind. Somewhere between the first and thirty-eighth floor, the elevator abruptly stopped, bounced for about a minute, then hung motionless.

Everyone in the elevator looked around and laughed nervously. As I stood there surveying the situation, I remained calm and made some humorous comment. But I was relieved when the doors finally opened. Some people got out, deciding to take another elevator. Others opted to continue their upward journey on the elevator that had just stopped. I was in the first group, figuring that there was no downside to avoiding an elevator that had just engaged in questionable behavior.

I knew that the elevators in this building were newer than the creaky ones that had killed the advertising executive. But those older elevators had passed safety inspections, and there were no violations relating to the tragic accident. How did it happen? And what about the other two fatalities? Were they in more modern elevators, like the one that had just stopped unexpectedly with me in it?

I've had a fair amount of exposure to risk and danger. I have survived automatic weapons, snipers, recoilless rifles, IEDs, a lightning strike, leopard seals in Antarctica, sharks, barracuda, poisonous cone shells, and the Sydney to Hobart Race. But when I read a *Time* magazine article that says, "It would be a lot easier to enjoy your life if there weren't so many things trying to kill you every day,"[3] I nod my head. There's a lot of scary stuff out there.

The reality is that life is filled with threats of various kinds. There are serious, life-threatening risks. And there are hazards that may not be life-threatening but are still significant: running out of money, having a password hacked, or having your reputation damaged. As long as people are alive and engaged in deliberate goal-directed efforts—such as running a business or a race—there will be danger. The challenge is to understand what to worry about, how to mitigate risk, and which risks are worth taking.

Tactics for *Teamwork at The Edge*

Know what you are getting yourself into

There were six fatalities in the 1998 Sydney to Hobart Race, bringing the total number of people who died in the history of the race to eight. The Hobart is one of the most challenging ocean races in the world—the Mount Everest of sailing. It is a tough, brutal event. But thousands of sailors have raced for over half a century, and the overwhelming majority have made it safely to Hobart.

On Mount Everest itself, more than 200 people have died since the first recorded fatalities in 1922. In 1996—the most deadly year, chronicled by Jon Krakauer's *Into Thin Air*—nineteen people died. For every successful summit attempt, about four people die, and the odds of not coming back alive are about 1 in 20.[4]

Each sport has some inherent risk, but some are more dangerous than others. There are also differences in the potential consequences when things go wrong, and choices to be made about safety precautions. If you're going to do the Sydney to Hobart Race, do you wear a life jacket? Do you tether yourself to the boat? And if you're climbing Everest, will you do it with or without supplemental oxygen? These are all choices that change the odds.

The financial meltdown that began in 2008 is a prime illustration of the risks associated with different businesses. The inherent dangers encountered by teams dealing with the subprime mortgage market were significantly greater than for the traditional real estate mortgage industry. And teams aggressively trading credit-default swap positions were doing more than climbing Everest without oxygen. They were the wing-suit flyers of the financial world—soaring past cliffs in Batman suits. Wing-suit flying may provide an adrenaline rush, but it is one of the most dangerous of extreme sports.

Beyond legal prohibitions, there are no rules governing what people are allowed to do in the world of business and in the world of some sports. But it is important to understand what you're getting yourself into and to decide what measures—if any—you will take to mitigate the inherent risks.

Be realistic about the capabilities of your team

Each boat caught in the '98 Sydney to Hobart storm had a choice to make. Some, like *Sayonara* and the other maxis, were fast enough to make it across the Bass Strait before the worst of the storm. They still hit big waves, and some people were injured. But because of their speed, the danger of sailing to Hobart was diminished—the option of turning back was much less attractive.

Other boats, like John Walker's *Impeccable,* were behind the *AFR Midnight Rambler* and closer to the Australian mainland. The crew of *Impeccable* had no appetite for continuing into the Bass Strait, and all agreed that the right choice was to turn around and sail for safety. Their decision was relatively straightforward.

The real problem arose for boats of moderate speed like *Sword of Orion, AFR Midnight Rambler, Midnight Special,* and *VC Offshore Stand Aside.* These boats had a tough decision to make, and the choice wasn't easy.

There were a number of factors that gave the Ramblers a wide range of real options. They had trained hard and, though the boat was new to them, the crew had worked together for years. The team was cohesive.

They had prepared thoroughly for all conditions, including the most difficult task of sailing at night. They had a superb helmsman, Ed Psaltis, and others who could also steer and give him some relief. Finally, they had a rugged boat that could take punishment, and they had tested the limits of the boat in their lightning-fast sail down the coast.

On the other side of the balance sheet, they had an injured crewman, Chris Rockell. But Chris appeared to be stabilized, and in order to get him medical help they needed to keep *AFR Midnight Rambler* afloat. That meant that the decision that was best for the Ramblers who weren't injured was also the best decision for Chris. Whatever their choice, it needed to be made with safety for all in mind.

Each crew had a different profile of capabilities and choices. The wording of this strategy is deliberate: *Be willing to sail into the storm.* Not every boat should sail into every storm. But boats that have the capability to deal with big waves should be willing to sail into the storm when the time is right.

To borrow a term from statistics, the Ramblers had more *degrees of freedom* than boats that were less well prepared, where the team was less cohesive, or where the boat itself was not as capable. Teams need to fully understand their true capabilities—both strengths and limitations—to be able to make the right decision when they are caught in a storm.

Test your limits before the storm hits

The Ramblers knew what they, as a team, were capable of. They had sailed together for years, and they were fully prepared for the race. But they needed to know how their new boat would perform as well.

The Ramblers deliberately pushed their limits well before the storm hit. As they were smoking down the coast of Australia on the first day, it was knife-edge sailing. They could have played it safe and slowed down with a smaller sail. Instead, they pushed hard until the *Rambler* broached as it was knocked over by the powerful wind.

They broached twice, and each time the team recovered seamlessly. They were traveling at high speeds, over 20 knots, but the sea was relatively flat. So their sail down the coast acted as a safe testing ground. And because they had taken relatively small risks early on, they knew what their boat could do and were prepared when the worst of the storm came.

Many organizations are surprisingly unwilling to undertake even small risks that might take on the appearance of failure. I once worked with a company that manufactured jet engines for military and commercial aircraft. As part of the testing process, engineers were expected to put the engines through a "stall test." Although this was a normal part of the testing process, as strange as it may seem, one engineer could not bring himself to actually watch the engine stall. It felt like a failure.

Teams need to test themselves incrementally in controlled conditions—the metaphorical equivalent of flat water or a laboratory. Only by taking small risks will teams be able to assess their ability to take on big ones—and to sail into the storm when they need to.

Be aware of what's happening around you

Situational awareness is a term originally used by the military as a way of understanding the critical success factors involved in air combat.[5] In a dogfight, pilots need to be aware of everything around them. They need to understand where enemy planes are located and anticipate what their next moves will be. They also need to be aware of everything that's happening inside the cockpit—for example, monitoring instruments that measure altitude and airspeed and listening to message traffic from ground stations and other aircraft.

The use of the term *situational awareness* has since been expanded to encompass not only military applications but other complex tasks. In health care, for example, *situational awareness* can improve patient safety and emergency management.

Situational awareness is more than simply gathering information. It involves collecting just the right amount of information (avoiding data overload), analyzing data to understand its implications, and then acting on the analysis.[6]

At first glance, *situational awareness* appears to be exactly the opposite of the *tunnel vision* required to focus on a winning scenario. Probing deeper, however, the tactics are complementary and can work together.

A team needs to take everything that's happening in the environment into account before committing to a course of action. But the team needs to demonstrate *situational awareness* even after a choice is made. *Tunnel vision* is useful, but everything related to the success of the mission needs to be brought into the tunnel. Distracting thoughts, or information not directly connected to the goal, should be left out of the tunnel.

The Ramblers demonstrated extremely high *situational awareness.* They were acutely conscious of everything that was happening around them, including the height and direction of the waves, the velocity of the wind, and the plight of other boats. They watched boats that had turned around and were surfing out of control, with the waves coming from behind. They gathered whatever information they could from radio transmissions, and they used whatever navigational instruments were working to guide their decisions.

When the Ramblers decided to sail into the storm, they were completely focused on the goal of sailing through the Bass Strait. They applied *tunnel vision,* but they continued to demonstrate *situational awareness* in spite of fatigue, physical discomfort, and fear.

When faced with adversity, individuals need to identify, process, and comprehend everything related to the team mission. They need to be aware of everything associated with their individual roles and also with the needs of other team members. Developing and maintaining a high level of *situational awareness* is a critical requirement for team success at *The Edge.*

Separate psychological risk from statistical risk

In recounting the story of the *Midnight Rambler* to one team, I described the Ramblers' decision to sail into the storm as taking "a big risk." One thoughtful person asked why I had characterized this decision as a big risk. The greater risk, he observed, would have been in turning around and running for safety.

In the case of the Ramblers, his observation was absolutely correct. When everything was taken into account, the safest course was, in fact, to sail into the storm. But for most people in a 35-foot boat facing waves twice that size and hurricane force winds, sailing hundreds of miles into a storm would have felt like an enormous risk.

The Ramblers were able to weigh the odds and—in spite of the perceived danger—choose the option with the lowest risk. The issue is that there can be a tremendous difference between the *psychological risk*—what feels like the greatest threat—and the *statistical risk* based on a rational calculation of probabilities.

After the terrorist attacks of 9/11, there was a significant increase in the number of fatal car crashes when compared with the previous year. It seems clear, and completely understandable, why more people would take to the highway because of their fear of terrorists. Air passenger miles fell, and vehicle miles rose.

A plausible explanation for this change in behavior is that people were responding to *dread risks*: low-probability but high-consequence events.[7] Though it's hard to know the precise impact of this response to *dread risk,* estimates are that hundreds of people died on the highway because of their fear of another terrorist attack. This *dread factor* creates anxiety. And the more anxious we get, the less likely we are to correctly assess the odds.

Although a great deal has been done to manage risk, whether sailing or investing, we are still influenced by emotions that are instinctive and automatic. We fear catastrophic, low-probability events. Unfamiliar threats scare us more than familiar ones. And we feel good when we have the illusion of control, even if our decision leads to a more dangerous path.

In his best-selling book *Blink: The Power of Thinking without Thinking*, Malcolm Gladwell explores the topic of rapid cognition, arguing that decisions made very quickly can be every bit as good as decisions made cautiously and deliberately. He also explores moments when our initial instincts can go wrong and suggests that these errors arise when our feelings of intuition are thwarted.

Our internal computers, Gladwell argues, can become distracted or disabled. But this happens for very specific reasons that can be identified and understood. He believes that snap judgments and first impressions can be educated and controlled.[8]

Others are less convinced that rapid cognition can be improved and cultivated. Nobel Laureate Daniel Kahneman, for example, argues that intuitive solutions fail when we're faced with difficult problems. He explores the distinction between fast and slow thinking, calling them *System 1* and *System 2*—or, perhaps, *Blinking* and *Thinking*.[9]

System 1 is automatic and generates ideas and feelings quickly. *System 2* undertakes the difficult tasks of comparing, choosing, and reasoning. In Kahneman's framework, *System 1* is the "secret author" of many choices and judgments. It's more influential than we realize.

We rely on *System 1* for most of our decisions and impressions, and it generally works. But *System 1* also gives us a lot of incorrect information and causes us to make mistakes. It doesn't always have the right answer, but it's always quick to respond—and it's never at a loss for words.

Kahneman is much less confident than Gladwell about the potential to eliminate the biases and errors inherent in *System 1* ideas. He argues that intuitive thinking will always be prone to overconfidence, but he does believe it's possible to recognize situations in which errors are likely. When we enter these cognitive minefields, we can slow down and ask for reinforcement from *System 2*—the voice of reason.

When teams are faced with decisions at *The Edge,* there is no need to choose between *System 1*, Blinking, and *System 2*, Thinking. Our intuitive *System 1* will always be shouting out ideas and recommendations. It is harder to engage in the more difficult task of activating *System 2*—especially when we are faced with the stress of major decisions with potentially dire consequences.

In *Surviving and Thriving in Uncertainty: Creating the Risk Intelligent Enterprise*, Frederick Funston and Stephen Wagner explore the concept of *risk intelligence*.[10] And they provide a blueprint for moving beyond conventional risk management by creating a *Risk Intelligent Enterprise.* They argue persuasively that a risk intelligent organization will thrive and make better decisions under conditions of uncertainty and turbulence.

What's true for a larger enterprise is also true for a smaller team dealing with decision making under adversity. What teams can do better than individuals is counteract the tendency to react to the emotions of the moment and make hasty, bad decisions. Every member of the team will *Blink* and generate ideas. But together, the team can collectively weigh the options and *Think,* drawing on the power of *team risk intelligence.*

Get everyone on board and commit fully to your decision

The process of decision making doesn't have to be protracted. In the case of the *AFR Midnight Rambler* sailors, their decision had to be made quickly—though it wasn't an easy decision to make. Ed Psaltis was concerned about Chris' injury, and he was worried about endangering the crew.

Recalling the moment of decision, Chris Rockell remembers that:

> We didn't have time for a sit around, show of hands team meeting or that kind of thing. But Ed did go around the crew over a relatively short time and say, "Look, what do you think? What should we do? Should we go back to Eden, or should we carry on?"[11]

By the time the final decision was made, the rationale for sailing into the storm was clear. Arthur Psaltis recalls that the choice "was rationally discussed and there was clear logic in the thought process. That logic was articulated to each member of the crew. There was a buy-in, because it made sense and it was explained."

The decision of the Ramblers was reminiscent of the process used by Shackleton and the *Endurance* Expedition. When the crew was stranded on Elephant Island, Shackleton realized that their only hope was for a small party to take the one seaworthy boat and sail 800 nautical miles so that they all might be rescued. The alternative was for everyone in the crew to remain on the island and slowly starve to death. But this choice would mean splitting the expedition and leaving a large group of "castaways" behind.

By the time Shackleton and five others sailed for rescue, the options had been so thoroughly discussed that the choice was clear to everyone.

There was complete consensus about a decision that involved risk for both those who would leave and those who would stay behind.

The crew of the *Endurance* had more than a week to contemplate their options and make a decision. The crew of *AFR Midnight Rambler* had only a matter of hours. But in both cases, each member of the team was fully aligned behind the decision, committed fully to making their choice successful.

Sail 60 degrees when the waves get high

Sail 60 degrees was the phrase that Ed Psaltis kept repeating when steering through the huge waves in the Bass Strait. Ed would direct the boat 60 degrees relative to the oncoming waves. Sailing zero degrees would be heading directly into the waves, and sailing 90 degrees would mean having the side of the boat parallel to the oncoming waves.

The danger of sailing directly into the waves is that the boat could be pitchpoled, and thrown backward—catapulted end over end into the trough of the wave. The danger of sailing 90 degrees—or *beam-on*—was that the boat could be easily rolled 360 degrees. This had happened to the Ramblers before, and Ed was intent on avoiding another catastrophic roll.

When I apply this *60 degree* metaphor to teams, I think about tasks that are so daunting that they need to be approached indirectly—but with clear forward motion. This might translate into taking on easier parts of the assignment first to gain traction. It also might mean changing timelines so there is less stress on the team.

Sailing a team into a challenging assignment is not exactly like sailing a boat into rogue waves. But I find the concept helpful when thinking about ways to take on the most difficult tasks. Introducing the metaphor of *sailing 60 degrees* in a team discussion can stimulate new ways of thinking about solving tough problems.

Navigation Points

1. Do you understand the inherent challenges and risks of the game you are playing—the business or sport you are competing in?
2. Have you made a realistic assessment of the capabilities of your team? Do you know how individual members will respond to challenge and risk?

3. Do members of your team demonstrate *situational awareness?* Is your team able to track, comprehend, and act on the important events in your internal and external environments?

4. Do you have a systematic process for discussing potentially risky decisions?

5. Is your team able to separate the emotional perception of risk from a rational assessment of danger? Can the team *blink* and *think* at the same time?

6. Is your team aligned and committed to decisions involving risk?

7. Is your team able to take on big challenges in ways that don't *break the boat?* Are you able to *sail 60 degrees* into the really big waves your team will encounter?

36

Stay Connected

Strategy #6
Cut through the noise of the wind and the waves.

I t's hard to imagine a bigger communication challenge than that faced by the Ramblers in hurricane force winds. The noise was horrific. The shriek of the wind, the crash of the waves against the hull, and the screeching static from the radio made verbal exchanges almost impossible.

Storms are not conducive to good communication. Yet the Ramblers found ways to stay connected and cut through the noise. Teams in more traditional settings may not have hurricanes to deal with, but organizational crises create their own forms of noise. These virtual storms can easily garble, mute, and discourage effective communication.

Team members are often geographically scattered, and demands on time and attention become overwhelming, leaving very few opportunities for casual communication. Communication within the team can also be clouded by political concerns and turf battles. In spite of these obstacles, however, teams need to figure out how to stay connected and cut through the noise.

Tactics for *Teamwork at The Edge*

Know your mates and tailor your message

People are increasingly deluged with messages from social media, and a recent study revealed some fascinating patterns. Researchers comparing Twitter and Facebook, for example, have found significant differences between the two message platforms.

On Twitter, the best time to tweet is midafternoon early in the week. One tongue-in-cheek theory is that "people in their Chipotle-induced stupor are more compelled to click on Tweets arriving after lunch."[1] And for businesses that want to drive traffic to their content, it's apparently a waste of time to post messages after 3 p.m. on Friday. On Facebook, however, optimal posting times are slightly different. Traffic spikes a little later than Twitter, and Wednesday at 3 p.m. may be the best time to post on Facebook.

These patterns may change over time, but the research becomes more intriguing when we think of social media as a metaphor. As the researchers point out, "It's easy to see that, just like your neighborhood restaurants, each social network has its own culture and behavior patterns. By understanding the simple characteristics of each social network you can publish your content at exactly the right time to reach the maximum number of people."[2]

Few of us rely on social media to communicate with members of our immediate team, but the central point remains. We are most likely to get our point across and cut through the noise by tailoring our messages to the audience. And it's worth taking the time to understand what works for individuals and for the team as a whole.

While there will be some individual differences, one thing is frequently overlooked: the positive impact of personalizing communication. In the increasingly sterile world of e-mail, blog posts, and Twitter—or the equivalent in your organization—messages seem to blend together. In-boxes fill up with requests, demands, and complaints—or needless CCs and REPLY ALLs. Over time, it all becomes a blur.

In spite of this information blizzard, changes in a few phrases or a sentence can dramatically alter the impact of an e-mail. The same core message, written in slightly different ways, can produce widely differing reactions. *We know what we intend to say, and we think we are saying what we mean.* But the message actually received can be quite different than the message we intended to send. Much can be lost in translation—sometimes with unintended negative consequences.

For important written messages, I ask one or two colleagues to take a look at what I've done and give me their impressions. In one difficult situation, for example, changing "I know you were upset" to "My sense is that you were upset" made a big difference. It softened the message, and it turned out that I hadn't read the situation properly. I overstated what I thought I knew, and the original wording would have been presumptuous.

For busy people who are stressed, this extra effort may seem excessive. But tailoring the message and adding an element of warmth contributes to a feeling of mateship. The messages of one colleague—who somehow manages to reply to my e-mails within ten minutes—almost always leave me with a smile.

He is a very senior executive in a large global organization, yet he finds a way to respond in a personal way. The topic of our discussion may be serious, but a simple "Cya soon" concludes on a warm note. However challenging the situation, I always look forward to seeing him soon.

Although the workplace is moving inexorably toward virtual communication, the most personal way of connecting continues to involve direct contact. I am always struck by the contrast between a face-to-face meeting and an e-mail or phone conversation—especially when there are conflicts or when tough messages need to be delivered.

In those difficult situations, it is fast and convenient to text or leave a voice mail. If meeting in person is out of the question, other video-conferencing options—such as Skype or FaceTime—can be used. But there is no substitute for looking a team member in the eye and speaking authentically. These direct conversations may be difficult to arrange and harder to manage. But when tensions are high, the most direct path to resolution almost always involves face-to-face communication.

Warn people below deck about big waves

People above deck in a storm are exposed to the elements—but they know what's going on, and they can see what's coming. People below have a different set of challenges. As Chris Rockell noted:

> Being below in the storm was both a bit of a blessing and a curse. You're certainly warmer than the people up top. But you can't see

what's coming. The only way you have any idea about what's ahead is when the guys up top are warning the helmsman that a big wave is on its way. I could hear those cries as well. And it gave me a signal that it was time to hold on and make sure I didn't fall off the bunk.[3]

As Chris described the experience of being trapped below deck, I couldn't help but think of the parallels I have seen in organizational settings. There are team members in a position to know what's coming—the good and the bad. They are the first to get notice about impending changes and problematic issues. And they may or may not remember what it's like for team members who are metaphorically down below.

With the noise of the storm, the Ramblers had to yell, "Big Wave!" And they also banged on the side of the cabin to alert the crew down below to brace for the next onslaught. That unmistakable warning made all the difference. It kept the crew connected and helped ensure that their teammates had enough time to brace and hang on.

Warning others about big waves is important for team members in any organization. And those on deck who have greater visibility need to constantly be aware of their mates down below.

Reach out to those at the helm

Although people on deck had the advantage of seeing the big waves that were coming, they didn't have the full picture. People below had other sources of information—information that was vitally important to the people on deck steering the boat.

Michael Bencsik recalls:

The information that people had below deck was quite critical—particularly when we found out through the radio about the things that were happening around us. People below needed to relay what they knew to the people who were on deck so they understood the weather conditions ahead of us, and what was happening with other boats like the *Sword of Orion*. Even if the news wasn't positive, at least the people on deck had the full picture.[4]

So the Ramblers down below had important information that those on deck needed to do their jobs. And, just as people on deck needed to bang on the cabin to warn about big waves, people below had to take the initiative as well. They passed along essential news about the weather, the fate of other boats, and other information that only they could hear.

In some cases, the metaphor of crew above and below deck corresponds to levels of organizational hierarchy. People in less visible positions may be reluctant to intrude on those above. But every member of the team sees a part of the picture. It is the responsibility of each team member to take the initiative and to stay connected with their mates in other parts of the boat.

When the situation calls for it, break protocol

The Sydney to Hobart Race has well-established procedures for scheduled check-ins—or *skeds,* as they are called. Each boat is authorized to report only its latitude and longitude, and transmissions are broadcast in alphabetical order. This information gives the coordinating vessel information about the safety and location of each racer, but other data that might give anyone a competitive edge is off limits.

During the 1998 storm, Rob Kothe—the owner of *Sword of Orion*—realized that the conditions he was encountering were extraordinary. At the 2 p.m. sked on the second day of the race, Kothe took the unusual step of requesting permission to report on the weather. And Lew Carter, who was coordinating the skeds from the radio relay vessel, authorized the departure from protocol saying, "*Sword of Orion,* I would appreciate that for ourselves and all the fleet."

Kothe then broadcast his alarming message: *Sword of Orion* was experiencing wind gusts of 78 knots. This warning helped alert other boats to the severity of the situation. And it framed Carter's message to the rest of the fleet, as he requested "that all skippers, before proceeding into the Bass Strait . . . give utmost consideration to what you're doing and talk with members of the crew."

For the benefit of others, Rob Kothe decided to break protocol and cut through the noise of the storm. But he was not the only skipper who made that choice. Earlier that day, *Doctel Rager* reported severe weather ahead with gusts over 70 knots. And shortly after that, three other boats—*Secret Men's Business, Wild One,* and *She's Apples II*—also broadcast warnings.

There are times when normal communications procedures and channels are simply insufficient to ensure that important messages get through. If the information is important and the noise of the storm is high, team members need to do things differently—think creatively, even break protocol so that others are alerted to critical information.

Navigation Points

1. Have you taken the time to think about the most effective way to reach individual members of your team? Have you considered their preferred communication styles and patterns?
2. How effective are your communication methods for the full team? Are messages sent in ways that keep people connected and encourage collaboration?
3. Does your team draw on a combination of techniques to ensure clear communication?
4. Are face-to-face meetings and conversations used to deal with important topics or emotional situations?
5. Do people on deck—in positions with greater visibility—reach out to warn those below about oncoming problems and issues?
6. Do people below deck take the initiative to communicate with people topside?
7. Are team members willing to break protocol, or devise creative or unusual methods, to ensure that their messages get through?

37

Step into the Breach

Strategy #7
Find ways to share the helm.

Steering a boat through a furious storm is exhausting work. The concentration and stamina required to maneuver through howling winds, towering waves, and drenching downpours takes an immense physical and mental toll.

Steering a team through other kinds of adversity—economic setbacks or tight deadlines, for example—can be just as strenuous and emotionally draining. Without some kind of support or relief, the burden can be too heavy for one person to carry. Rather than rely on one person's heroic efforts, teams at *The Edge* need to draw on each other's strengths. They need to share the load.

Sharing the load involves two different but related concepts. The phrase *stepping into the breach* is perhaps best known because of Shakespeare's play *Henry V*. With England at war with France, King Henry encourages his countrymen to step "unto the breach" by attacking a gap in the walls of a fortified French city. In combat, stepping into the breach can mean plugging an opening in a defensive perimeter. When applied to business teams, stepping into the breach means finding a gap in the performance of the team, then taking the initiative to fill it.

Team members on a sailboat can *share the helm* by taking turns steering the boat. In other teams, individuals can figuratively share the helm by providing direction or helping in other ways. This *distributed leadership* can be extremely effective, taking the burden off the formal leader and spreading the load.

Tactics for *Teamwork at The Edge*

Scan for gaps in team performance and fill the holes

After his "hard or squishy" self-examination, Chris and the other Ramblers were satisfied that the injury wasn't life-threatening. But Chris was prohibited from climbing back on deck and standing his watch—so there was a key role that needed to be filled.

Gordon Livingstone stayed on the rail without complaint, filling in for his injured teammate. Ed Psaltis describes the scene:

> When Chris was injured, Gordon was sitting up on the side of the boat. I was so busy doing my steering that I wasn't even aware of him. Gordo sat there on the rail for hours without complaint. Even one hour in those conditions was tough physically, but he never complained.[1]

Why did Gordo do it? Because he was part of the team, and he was determined to stay there until someone told him to move. There was no "Come on, guys, give me a break." He was simply determined not to budge until someone told him to budge. He was not going to be a weak link.

Gordo finally asked politely, "Hey, Ed, do you reckon I might be able to go down below now?" But when he saw the gap left by Chris' injury, Gordo had been more than willing to pitch in without complaint.

Monitor your own stamina and that of your teammates

Gordon had filled the void created by Chris' injury, but there was another gap that needed to be plugged: a system for managing the crew under the extraordinary conditions. Ed was completely focused on getting over the mountainous waves, and no one was thinking about crew management. When Arthur realized what had happened to Gordo, he thought:

> We've got to get a grip because we can't go on like this. Ed had been sailing far too many hours, and the thing that struck me the most was that the storm is getting worse, and we're in daytime. What happens when it gets to be nighttime? We're going to need our best sailor, and Ed is our best helmsman in these conditions. We've got to rest him during the daytime, because the last thing we need is to have him fatigued at night.[2]

Arthur realized that the crew was not being managed well and that Gordon had suffered because of it. That insight was the catalyst for creating a new system that would spread the load more evenly. Arthur felt that there were three people capable of steering the boat and three who were capable of wave spotting. Both roles required different skills, but people needed to be rested to do either well.

Arthur took the initiative and spoke with Bob. They discussed a watch system that would give Ed some time to rest. They would also limit others to an hour on deck with two hours down below. With the new system, the Ramblers were able to have a fresh wave spotter and helmsman on deck at all times.

By monitoring each other's limits, the Ramblers saw the gaps and took action to fix the shortfall in crew management. The new system was critically important to their survival. It was a psychological boost to know that their time in the maelstrom was limited to an hour. And the new system meant that they were going to be physically ready for their exhausting jobs and capable of dealing with the storm.

Find out what people can do before the storm hits

Everyone on *AFR Midnight Rambler* had a clear understanding of their teammates' abilities. Many had sailed together for a number of years, and even those relatively new to the boat were intensely scrutinized during the ramp-up to the race. Ed Psaltis was the principal helmsman, but Arthur Psaltis and Bob Thomas had also shown their skill at steering. When the critical point of decision came during the storm, Ed had confidence that others could take the helm and give him some relief.

On boats with crews that have had less time working together, it is still possible to let people try different positions—and to see how well they perform. Some skippers make a point of systematically letting each crew member steer to assess their skill at the helm. With these trial runs in relatively calm conditions, the skipper and crew are able to inventory the full range of their capabilities.

I've sailed on boats where crew members are given a chance to show their stuff, and I've sailed on others where important tasks are limited to a select few—the people who are close to the skipper. Their capabilities, and their limitations, are a known quantity.

The problem with this approach is that newer members of the crew may have talents that are overlooked or unappreciated. In some instances, I've seen team members with limited skills given preference over others who were more talented but untested. The result of this narrow selection process was poor race performance—and frustration on the part of those in the crew whose abilities had been overlooked.

Leaders may feel more comfortable assigning tasks to members of their inner circle. But this insular approach fails to account for the full potential of the team. Under normal conditions, playing favorites will result in subpar team performance. But in crisis conditions, an inability to draw on the full potential of the team can be disastrous.

The implications for *Teamwork at The Edge* are clear. Teams need to provide opportunities for newer or untested members to demonstrate their skills in safe waters. Junior partners, for example, can do presentations, show what they are capable of, and get coaching from more experienced team members. Over time, these opportunities for broader participation encourage initiative, increase motivation, and—ultimately—strengthen the team.

Be willing to let go

In the middle of the storm, Ed Psaltis thought to himself, "I'm at the end of my tether." Yet it never occurred to him to ask for help. He was focused on only one thing:

> I was intent on steering the boat, because this was life and death stuff. If you get this wrong, people are going to die. It wasn't that I didn't care about other things, but I didn't have time to think about them.[3]

Ed wasn't going to tell the crew, even though he knew he couldn't keep going on like this. He felt that there was no one else who could steer the boat.

When Arthur came up to confront his brother, he interrupted Ed's fixation on driving the boat. Arthur's confidence that he and Bob could steer, combined with his insistence that Ed had to get off the helm, was persuasive. Still, in the middle of the storm, Ed needed to take his hand off the tiller and let go.

The process of letting go can be difficult. It can be hard for a team leader to let others step into a leadership role and provide direction. It can be hard for any team member who excels in a particular role to let someone else "give it a go." But to develop the full capability of the team—to bring other resources to bear on a problem—people need to move out of their familiar space. They need to take their hands off the tiller—to let go of something at which they excel. Letting go may not be easy. But for teams that aspire to the highest level of performance, it's a skill that needs to be mastered.

There are many ways to contribute—and small things make a difference

The most visible ways the Ramblers shared the load involved steering and protecting the helmsman as wave spotters. But that was not all they did to contribute to the team, and the less dramatic actions were important, too.

People down below could have retreated to their bunks. But attuned to the needs of those on deck, they got out of their berths and stood by the hatch, passing water up to the crew above. They asked if crew members on deck needed food or something else—anything—to ease the strain. It was comforting for those exposed to the waves to know that their mates down below stood ready to lend a hand.

They were all terrified. At times, their faces were ashen white with fear. They knew they might die. Yet the crew still did everything they could to minimize the suffering of their teammates.

Those who were most seasick were truly at the depths of despair. They felt like they wanted to die, and at the same time they were frozen with fear that they might die. But those who were most sick were comforted by those who were less so. Those who were most able to help gave water to those who were immobilized. And somehow, in spite of the terror, they summoned the energy to provide a few words of encouragement to those who were at their limits.

Everyone made a difference, and everyone contributed. Even with the blur of their fight for survival, people saw the small things. And even small actions reinforced their shared belief that they were in this together. Chris may have been injured, but he shifted his weight and held on to the pipe as ballast. He did everything in his power to help the team.

Some team roles are more visible than others, and some efforts are more dramatic. But the impact of small contributions cannot be overestimated. A word of encouragement can help a teammate regain confidence. And the smallest contribution is symbolically powerful. As Ed put it: "If we had simply been seven individuals, there is no way we could have gotten through the storm. But the teamwork made us so much more powerful. We were more than seven individuals. We were a team."

Navigation Points

1. Do team members look for gaps in team performance? Do they take the initiative to *step into the breach* and fill in for others?
2. Are team members aware of their own stamina—both physical and psychological? Do they keep an eye on how others are holding up?
3. Are people given the opportunity to test their abilities in different roles and positions? Is there a shared understanding of team members' capabilities?
4. Are team members willing to step aside and let others help them out when needed?
5. Do team members encourage and value all contributions, both small and large?

38

Eliminate Friction

Strategy #8
Step up to conflict—and deal with the things that slow you down.

W hen I was in graduate school, a professor related an interesting story about a potential research pitfall. During World War II, as the story goes, the U.S. military wanted to determine the optimal placement of armor on aircraft. Their approach involved studying planes returning from bombing missions over Europe, then recording the location of shrapnel damage and bullet holes. It seemed logical that additional armor should be placed where the damage was the greatest.

A group of operations researchers were called in to confirm the military's findings. After studying the problem, the researchers came to a surprising conclusion: The areas of the bombers that were *not damaged* should have the highest priority for armor.

The researchers realized that the returning bombers represented a biased sample. Aircraft that made it back may have been riddled with bullet holes, but the damage was survivable. The aircraft that really needed help were the ones that didn't make it back. They were the ones that had been hit in the most vital parts of the aircraft—the sections containing the most critical components needed to keep the bombers flying.

If I had focused only on successful ocean racing crews such as *AFR Midnight Rambler,* this same sort of sampling error problem might have led to other mistakes. On the best boats, for example, unresolved conflict and other destructive interpersonal problems were relatively rare. But when the sample included the entire fleet, a different picture emerged.

Accounts of the 1998 race, for example, illustrate what can happen when the crew is not aligned—and when conflicts fester unresolved. I would never presume to make a direct connection between failure to manage conflict and any specific outcome or consequence. There were many forces at play in the storm, and there were cohesive teams that still ran into problems.

But I am confident in this assertion: Boats that consistently win do not have chronic problems with alignment and conflict. They win because they have eliminated anything and everything that slows them down. Whether the drag is created by interpersonal problems or mechanical issues, winning boats find and fix the underlying cause.

Tactics for *Teamwork at The Edge*

Fix the problem, not the blame

I asked *Rosebud's* Malcolm Park if he could think of an example where seamless teamwork had made a difference in a memorable race. Park said that he could think of numerous instances where teamwork *wasn't* visible because it was seamless. From start to finish, decision after decision, and from watch to watch, people worked together so well that teamwork produced results. But nobody thought about teamwork, because it was so smooth that it was virtually invisible.

There was rarely one momentous event where seamless effort resulted in a victory. But there were numerous examples of teamwork falling apart. These were cases where a crew didn't work together smoothly, and the result was a failure in a race. When I probed further and asked Park for an example, he had no trouble coming up with illustrations of things that he had seen go wrong.

The example that Park came up with involved two identical boats battling for position at the finish of the Sydney to Hobart Race. They couldn't sail directly to the finish line, so they needed to zigzag toward the destination. Park saw the action from his hotel room, and, though the boats were some distance away, he was in a perfect spectator's seat:

> I was watching the boats coming across the finish line. And they were jibing [zigzagging with the wind from behind] across from each other. On one jibe, one boat was ahead. The next jibe the other boat was ahead. And from about a mile out I said, "I bet you anything I can guess which boat is going to win."
>
> I saw that one boat was having constant breakdowns in teamwork on every one of their jibes. The crew would make an error, and then compensate with good tactical decisions. But the crew work was falling apart. I could see the guys yelling at each other and arguing with each other, fingers pointing. And sure enough they didn't win. It all fell apart. *But you could see the breakdown from a mile and a half from the finish line.*[1]

I know what it's like to sail on a boat where people are more concerned with fixing blame than fixing problems. Things would go wrong, and the skipper would naturally be frustrated. But because we never took the time to figure out how or why something went wrong, we repeated the same mistake on numerous occasions. Each time, there would be yelling, shouting, and blaming, but the problem remained.

Winning teams direct their energy to dissecting problems and figuring out how to keep them from happening again. Losing and mediocre teams spend time blaming individuals and shouting.

Confront differences in ability

Previous chapters emphasized the importance of selecting people who have the right skills and who are committed to the challenge. Then, when the team is configured, individuals need to be given a chance to demonstrate their capabilities in as many roles as they might reasonably be expected to fill. This systematic process helps to ensure that the team will be composed of motivated people who are fully capable of doing their jobs.

There are times, however, when shortcomings surface later in the game. In spite of everything that has been done to choose the right people and give them a chance to try their skills, people can wind up in the wrong positions. And when that happens, the team suffers.

These situations can be awkward, especially when individuals are oblivious to their limitations. And it can be especially difficult when people have been in their roles for some time, and they feel comfortable and secure. But for a team to reach its potential, fundamental performance problems need to be addressed and resolved.

This is not a question of blaming an individual for a specific mistake or problem. It is a more fundamental question of long-term team effectiveness. And confronting a capability problem does not automatically mean that an individual needs to be removed from the job. It means that performance issues need to be clearly identified and fixed.

The corrective action starts with an honest conversation about performance. The next step can involve training, coaching, or education designed to develop the required skills. Team members who want to perform in a role should be given every opportunity to excel. But people who can't develop the skills to perform need to find another role—or another boat. Teams at *The Edge* rely on everyone's ability to perform at the highest level. Shortfalls need to be confronted and corrected.

Count the bolts and lighten the boat

In preparing for the Sydney to Hobart Race, I accumulated quite a collection of equipment and special-purpose clothing. I left the States for Australia with a large suitcase and a big sea bag, thinking that I would take the sea bag with me when we sailed south to Hobart.

A few days before the start of the race, the skipper, Goldy, gave everyone on the crew a small waterproof bag. He made it quite clear that everything that we would be allowed to take on the boat had to fit into these standard issue bags.

The bags we were authorized to use were about one-tenth the size of the bag I had thought I would be taking. In retrospect, it was pretty funny that I could have ever imagined fifteen people taking full-size sea bags on this race. Even though this was a 60-foot boat, there just wasn't that much space in the cramped quarters below.

There was room for the things needed to sail the boat, and some of the equipment was heavy. I hesitate to guess how much the giant Anaconda sail weighed. But everything aboard the boat was functional, and crew comfort was not a primary concern. On race day, I stood in line with the other sailors to check in both my suitcase and my sea bag. I wasn't sure how they would get to Hobart, but I knew it wouldn't be aboard the boat that I was sailing on.

Having spent time with the crew of *AFR Midnight Rambler,* I should have realized long before that speed was good—and excess weight was bad. According to Bob Thomas:

> We stripped as much weight out of the boat as we could. . . . Weight's crucial, and we count the nuts and bolts. We go through everything in that toolbox. We scour the whole boat, looking everywhere. It's amazing how much weight we can get off the boat each year, even though we've owned it for years.[2]

The fanatical commitment that the Ramblers have to reducing weight holds a lesson for teams. Just as polishing the stove symbolizes the Ramblers' dedication to careful preparation, counting the bolts represents their commitment to removing anything that might slow them down.

The responsibility for eliminating excess weight belongs to every member of the crew. Teams that aspire to the highest levels of performance need to be on the alert for anything that might hold them back. Even one extra bolt can make a difference.

Use humor to defuse tension

Ed Psaltis is the first to admit that he can get overly excited with the pressure of the race—and he becomes frustrated when things aren't happening fast enough. Although this can lead to some shouting, everyone understands what's going on. Ed's passion to win energizes the team, but he gets carried away. Over time, the crew has learned to handle Ed's outbursts in a good-humored way.

Some of Ed's excited expressions have become standing jokes. *Give me 60 feet of rope!* is a particular favorite. As Gordo tells it:

> Ed will occasionally ask for a sail to come down at the speed of light, and he'll scream "Mix, give me 60 feet!" Mix will be doing his best to manage the process. We'll go around the mark and we'll

pack the sail away. Then we'll be sitting up on the rail and Mix or
Arthur or I will imitate Ed's performance from a couple of minutes
ago. It's a good way to settle the crew down, get everyone back on
the same plane, and away we go.[3]

Give me 60 feet of rope eventually became an all-purpose phrase that, in
Ed's vocabulary, translates to *Do it now!*

Though humor can defuse tension under many circumstances, it can
be especially important when the stakes are high. When the Ramblers
were fighting constantly changing winds in the Derwent, the pressure
was exceptionally intense. They were exhausted from battling the waves
and the winds in the Bass Strait, and from incessant sail changes. Pressure
was building and frustration was growing.

They had started the race with four winch handles—an essential piece
of equipment on a sailboat. Mix had dropped three over the side—or, at
least he was alleged to have lost them. So they were left with only one
winch handle for the remaining part of the race.

Mix recalls that at one point:

Gordon, the *court jester,* looked me in the eye said, "Just chuck this
one over the side, will you, Mix?" And it made everyone burst into
laughter because it was the worst thing I could've possibly done. If I
had thrown the last winch handle over the side, we would have had
to grind with our fingers—and that would have been a disaster.[4]

Gordon remembers the incident somewhat differently:

It was a good moment because it really reflected how important
that winch handle was and yet, we were having a little bit of a joke
about it as well. I would state for the record that I don't believe Mix
had tossed any winch handles over the side during that race. They
just fell over by themselves.[5]

Regardless of whose recollection is more accurate, the point remains:
Humor can help alleviate anxiety and mitigate conflict, two strategies
necessary for winning teams. As Arthur observed, "You need people on
a boat who can recognize the seriousness of a situation, but still be lighthearted. It realigns their concentration!"

Navigation Points

1. When something goes wrong, does your team focus on solving the problem or finding someone to blame?
2. Does your team have the right people in the right positions? If there are performance problems, are these issues confronted and addressed?
3. Does everyone on your team look for things that could slow you down or interfere with performance? Do you *count the bolts* and lighten the boat?
4. Is your team able to lighten up and use humor to diffuse tension?

39

Practiced Resilience

Strategy #9
Master the art of rapid recovery.

Psychologists have long been interested in trying to understand why
some people flourish under stress, while others collapse. Those who
thrive under tremendous pressure are described as *resilient,* or high
in *stress hardiness.* They enjoy change and look forward to dealing with
problems. For these resilient people, the tougher life gets, the more they
enjoy it.

Though stress hardiness may have a genetic component, other explanations involve early childhood experiences and family structure. But
whatever individuals bring to the workplace, there is reason to believe
that they can learn to increase their ability to deal with difficult situations.

Just as people vary in their ability to deal with stress, so do teams.
And like individuals, teams can also develop the capacity for rebound-
ing from pressure and setbacks. They can increase their level of *team
resilience.*

By consciously working together, teams can pool their individual resources and strengthen their shared ability to deal with stressful situations. This increase in team resilience will enable them to overcome setbacks. It will enhance their ability to recover rapidly so that they are prepared to deal with the next challenge.

Tactics for *Teamwork at The Edge*

Anticipate problems as normal occurrences

By the time the Ramblers got to the '98 race, they had overcome numerous obstacles as a team. They had capsized, torn sails, and dealt with a host of other problems that accompany ocean racing. Some of the difficulties were totally unexpected, and some occurred because they were pressing the limits. But throughout their history one thing was clear: There would be problems.

Problems will occur even when all of the *Teamwork at The Edge* strategies outlined in this book are put into practice. Teams can be clear about what it means to win; select the most capable, talented members; put the right people in the right roles; prepare meticulously with checklists; encourage each other with a sense of mateship; and take only measured, calculated risks. They can do all of those things—and things will still go wrong.

Teams that win races at *The Edge* know that they will encounter problems with regularity. They anticipate setbacks with the confidence that, when things go wrong, they can deal with any problem that comes their way.

Calmly put the pieces back together

When a boat broaches or is knocked down by a wave, anything can happen. Those on deck need to keep their heads down, because the boom can swing rapidly. Ropes and lines flap everywhere, and the mast is often submerged. The challenge is to get the boat under control and to move quickly back into racing mode.

Some crews accomplish this better than others, and the Ramblers are one of the best. Samantha Byron—a relative newcomer to the *Rambler* team—had the advantage of observing their teamwork with fresh eyes. She was struck by their ability to execute a seamless recovery:

> The first offshore race I did with the Ramblers lit a fire as to why I wanted to join them as a team member. On our way back to Sydney after the Bird Island Race, we were hit by some really bad weather and very high winds. We had the wrong sails up for those conditions and the boat was flattened.
>
> The reaction by Ed and the crew was so fast, and so quick. Equipment had failed, crew members were all over the place, yet we all managed to pick ourselves up. Within minutes everything was back under control. The old sails were down, we had new sails up, and we were off. In no time, we were powering off again to finish the race.[1]

Samantha had sailed on other boats, but she was taken aback by the speed and seamless recovery exhibited by the Ramblers. Teams at *The Edge* need to start recovering while they're still in the water, and then move quickly to finish the race.

Measure success in terms of recovery time

Once problems are accepted as inevitable, it follows that setbacks do not equal failure. To maximize performance, teams need to take risks—and some of those risks may flip the boat.

Because the team's focus should be on its ability to recover from mistakes, the amount of time needed for recovery is a key metric for judging performance. While recovery will never be instantaneous, teams can aspire to spending an ever decreasing amount of time putting the pieces back together.

Don't break the boat

Once the *Midnight Rambler* made it through the storm, the crew started pushing the boat hard again. The winds were still blowing at gale force, and the seas were rough. But after what the Ramblers had been through, Ed thought it was "like a walk in the park." And he was determined to press the limits and make up for lost time.

Bob Thomas went below and charted the position of every boat he could locate. He found that *AFR Midnight Rambler* was winning the race by a very large margin. The news was uplifting, and as Bob recalls:

> I came on deck. We were sailing with a full main. We were a little bit overpowered, and I said to Ed, "We're in a bit of a hammer position here. If we can stay in one piece, we should be able to win this race." Then I said, "I think we could probably use a reef in the main now." I thought if we could keep the boat in one piece, we'd be very difficult to beat.[2]

Ed Psaltis has a slightly different recollection. He knew that they were sailing hard. It was exciting that they were sailing past bigger boats, and they were speeding past boats that were their own size. Ed remembers:

> I was thinking, *keep pushing, pushing, pushing*—push as hard as we could. And Bob came up on deck and said, "Look, don't do this. Don't crack any gears, just maintain. Don't lose it. *Don't break the boat* because we are in such a fantastic position!"[3]

Whether Bob actually said "Don't break the boat," or whether that's what Ed heard, makes little difference. What is important is that Ed took Bob's advice. For the next twelve hours they were still racing hard—but also making sure that they stayed in one piece and finished the race. In spite of his passion to win, Ed understood that it was important to "never lose sight of the ultimate goal." He adds, "I had to avoid getting too excited, pushing too hard, and cracking something!"

As important as it is to seamlessly recover from setbacks and shift back into racing mode, it is equally important to avoid overcorrecting. Recovery needs to be rapid but also measured. Teams at *The Edge* have to be able to put the pieces back together and then calmly push as hard as they can, without breaking the boat.

Navigation Points

1. Does your team accept problems and challenges as part of doing business—something to be anticipated and overcome? Or do they see setbacks as cause for alarm and panic?

2. Can your team assess the situation when things go awry and calmly take corrective action?
3. Does your team track recovery time as a metric for success?
4. If problems occur, does your team respond without overcorrecting when trying to make up for lost time? Can they push hard *without breaking the boat*?

40

Tenacious Creativity

Strategy #10
Never give up—there's always another move.

Teams that succeed in the face of extreme adversity share two complementary characteristics: They persevere in the face of enormous odds, and they devise imaginative solutions to problems. These two elements—determination and creativity under pressure—make a team unstoppable.

All the Ramblers brought their own sense of resolve to the team. For Ed Psaltis, his determination started in sports:

> I played rugby football and was reasonably good. I might not have had as much talent as my other schoolmates, but I had a lot of tenacity. I never gave up. If we lost a game, I came back twice as hard the next time. Tenacity is something I've always had in anything I've done in life—business or sports. I don't give up. I keep at it until I get to the goal.[1]

Individual tenacity was important, but it was the combined effort of the team that enabled them to not only persist but also to innovate in the most stressful and life-threatening situations.

In the '94 Hobart, when *Nuzulu* was rolled and lost its mainsail, things seemed truly hopeless. The Ramblers were disappointed and demoralized. They had come close to drowning, and they had no chance of winning the race. It would have been easy to pull out.

Yet they came together as a team, and they found the determination to persevere. Mix Bencsik created a catalytic moment with his resolute statement: "Don't even think about pulling out of this race. We have gotten this far and we have to finish the race. If we do, we will remember this as one of our proudest moments."

The race became a milestone for the Ramblers—but only because they were able to combine tenacity with creativity. Arthur Psaltis recalls:

> We tried a number of different jury-rigged systems that didn't work. But the solution was staring us in the face: We could create a series of knots that we could put into the mast, and then tie some knots onto the sail. Once we'd done it, it was obvious how it could work. But it took hours of thinking to come up with the solution, and we were going sideways all that time. It looked hopeless, but we really wanted to finish. By constantly thinking about what we needed to do, the solution finally came.[2]

The solution did emerge, but it didn't come from a think tank in Silicon Valley. It came from a group of guys who had just recovered from a capsize. It came from their determination to devise a way to finish a race they knew they couldn't win. And it was one of their proudest moments.

The unyielding tenacity that the Ramblers demonstrated in 1994 stayed with them through other daunting times. It was there in 1998, when they encountered hurricane force winds and walls of water twice the size of their boat. It was there when they needed to devise a crew management system to survive the storm. And it was there near the end of the race, when they lost their navigation instruments and were fighting dying winds in the Derwent River.

The same spark of creativity that had enabled them to devise a makeshift sail on *Nuzulu* helped them on the Derwent. Improvising once again, the Ramblers created a makeshift wind instrument by breaking a cassette and fastening the tape to the mast so they could judge the wind direction. It wasn't elegant—but it worked.

The Ramblers' ability to persevere has been displayed on many occasions, and one of the most memorable examples came in a 2007 race. On a pitch-black night, with a hard southerly wind and big seas, their mainsail burst. They could have turned around—numerous other boats did. But surrender is not a word in the team's vocabulary. The Ramblers sailed on through the night to Flinders Island, turned around, and made it home, completing the "out and back" race that was part of the *Blue Water Point Score* series.

Because conditions were so difficult and so many boats retired, even with their small storm sail the Ramblers still finished in third place. When the season was over, *AFR Midnight Rambler* had won the coveted *Blue Water Point Score* by two points. If they had retired, they wouldn't have won the series.

Tom Barker—another newcomer to the team—shared his observations on the 2007 competition:

> That race was a good metaphor for the crew's approach to racing. Even when conditions are tough and everything is stacked against us, we find an answer to make our way through. Finishing the race was important and it is a testament to the crew. When those other boats turned around and retired and headed home, we were still out there.[3]

This strategy, then, is a state of mind—a set of lenses for viewing the world. It is grounded in the belief that the team will succeed, but it is much more than stubborn persistence. It is based in reality. If a solution isn't working, then it's time to try something else.

The Ramblers—and other teams that succeed at *The Edge*—maintain an unshakable belief that somehow, somewhere, there must be a path that will get them to the finish line. As Ed Psaltis observed, "*When the chips are really down, our mentality is—never give up. There is always another move, and always another option.*"

Navigation Points

1. Does your team persevere in the face of adversity?
2. When faced with setbacks, is your team able to think creatively and develop innovative solutions?
3. Are there "proud moments" in the history of your team—times when the team has come together and exhibited tenacious creativity?
4. Do you draw inspiration from stories of other teams that have worked together to overcome daunting challenges? Does your team share stories as a source of inspiration?

A Note to the Skipper

There are two central themes in this book. The first is the importance of *exceptional teamwork* in overcoming challenges at *The Edge*. The second is the value of *distributed leadership*—a team culture that allows every person to provide direction when he or she has expertise that will help the team succeed.

The story of *AFR Midnight Rambler* exemplifies the power of exceptional teamwork and distributed leadership. But where does this leave a formal team leader—the skipper of a boat, the CEO of a corporation, the commanding officer of a military unit, or the President of the United States, for that matter? Is there a unique role that he or she needs to play?

I believe there are unique responsibilities that come with the territory of being the formal leader. This is not to suggest that the leader needs to be an imposing, charismatic figure. As Rakesh Khurana notes in *Searching for a Corporate Savior*,[1] the irrational quest for charismatic leadership places a premium on fame and personality rather than experience and ability. And he goes on to argue that this misplaced focus can lead to a decline in corporate performance, with long-term consequences.

I agree with the fundamental premise. Charisma and force of personality are hardly the most important characteristics for a skipper in an ocean race—or for the leader of a business team. But personality aside, there are some critical things—some unique responsibilities—that fall to the skipper.

The leader needs to keep the team aligned.

The varied performance of boats in the Sydney to Hobart Race—
particularly in 1998—underscores the importance of having a coherent,
unified team. Some boats, like the *Midnight Rambler,* demonstrated extraordinary cohesiveness even under the most terrifying, life-threatening conditions. At the other end of the alignment continuum, some crews were
fragmented, with key team members at odds with each other—in a leadership vacuum.

Other boats, like *Sayonara,* were somewhere in the middle. Larry Ellison, as the owner, could impose his will on the crew, and everyone acquiesced to his decision. But this is not the same level of alignment that we
saw in the *Rambler.* Resigned acquiescence is not the same as aligned
commitment, and gaining that commitment requires leadership.

Adrienne Cahalan, considered one the world's best navigators, has had
a chance to observe the role of the leader in more than twenty-five years
as a professional competitive sailor. She has been named *Australian Yachtswoman of the Year* twice—and has been nominated four times for *World
Yachtswoman of the Year.*

Adrienne characterized the leader's role:

> Skippers need to keep the team focused and pull everybody
> together. They need to keep an eye out to see if someone is waver-
> ing, or a faction developing. They need to have the skill to man-
> age all the personalities, to bring them together and to get them
> focused on the common goal. Not everybody's perfect, so a good
> leader is able to deal with imperfections. And they need to be able
> to do it all under pressure.[2]

Managing personalities and bringing people together can be challenging in any situation. But the pressure of a race—or, even worse, a
storm—calls for exceptional leadership.

The leader needs to demonstrate passion.

The leader's passion is a magnetic force that pulls other people in. And
Ed Psaltis' passion stands out, especially to relative newcomers to the crew.

Describing the impact of Ed's will to win, Samantha Byron said:

No boat had ever won both the *Blue Water Point Score* and the *Short Ocean Point Score* in the same year. It was a bold goal that had never been achieved before. But it was Ed's vision, and it became the team vision, and then it became my vision.

I think what makes Ed an exceptional leader is his complete drive to win. He is committed to driving the boat as fast as it can go. And he can take risks because of his comfort and trust in the team.[3]

No one who has ever sailed with Ed Psaltis has any doubt about his absolute, total commitment to winning. He is so passionate that his excitement sometimes needs to be offset—by humor, or by the composure of others. But there is no mistaking the electric spark that comes from a leader who is excited to win. That enthusiasm is contagious, and it is a contagion that leads to victory.

The leader needs to instill optimism and confidence that the team will succeed.

Ed Psaltis and Bob Thomas had a close relationship—reminiscent of Ernest Shackleton and Frank Wild, the second in command on the *Endurance* Expedition. They had complementary personalities, with Bob's cool demeanor balancing Ed's passion.

Both Ed Psaltis and Bob Thomas joined forces during the storm, and their combined leadership provided a reassuring presence for the crew. Mix Bencsik recalls:

The leadership example set by Ed and Bob was quite symbolic. Their leadership played a large part in keeping our motivation going, and in making sure that no one gave up.

Bob is a noble seaman by trade. He understands storms, and he has been through a lot at sea. We have a lot of confidence in his ability.

Ed and Bob constantly instilled optimism and confidence that we could handle the conditions, and that the crew had the ability to win.[4]

While there was no question about Ed Psaltis' formal role as skipper, Ed and Bob together reinforced a sense of unified leadership. And because of their close personal relationship, they were able to send a joint message of reassurance and optimism.

The leader needs to set an example.

It may seem somewhat ironic that Ed Psaltis—one of the best amateur sailors in the world—gets seasick. But being a great sailor doesn't inoculate him, or anyone else, from a physiological response to motion. As Ed sees it:

> Being seasick isn't a problem. If you are sick, no one is going to be upset about that. We are only going to be upset if you don't do your job—if you start missing watches and letting your team down, that's when it's a problem.
>
> When I'm sick, I always try to make sure that I get up very, very quickly, because everyone is watching me. Then I'll smile and make a joke and people will go, *Well, okay, he's not too bad after all.*[5]

Ed realizes that people are watching him in his role as the skipper. And how he reacts to being sick is the critical issue, not the seasickness itself.

This is true for a number of other things that Ed does in a conscious effort to set an example. Coming off his watch as helmsman, Ed will take a forward position on the rail. In this exposed position, he is subjected to the first onslaught of water and spray. It is cold and uncomfortable, but it is clear that Ed is not afraid to do his share.

Ed will also take his turn in "the bad bunk." It seems that every boat comes equipped with a berth that—for one reason or another—is undesirable. Nobody wants the bad bunk, but Ed makes sure that he takes his turn. He is sending a message.

In his compelling book, *In Extremis Leadership,* Colonel Thomas Kolditz makes the point that leaders need to avoid elitism and share a common lifestyle with other members of the team:

> We believe that in extremis leaders accept, even embrace, a lifestyle that is common to their followers as an expression of values, and that such values become part of their presence and credibility as leaders. There is an inspirational Quaker saying that underscores the value of a transparent lifestyle: "Let your life speak." The idea is that followers come to understand values by watching the leader.[6]

Leaders need to set an example through lifestyle and the normal course of simply getting the job done. But there are some moments that are different. There are times when leaders need to inspire others though fortitude, courage, and skill. One such moment came for Ed Psaltis in the 1998 Sydney to Hobart Race.

I spoke with Michael Bencsik about his impressions of the '98 race, and Mix described this vivid moment:

> I've been through a lot of storms with Ed. Sitting on the side of the boat—wave spotting while he was helming in those conditions—was something that made me feel really proud. I thought, *Here's a person who has my life completely in his hands.* He was performing extraordinary feats of strength and seamanship, holding a 35-foot boat on the right course in those conditions.
>
> Ed was giving more than 110 percent. The well-being of the boat and crew were in his hands, and he didn't falter. It was an outstanding feat of seamanship. Even to this day, it's quite emotional to talk about. That was his finest moment.[7]

Not every leader has the ability to steer a boat through a storm like Ed Psaltis. But there comes a time when every leader needs to be willing to step up and give "more than 110 percent." For every leader, there can be a finest moment.

The Parts of a Sailboat

Lane Scarano

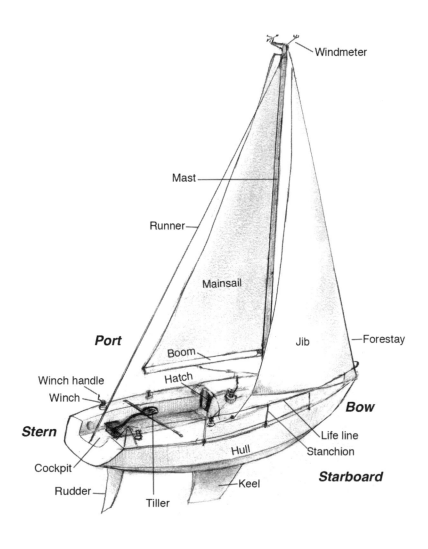

Windmeter

Mast

Runner

Mainsail

Port

Jib — Forestay

Boom

Winch handle

Hatch

Winch

Bow

Stern

Life line

Stanchion

Cockpit

Hull

Rudder

Starboard

Keel

Tiller

Acknowledgments

've always believed that acknowledgments are one of the most important parts of any book—and especially so for a book on teamwork. This has been an extraordinary team experience, and I'm delighted to be able to thank the many people who have helped me "make it to Hobart."

Working with Laura Gardner and Jillian Murphy transformed the daunting book race from *impossible* to simply *challenging*. With Laura in the "pit"—organizing our ropes, lines, bills, and permissions—I had no doubt that every assignment would be completed competently and with good cheer. And with Jillian on the bow as the forward hand, I was confident that she would fearlessly endure the cold waves that kept crashing into our literary vessel. Without Jillian and Laura, we would still be in the Bass Strait!

I also appreciate the many contributions made by Kathryn Fallon, the Editor's Editor, whose careful research and thoughtful editing were invaluable. With our *Rock Star Book Team*—one of the finest teams I have ever been a part of—I felt like the skipper of a winning boat.

I am grateful for the experience of getting to know, and learning from, the Ramblers. Their willingness to share the story of *AFR Midnight Rambler,* and their formula for *Teamwork at The Edge,* made the book possible. My thanks go to the '98 team—Mix Bencsik, Gordon Livingstone, Ed and Arthur Psaltis, Bob Thomas, Chris Rockell, and John Whitfeld—and to newer members, Tom Barker and Sammy Byron, who also shared valuable insights. And of course, the story would not have been complete without the perspectives shared by Bill Psaltis and Ed's wife Sue.

I learned much from other sailors who—though they compete against *AFR Midnight Rambler* in the Hobart—generously shared their insights about teamwork. In a folder marked "Sailing Greats," I have pages of notes from interviews with Adrienne Cahalan, Neville Crichton, Roger Hickman, Malcolm Park, and Jim Slaughter, all of which guided my thinking. And I was inspired by Kristy McAlister, whose story stands out as a remarkable example of teamwork and courage.

I deeply appreciate those who helped me make it to Hobart when I did the 2006 race: Peter Beekman, James ("Jungle") Craddock, Ben Feeney, Johno Fullerton, Brian Griffin, Scott Jug, Steve Kellaway, Pete Le Masurier, Robyn Lindley, Sam Price, Andy Pryor, Peter Tarimo, Matt Whitmell, and our skipper, Peter Goldsworthy. I am especially thankful for the hospitality shown by Brett McIntyre and his family, who made me feel so welcome over the holidays in Australia.

Special thanks go to Edgar ("Eddo") Smith—a key partner in all aspects of the book race. Edgar accompanied me on the race as the official videographer, and he has skillfully edited numerous videos—including the promotional trailer for the book and the "We're No Rockstars" documentary of the *AFR Midnight Rambler*. Eddo's watchful eye was especially appreciated on the Sydney to Hobart Race, when I did an unexpected re-creation of Chris Rockell's flight through the air. After I cracked my head on the side of the boat, Eddo waited patiently while I recovered—making sure that my skull was still hard, not "squishy."

Art Vasenius, of the Sailing Pro Shop in San Diego, and Martha Parker, of Team One Newport in Rhode Island, helped me get the right equipment for the Sydney to Hobart Race. Zach Leonard shared valuable insights about safety and endurance in ocean racing. Others who helped make the book possible include Mark Wolfe, CEO of the Cruising Yacht Club of Australia; Richard Bennett, with his spectacular photography; and Lisa Ratcliff, who contributed her great photo of Ed Psaltis and Bob Thomas.

I appreciate the lessons in teamwork shared by fellow Marines. General John Arick's skillful recon extract in Vietnam has always been a source of pride for me, especially during the years when the service of combat veterans was little understood and largely unappreciated. And as General Rich Natonski recounted his more recent experiences, I realized that—though technology and tactics may have changed—Marines of all ranks and all generations have much in common. John Arick, James "Crash Kimo" Andrews, Rich Natonski, Aaron Jensen, and Brody Savoie have answered the call to defend freedom "in every clime and place," and Marines will always continue that proud tradition.

The concept of this book has taken shape over a number of years, and I have been influenced by many thoughtful people. Mark Nadler wrote the first article to capture the story of the Ramblers. Chuck Raben helped me think about the role of the skipper. Michael Simon and Peter Economy shared their views on teamwork. Jillian (Caracciolo) Savoie and Brian Keady helped launch the book. And Diana Vienne made a number of helpful suggestions about the proposal.

There were times during which I wondered if I would ever make it to the finish line, and friends and colleagues made all the difference. Martha Miller read an initial draft of the book, and reassured me that I had a powerful message. Melanie Kirkpatrick, Molly Powell, and Micah Morrison all made helpful and timely suggestions.

I'd like to recognize our *Expedition Leaders,* especially Ron Jungalwalla and Mike Boyle—who have been presenting the story of the *Midnight Rambler* in Australia for years. Ron thoughtfully reviewed the manuscript, and even came to meet us in Connecticut—all the way from Melbourne! A number of other *Expedition Leaders* have also played an important role in our journey, including David Ellis, Hazel Rosin, Piotr Wisoky, and all our colleagues at the Korea Syncretics Leadership Center.

Others who deserve credit include Deb Abildsoe, David Bliss, Jen Chobor, Andy Corea, Pete Dayman, Andy Errato, Paul Fedorko, John Michalak, Mike Kennedy, Rick Ketterer, Nick Lopergalo, Seth Meskin, Camille Murphy, Robert Ostroff, Mike Rubenstein, Carl Swope, and Dave Wygant. I also appreciate my friends at Sunset Limo who have helped me get to the airport at the start of almost every adventure, and the experts at TNS who have kept my technology afloat so I could write about my experiences at *The Edge.*

Dewitt Keith has also aided in my travels, and has helped me reach meetings in a number of disparate locations. These trips have frequently involved meetings with the men and women who work tirelessly to protect our national security. I am honored to be able to help with their critical mission.

I appreciate the hard work and dedication of the AMACOM team. Christina Parisi has been a longtime supporter of *The Edge,* endorsing both a second edition of *Leading at The Edge* and this book as well. Her editorial suggestions substantially improved the manuscript, and I know I have a better book because of her insights. Irene Majuk made great contributions in promoting both editions of *Leading at The Edge.* And the photo of her spunky dog, Spike—wearing a party hat while celebrating his eighteenth birthday—never fails to bring a smile to my face. He will always be a member of the expedition.

Others at AMACOM have also helped with the complex and often tedious work of publication. Erika Spelman's thoroughness, patience, and unflappable style made a tremendous difference. And thanks go to Jenny

Wesselmann Schwartz, Cathleen Ouderkirk, James Bessent, Janet Pagano, and Kama Timbrell for their support and assistance.

The folks at North Market Street Graphics brought the book over the finish line. I deeply appreciate the work of the NMSG Team, including Ginny Carroll, Dennis Bicksler, Mike Dunnick, Ginny Landis, Sue Miller, Rhonda Stough, and Stewart Smith. Ginny Carroll served as copy editor and "point person" for the mission, and her genuine enthusiasm for the story provided much needed encouragement when we were becalmed in the Derwent.

As always, I am grateful for the support of my family. My daughter, Holly, fearlessly ventured out to sail on cold winter days, and a photo of granddaughters Juliana and Liya provided constant inspiration. I appreciate the support of my son, Jonathan, his wife Karla, and their children. Hearing Alicia, Joshie, and Samuel talk about their *Abuelo Don Dennis* is a never-ending source of joy. The Oregon Perkins Clan—my brother Bob, his son Rob and wife Melissa, and grandson Ryan—all deserve recognition for their help.

Once again, I express my deepest appreciation for the support, love, and encouragement of my wife, Susan, and her son, Ryan. Although writing a book requires extraordinary commitment, and discipline, other family members make sacrifices as well. And I know full well that being the spouse of an author is "no picnic either"! I appreciate Susan's encouragement, her faith in my ability, her New York wit, and her smile. I am so thankful that I found her.

Toward the end of the book, there were difficult days when it seemed as if the task would be never ending. But I kept inspired with two photos next to my computer monitor. The first was my friend Reggie Higgins, who was photographed in a ferocious pose. Reggie is a Mixed Martial Arts, heavyweight fighter—and his ferocity is real. I have seen him in action. The second photo was of my grandson, Joshie. It shows him swinging a croquet mallet at a piñata—a green dinosaur created with papier-mâché.

The piñata was part of Joshie's fourth birthday party, and it was filled with candy. Though much smaller than Reggie, Joshie went after the piñata with equal ferocity. Again and again, Joshie bashed the piñata—but to no avail. The piñata seemed to be made of steel, or possibly concrete.

It was quite a show. Joshie attacked the piñata with the determination of an MMA fighter. At times I felt as if I were watching Reggie at Foxwoods Casino. I often expected Joshie to put a submission hold on the dinosaur. Sometimes Joshie missed and swung round in a complete circle, falling down with his mallet. But he didn't stop. He was relentless.

Finally, the piñata fell to the ground. It was still intact, but Joshie pounced. He was not to be denied. After a final, furious series of attacks, the piñata cracked. After all that, Joshie had his candy. His determination was inspirational.

With the help of Joshie and Reggie, and the support of all those included in the acknowledgments, I finished the book, made it to Hobart, and cracked the piñata. I know that I would never have made it without your help.

Notes

Preface
1. The measurements used in the book are nautical miles for distance and knots for speeds. One nautical mile is equivalent to 1.15 statute miles. A knot is equivalent to 1.15 miles per hour. In some cases, statute miles and miles per hour are also shown.

PART ONE: THE STORY OF THE *AFR MIDNIGHT RAMBLER* AND THE SYDNEY TO HOBART RACE
Chapter 2: The Patriarch of a Sailing Family
1. Bill Psaltis, personal communication.

Chapter 3: *Nuzulu* and the Start of a Winning Team
1. Arthur Psaltis, personal communication.

Chapter 6: The Aussie Competitors
1. Information about Australian competitors was derived from the following books: G. Bruce Knecht, *The Proving Ground* (New York: Grand Central Publishing, 2002); Kim Leighton, *A Hard Chance: The Sydney Hobart Disaster* (Minocqua, WI: Willow Creek Press, 1999); Rob Mundle, *Fatal Storm: The Inside Story of the Tragic Sydney-Hobart Race* (Sydney: International Marine McGraw-Hill, 1999); and Debbie Whitmont, *An Extreme Event: The Compelling, True Story of the Tragic 1998 Sydney-Hobart Race* (Sydney: Random House Australia, 1999).

Chapter 7: *Sayonara*—The Big Yank Tank
1. Information about Larry Ellison and *Sayonara* was taken from Matthew Symonds, with commentary by Larry Ellison, *Softwar: An Intimate Portrait of Larry Ellison and Oracle* (New York: Simon & Schuster Paperbacks, 2003); Mike Wilson, *The Difference between God and Larry Ellison: Inside Oracle Corporation* (New York: Harper, 2003); and Knecht, *Proving Ground*.

2. Symonds, *Softwar,* p. 311.
3. Ibid., p. 305.
4. "I Never Ever Mooned Larry Ellison," *Sailing World,* March 14, 2003.
5. Symonds, *Softwar,* p. 315.

Chapter 8: Uncertain Weather—Buster or Bomb?
1. Information from this chapter was derived from sources including *Preliminary Report on the Meteorological Aspects of the 1998 Sydney to Hobart Race,* (Australia: Bureau of Meteorology, February 1999); New South Wales State Coroner's Inquest, 1998 Sydney to Hobart Yacht Race—Testimony and Evidence, April 2000; "Storm Warning," *Vanity Fair,* May 1999; Knecht, *Proving Ground.*
2. Speech by John Mooney, Sydney to Hobart Race Awards Ceremony, January 2, 1999.

Chapter 10: *Sayonara*—The Best Professional Sailors on the Planet
1. Information for this chapter derived from Knecht, *Proving Ground,* and Symonds, *Softwar.*
2. Symonds, *Softwar,* p. 312.
3. Knecht, *Proving Ground,* p. 24.
4. Symonds, *Softwar,* p. 316.
5. Ibid.

Chapter 12: *Sayonara*—Temporary Humility
1. Symonds, *Softwar,* p. 317.
2. Ibid., p.318.

Chapter 14: *AFR Midnight Rambler*—Hard or Squishy?
1. Arthur Psaltis, personal communication.
2. Chris Rockell, personal communication.

Chapter 15: *VC Offshore Stand Aside*—A Twist of Fate
1. Interview with Ian Moray, Coroner's Inquest.

Chapter 16: Rescue from the Sky—Angels on Winches
1. Kristy McAlister, personal communication; Coroner's Inquest.

Chapter 17: *AFR Midnight Rambler*—Hell on White Water
 1. Interview with Darryl Jones, Coroner's Inquest.
 2. Statement from Darryl Jones, Coroner's Inquest.

Chapter 19: *Sword of Orion*—Out of Control
 1. Material from this chapter derived from Coroner's Inquest and interviews with Rob Kothe, Steve Kulmar, and Adam Brown.

Chapter 20: General Mayday—An Official Catastrophe
 1. Statement from John Hope Gibson, Coroner's Inquest.

Chapter 22: *Sayonara*—Tack the Boat
 1. Information in this chapter derived from Symonds, *Softwar*; Knecht, *Proving Ground*; and "Storm Warning," *Vanity Fair.*
 2. Symonds, *Softwar,* p. 320.
 3. Knecht, *Proving Ground,* 2nd edition, (Las Vegas, NV: Amazon Encore, 2011), p. 257.
 4. Symonds, *Softwar,* p. 321.
 5. Ibid.

Chapter 24: *Sayonara*—A Thousand Years
 1. Mundle, *Fatal Storm.*
 2. Leighton, *A Hard Chance,* p. 241.
 3. Ibid., p. 243.
 4. Symonds, *Softwar,* p. 321.
 5. Ibid.

Chapter 25: Go the *Rambler*!
 1. Ed Psaltis, personal communication.

PART TWO: CRITICAL STRATEGIES FOR *TEAMWORK AT THE EDGE*
Chapter 28: Introduction to the Strategies
 1. Roger Hickman, personal communication.

Chapter 29: The Research Challenge
 1. Phil Rosenzweig, *The Halo Effect . . . and Eight Other Business Delusions That Deceive Managers* (New York: Free Press, 2007).
 2. Michael Raynor, et al., "Are 'Great' Companies Just Lucky?" *Harvard Business Review,* April 2009.

3. Nassim Nicholas Taleb, *Fooled by Randomness: The Hidden Role of Chance in the Markets and in Life* (New York: W.W. Norton & Company, 2001).

4. B.F. Skinner, " 'Superstition' in the Pigeon," *Journal of Experimental Psychology* 38:2 (April 1948), pp. 168–172.

5. "Medical Studies' Claims Irk Profession's Skeptics," *Wall Street Journal,* July 12, 1993.

Chapter 31: Team Unity

1. Ed Psaltis, personal communication.

2. Geoff Smart and Randy Street, *Who: The A Method for Hiring* (New York: Ballantine, 2008), p. 168.

3. Psaltis, ibid.

4. Smart and Street, *Who,* p. 168.

5. Deborah Ancona and Henrik Bresman, *X-Teams: How to Build Teams That Lead, Innovate, and Succeed* (Boston: Harvard Business School, 2007).

Chapter 32: Prepare, Prepare, Prepare

1. Michael Bencsik, personal communication.

2. Dennis Connor and John Rousmaniere, *No Excuse to Lose: Winning Yacht Races* (New York: W.W. Norton & Company, 1978).

3. Atul Gawande, *The Checklist Manifesto: How to Get Things Right* (New York: Metropolitan Books, 2009).

4. Ibid., p. 103.

5. Michael Useem, *The Leader's Checklist: 15 Mission-Critical Principles* (Philadelphia: Wharton Digital Press, 2011).

6. John Rousmaniere, *The Annapolis Book of Seamanship,* 3rd edition (New York: Simon & Schuster, 1999).

7. General Richard Natonski, personal communication.

8. Richard S. Lowery, *New Dawn: The Battles for Fallujah* (New York: Savas Beatie, 2010).

Chapter 33: Balanced Optimism

1. Ed Psaltis, personal communication.

2. Malcolm Park, personal communication.

3. Kenneth Kamler, *Surviving the Extremes: A Doctor's Journey to the Limits of Human Endurance* (New York: St. Martin's Press, 2004).

Chapter 34: Relentless Learning

1. R.B. Shaw and Dennis N.T. Perkins, "Teaching organizations to learn," *Organization Development Journal* 9:4 (1992).
2. John Wukovits, *American Commando: Evans Carlson, His WWII Marine Raiders and America's First Special Forces Mission* (New York: Penguin, 2009).
3. Neville Crichton, personal communication.
4. Malcolm Park, personal communication.
5. Vietnam Center and Archive at Texas Tech University.

Chapter 35: Calculated Risk

1. Jane Spencer and Cynthia Crossen, "Why Do Americans Believe Danger Lurks Everywhere?" *Wall Street Journal,* April 24, 2003.
2. Don Mays, "Furniture Tip-over Kills Two-Year-Old," *Consumer Reports,* September 21, 2010; http://news.consumerreports.org/safety/2010/09/furniture-tip-over-kills-2-year-old-1.html.
3. "How Americans Are Living Dangerously," *Time,* November 26, 2006.
4, Andrew Sutherland, "Why are so many people dying on Everest?" *British Medical Journal,* (2006) 333:452.
5. Barry D. Watts, *Clausewitzian Friction and Future War* (Washington, D.C.: McNair Papers/National Defense University, 2004).
6. Eric S. Toner, *Creating Situational Awareness: A Systems Approach,* white paper prepared for a workshop hosted by the Institute of Medicine Forum on Medical and Public Health Preparedness for Catastrophic Events, June 10, 2009.
7. Sharon Begley, "Afraid to Fly after 9/11, Some Took Bigger Risk—in Cars," *Wall Street Journal,* March 23, 2004.
8. Malcolm Gladwell, *Blink: The Power of Thinking Without Thinking* (New York: Little Brown, 2005).
9. Daniel Kahneman, *Thinking, Fast and Slow* (New York: Farrar, Straus & Giroux, 2011).
10. Frederick Funston and Stephen Wagner, *Surviving and Thriving in Uncertainty: Creating a Risk Intelligent Enterprise* (Hoboken, NJ: John Wiley & Sons, 2010).
11. Chris Rockell, personal communication.

Chapter 36: Stay Connected

1. "Time Is on Your Side," http://blog.bitly.com/post/22663850994/
   time-is-on-your-side, accessed May 8, 2012.
2. Ibid.
3. Chris Rockell, personal communication.
4. Michael Bencsik, personal communication.

Chapter 37: Step into the Breach

1. Ed Psaltis, personal communication.
2. Arthur Psaltis, personal communication.
3. Ed Psaltis, ibid.

Chapter 38: Eliminate Friction

1. Malcolm Park, personal communication, italics added.
2. Bob Thomas, personal communication.
3. Gordon Livingstone, personal communication.
4. Michael Bencsik, personal communication.
5. Livingstone, ibid.

Chapter 39: Practiced Resilience

1. Samantha Byron, personal communication.
2. Bob Thomas, personal communication.
3. Ed Psaltis, personal communication.

Chapter 40: Tenacious Creativity

1. Ed Psaltis, personal communication.
2. Arthur Psaltis, personal communication.
3. Tom Barker, personal communication.

A Note to the Skipper

1. Rakesh Khurana, *Searching for a Corporate Savior: The Irrational Quest for
   Charismatic CEOs* (Princeton, NJ: Princeton University Press, 2004).
2. Adrienne Cahalan, personal communication.
3. Samantha Byron, personal communication.
4. Michael Bencsik, personal communication.
5. Ed Psaltis, personal communication.
6. T.A. Kolditz, *In Extremis Leadership: Leading as if your Life Depended on
   It* (San Francisco: Jossey-Bass, 2007).
7. Bencsik, ibid.

Bibliography

Adams, David, with Caroline Adams. *Chasing Liquid Mountains: Adventures of a Solo Yachtsman.* Sydney: Macmillan, 1997.

Ancona, Deborah, and Henrik Bresman. *X-Teams: How to Build Teams That Lead, Innovate, and Succeed.* Boston: Harvard Business School, 2007.

Baghai, Mehrdad, and James Quigley. *As One: Individual Action Collective Power.* New York: Penguin, 2011.

Bailey, Maurice, and Maralyn Bailey. *117 Days Adrift.* Dobbs Ferry, NY: Sheridan House, 1992.

Bennett, Richard, with text by Bob Ross. *Ocean Classics.* Kingston, Tasmania: Richard Bennett, 1994.

Bickel, Lennard. *Mawson's Will.* New York: Avon, 1978.

Boukreev, Anatoli, and G. Weston DeWalt. *The Climb: Tragic Ambitions on Everest.* New York: St. Martin's Press, 1997.

Bruce, Erroll. *When the Crew Matter Most.* Oxford: Oxford University Press, 1961.

Calahan, Adrienne. *Around the Buoys with Champion Yachtswoman and Navigator Adrienne Cahalan.* Sydney, Australia: Random House Australia, 2006.

Connor, Dennis, and John Rousmaniere. *No Excuse to Lose: Winning Yacht Races.* New York: W. W. Norton & Company, 1978.

Dugard, Martin. *Knockdown: The Harrowing True Account of a Yacht Race Turned Deadly.* New York: Pocket Books, 1999.

Fredston, Jill. *Snowstruck: In the Grip of Avalanches.* New York: Harcourt, 2005.

Funston, Frederick, and Stephen Wagner. *Surviving and Thriving in Uncertainty: Creating the Risk Intelligent Enterprise.* Hoboken, NJ: John Wiley & Sons, 2010.

Gawande, Atul. *The Checklist Manifesto: How to Get Things Right.* New York: Metropolitan Books, 2009.

Gladwell, Malcolm. *Blink: The Power of Thinking without Thinking.* New York: Little Brown, 2005.

Gonzales, Laurence. *Deep Survival: Who Lives, Who Dies, and Why, True Sto-*

ries of Miraculous Endurance and Sudden Death. New York: W. W. Norton & Company, 2003.

Henderson, Bruce. *Fatal North: Adventure and Survival Aboard* USS Polaris, *the First U.S. Expedition to the North Pole.* New York: New American Library, 2001.

Herzog, Maurice. *Annapurna.* North Salem, NY: The Adventure Library, 1995.

Heyerdahl, Thor. *Kon-Tiki.* New York: Washington Square Press, 1973.

Isler, Peter, and Peter Economy. *At the Helm: Business Lessons for Navigating Rough Waters.* New York: Doubleday, 2000.

Junger, Sebastian. *The Perfect Storm: A True Story of Men against the Sea.* New York: W. W. Norton & Company, 1997.

Kahneman, Daniel. *Thinking, Fast and Slow.* New York: Farrar, Straus, and Giroux, 2011.

Kamler, Kenneth. *Surviving the Extremes: A Doctor's Journey to the Limits of Human Endurance.* New York: St. Martin's Press, 2004.

Khurana, Rakesh. *Searching for a Corporate Savior: The Irrational Quest for Charismatic CEOs.* Princeton, NJ: Princeton University Press, 2004.

Kiley, Deborah Scaling, and Meg Noonan. *Albatross: The True Story of a Woman's Survival at Sea.* New York: Houghton Mifflin, 1994.

Klaben, Helen, with Beth Day. *Hey, I'm Alive!* New York: McGraw-Hill, 1964.

Knecht, G. Bruce. *The Proving Ground.* New York: Grand Central Publishing, 2002.

Knecht, G. Bruce. *The Proving Ground,* 2nd edition. Las Vegas, NV: Amazon Encore, 2011.

Kocour, Ruth Anne, with Michael Hodgson. *Facing the Extreme: One Woman's Story of True Courage, Death-Defying Survival, and Her Quest for the Summit.* New York: St. Martin's Press, 1998.

Krakauer, Jon. *Into Thin Air: A Personal Account of the Mt. Everest Disaster.* New York: Villard, 1997.

Kuhne, Cecil, ed. *Near Death on the High Seas: True Stories of Disaster and Survival.* New York: Vintage Books, 2008.

Larsen, Paul C. *To the Third Power: The Inside Story of Bill Koch's Winning Strategies for The America's Cup.* Gardiner, ME: Tilbury House, 1995.

Leighton, Kim. *A Hard Chance: The Sydney Hobart Disaster.* Minocqua, WI: Willow Creek Press, 1999.

Leslie, Edward E. *Desperate Journeys, Abandoned Souls: True Stories of Castaways and Other Survivors.* Boston: Houghton Mifflin, 1988.

Lewis, Cam, with Michael Levitt. *Around the World in 79 Days.* Lincolnville, Maine: Team Adventure Press, 2001.

Lowery, Richard S., *New Dawn: The Battles for Fallujah.* New York: Savas Beatie, 2010.

Maclean, Norman. *Young Men and Fire: A True Story of the Mann Gulch Fire.* Chicago: The University of Chicago Press, 1992.

Mitchell, Richard G., Jr. *Mountain Experience: The Psychology and Sociology of Adventure.* Chicago: The University of Chicago Press, 1985.

Mundle, Rob. *Fatal Storm: The Inside Story of the Tragic Sydney-Hobart Race.* Sydney: International Marine McGraw-Hill, 1999.

Nalepka, James, and Steven Callahan. *Capsized: The True Story of Four Men Adrift for 119 Days.* New York: HarperCollins, 1992.

Nichols, Peter. *A Voyage for Madmen.* New York: Harper Perennial, 2001.

O'Neill, Helen. *Life Without Limits: The Remarkable Story of David Pescud and His Fight for Survival in a Sea of Words.* Sydney: Bantam Books, 2003.

Perkins, Dennis, with Margaret P. Holtman and Jillian Murphy. *Leading at The Edge: Leadership Lessons from the Extraordinary Saga of Shackleton's Antarctic Expedition.* 2nd Edition. New York: AMACOM, 2012.

Philbrick, Nathaniel. *In the Heart of the Sea: The Tragedy of the Whaleship Essex.* New York: The Penguin Group, 2000.

Potterfield, Peter. *In the Zone: Epic Survival Stories from the Mountaineering World.* Seattle, WA: The Mountaineers, 1996.

Read, Piers Paul. *Alive: The Story of the Andes Survivors.* New York: Avon Books, 1975.

Robertson, Douglas. *The Last Voyage of the Lucette.* Suffolk, England: Seafarer Books, 2005.

Robertson, Douglas. *Survive the Savage Sea.* New York: Sheridan House, 1994.

Rousmaniere, John. *After the Storm: True Stories of Disaster and Recovery at Sea.* New York: International Marine/McGraw-Hill, 2002.

Rousmaniere, John. *The Annapolis Book of Seamanship.* 3rd edition. New York: Simon & Schuster, 1999.

Rousmaniere, John. *Fastnet, Force 10: The Deadliest Storm in the History of Modern Sailing.* New York: W.W. Norton & Company, 2000.

Shaw, R.B., and Dennis N.T. Perkins. "Teaching organizations to learn," *Organization Development Journal* 9:4 (1992).

Smart, Geoff, and Randy Street. *Who: The A Method for Hiring.* New York: Ballantine, 2008.

Steger, Will, and Jon Bowermaster. *Crossing Antarctica.* New York: Alfred A. Knopf, 1992.

Stewart, George R. *Ordeal by Hunger: The Story of the Donner Party.* New York: Houghton Mifflin, 1988.

Sutherland, Andrew. "Why are so many people dying on Everest?" *British Medical Journal,* (2006) 333.

Symonds, Matthew, with commentary by Larry Ellison. *Softwar: An Intimate Portrait of Larry Ellison and Oracle.* New York: Simon & Schuster Paperbacks, 2003.

Toner, Eric S. *Creating Situational Awareness: A Systems Approach.* White paper prepared for a workshop hosted by the Institute of Medicine Forum on Medical and Public Health Preparedness for Catastrophic Events, June 10, 2009.

Trumbull, Robert. *The Raft: The Courageous Story of Three Naval Airmen against the Sea.* Annapolis, MD: Naval Institute Press, 1992.

Useem, Michael. *The Leader's Checklist: 15 Mission-Critical Principles.* Philadelphia: Wharton Digital Press, 2011.

Useem, Michael, et al. *Upward Bound: Nine Original Accounts of How Business Leaders Reached Their Summits.* New York: Crown Business, 2003.

Walters, Humphrey, Peter Mackie, Rosie Mackie, and Andrea Bacon. *Global Challenge: Leadership Lessons from "The World's Toughest Yacht Race."* Sussex, England: The Book Guild, 1997.

Ward, Nick, with Sinéad O'Brien. *Left for Dead: Surviving the Deadliest Storm in Modern Sailing History.* New York: Bloomsbury, 2007.

Whitmont, Debbie. *An Extreme Event: The Compelling, True Story of the Tragic 1998 Sydney-Hobart Race.* Sydney: Random House Australia, 1999.

Willis, Clint, ed. *Rough Water: Stories of Survival from the Sea.* New York: Adrenaline, 1998.

Wilson, Mike. *The Difference between God and Larry Ellison: Inside Oracle Corporation.* New York: HarperBusiness, 2003.

Index